No. 2462
$27.95

THE ILLUSTRATED BUYER'S GUIDE TO
USED
AIRPLANES

SECOND EDITION

BILL CLARKE

TAB BOOKS Inc.
Blue Ridge Summit, PA

SECOND EDITION
FIRST PRINTING

First edition copyright© 1985 by **TAB BOOKS Inc.**
Copyright © 1990 by **TAB BOOKS Inc.**
Printed in the United States of America

Library of Congress Cataloging in Publication Data

Clarke, Bill (Charles W.)
    The illustrated buyer's guide to used airplanes / by Bill Clarke.
    — 2nd ed.
       p.   cm.
    Includes index.
    ISBN 0-8306-9162-6   ISBN 0-8306-9462-5 (pbk.)
    1. Used aircraft—Purchasing. I Title.
TL685.1.C54   1989
629.133'34—dc20   89-34727
                                                          CIP

TAB BOOKS Inc. offers software for sale. For information and a catalog, please contact
TAB Software Department, Blue Ridge Summit, PA 17294-0850.

Questions regarding the content of this book
should be addressed to:

    Reader Inquiry Branch
    TAB BOOKS Inc.
    Blue Ridge Summit, PA 17294-0214

Acquistions Editor: Jeff Worsinger
Book Editor: Norval G. Kennedy
Production: Katherine Brown

Contents

Introduction

Sometime or another, everyone who has ever flown will entertain thoughts of owning an airplane. Like everything else, however, certain complexities must be known and understood. Dollar values and costs are perhaps the most important, but others exist.

In 1984, a new Cessna 172 displayed a price tag in the vicinity of $65,000. A couple of years later, when the model was priced out of existence, production stopped. At the same time, top-of-the-line planes such as the Beech Bonanzas were found with starting prices of nearly $200,000, even when equipped with only modest avionics. The effect of these hight prices has been the elimination of most fliers from the new airplane market. However, a viable alternative to an expensive new airplane exists: a good used airplane.

The Illustrated Buyer's Guide to Used Airplanes—2nd Edition is written to assist you, the prospective buyer, in the successful search for a suitable and cost-effective airplane. Part I of the book explains how to determine the size and type of aircraft best suited to fulfill your flying needs. Then it shows how to evaluate a used airplane and to read the cryptic used-airplane ads. This book explains where and how to find a good used airplane, and, more importantly, how to keep from getting burned in the process.

You will gain an understanding of the mountains of paperwork required for airplane ownership, learn how to select a home base, how to perform preventive maintenance, and how to provide other owner upkeep.

Although you may have a basic idea of what a particular used airplane looks like, or what some of the specifications are, you must have a ready source of review for additional information. Part II of this book is such a source. Part II contains historical information, photographs, and specifications for most airplanes that will be found on today's used market.

Part III offers interesting stories and other tidbits of information heard around the hangar. Alternative aircraft are investigated, including the fast powerful warbirds, sleek homebuilts, serene gliders, and float planes.

Appendices list many of the airworthiness directives that apply to airplanes described in this book. Examine the NTSB aircraft accident chart, and see where your dream plane rates. Appendices also list addresses for the FAA, state aviation agencies, and airplane clubs. Finally, you will find the all-important used airplane price list.

In summary, *The Illustrated Buyer's Guide to Used Airplanes—2nd Edition* was written to help you in economical decision making and to show you how to avoid many pitfalls encountered when buying a used aircraft.

Part I

Practical Used Airplane Buying

1

To Own or Not to Own

SOONER OR LATER nearly everyone who earns a pilot's license has the desire to own an airplane. You are probably no exception, and the fact that you're reading this book means you at least dream of having your own plane. Owning a plane brings pride of ownership, the freedom to fly anytime and anywhere desired, to equip the airplane as you wish, to care for it, love it, and most of all *to pay* for it.

Expense Of Ownership

Ask yourself this question: "Can I really afford to own an airplane?" Before you answer, consider the following:

Do I fully understand the overall costs of airplane ownership? Will I use the airplane often enough to justify ownership? Have I considered alternatives to ownership?

Although new airplane prices have gone straight through the roof, it is a fact that the prudent purchase of a used airplane will reduce the cost of flying.

The portion of ownership examined in this chapter is financial justification. In other words, is owning an airplane worth what it costs?

Let's examine the real costs of ownership, costs that are not included in the price of purchase. Assume that cash will be paid for the airplane because a discussion of aircraft financing would be too broad for consideration at this time.

Vocabulary

Aircraft ownership and operation abound with new words and phrases.

Fixed costs: The cost of ownership regardless of use. Included in fixed costs are hangar or tiedown fees, state or local property taxes on the aircraft, insurance premiums, and the cost of the annual inspection (sometimes a vague/gray area).

Operating costs: The cost of fuel per hour (gas and oil), an engine reserve account, and a general maintenance fund (to repair those small items that need a mechanic's or technician's attention), oil changes, periodic ADs, minor mechanical defects, avionics problems, etc.

Hourly cost: An overall figure based upon the annual total of fixed and operating costs, divided by the total hours of operation. Hourly cost is the all-important number that shows if ownership is practical.

Engine reserve: A monetary fund, built up on a hourly basis, to pay for the eventual engine overhaul. The hourly rate is figured as the cost of a major overhaul divided by the recommended overhaul time limit.

General maintenance fund: A cumulative savings used to pay for minor repairs and service. Normally, two to five dollars per hour of operation, depending upon complexity of the aircraft, will be adequate.

Worksheets

A worksheet will help figure the costs of ownership. Fill in the blanks and follow the instructions for computations.

Fixed Costs

12 months of storage	$_____
Annual taxes	$_____
Annual state license	$_____
Insurance premium (12 months)	$_____
Annual inspection (estimated)	$_____
Total fixed costs	$_____

Operating Costs

Fuel cost per gallon × GPH	$_____
Engine reserve per hour	$_____
General maintenance per hour	$_____
Total operating costs	$_____

Hourly Cost

Fixed costs	$_____
Operating costs × hours flown	$_____
Total costs	$_____
Total cost/hour	$_____

Examples

Let's examine a hypothetical case of ownership. The airplane is a Cessna 150.

This example is based upon $25 per month for outside tiedown, which is very modest. A one percent local tax is applied to the $6,000 value of the airplane, and a state license costs $9. The insurance cost is an estimate based on the value of the airplane and the pilot's experience. The annual inspection is a gray area, however, this was the average estimate made by several FBOs. The five GPH is an estimate for fuel usage. Fuel costs $1.90 per gallon.

An engine reserve of $2.50 per hour should be adequate to properly maintain the engine and assure a complete overhaul. The general maintenance rate of $3 per flying hour will allow a reserve to build up for normal mechanical difficulties (brakes, tires, nose wheel shimmy, flap actuator jack problems, radio failure, etc.) to be repaired. At the end computations, fixed costs total $1,379 per year and operating costs total $15 per hour.

Fixed Costs

12 months of storage	$ 300
Annual taxes	$ 60
Annual state license	$ 9
Insurance premium (12 months)	$ 660
Annual inspection (est.)	$ 350
Total fixed costs	$1,379

Operating Costs

Fuel cost per gallon x GPH	$ 9.50
Engine reserve per hour	$ 2.50
General maintenance per hour	$ 3.00
Total operating costs	$15.00

Hourly Cost

Fixed costs	$1,379
Operating costs x hours flown (assume 100)	$1,500
Total costs	$2,879
Total cost/hour (approx.)	$ 29

This example was for an airplane operated (flown) 100 hours during the year. Now try other times to see how usage affects the bottom line.

One Hour

(A worst-case scenario, only one flying hour for the entire year.)

Fixed costs	$1,379
Operating costs x hours flown	$ 15
Total costs	$1,394
Total cost/hour (approx.)	$1,394

Fifty Hours

Many privately owned airplanes are only operated 50 hours a year. This is a good average.

Fixed costs	$1,379
Operating costs x hours flown	$ 750
Total costs	$2,129
Total cost/hour (approx.)	$ 43

200 Hours

The fortunate owner who flies his plane 200 hours a year gets the most return from his investment.

Fixed costs	$1,379
Operating costs x hours flown	$3,000
Total costs	$4,379
Total cost/hour (approx.)	$ 22

More Examples

Let's see what a four-place airplane with a 225-hp engine and retractable landing gear will cost. The airplane is located in a metropolitan area.

This example is based upon $100 per month for outside tiedown, which is typical in major cities. Indoor storage could be as high as $350 per month. A four-percent local tax is applied to the $35,000 value of the airplane. A state license costs $60, and is based upon the plane's weight. The insurance cost is an estimate based on the value of the airplane and the pilot's experience (or lack of experience) in a retractable. The annual inspection reflects the increased costs of a more complex airplane over that of the original example. Fuel usage is calculated at 16 gph. Engine reserve is $4 per hour, based on the current overhaul costs for a 225-hp engine. The general maintenance rate of $5 per flying hour allows for a repair reserve.

Fixed Costs	
12 months of storage	$ 1,200
Annual taxes	$ 1,400
Annual state license	$ 60
Insurance premium (12 months)	$ 2,600
Annual inspection (est.)	$ 850
Total annual fixed costs	$ 6,110
Operating Costs	
Fuel cost per gal x GPH	$ 32
Engine reserve per hour	$ 4
General maintenance per hour	$ 5
Total annual operating costs	$ 41
Hourly Cost	
Fixed costs	$ 6,110
Operating costs x hours flown (assume 100)	$ 4,100
Total costs	$10,210
Total cost/hour (approx.)	$ 102

What Now?

Go forth and compare these figures—or figures based upon your selected airplane—with the straight hourly rental charged for a similar airplane at the local FBO. Keep in mind that you can sometimes purchase blocks of time from an FBO for a reduced rate, often as much as 20 percent. Just out of interest, my local FBO charges $45 per hour for a 152.

Against Ownership

The first part of this chapter mentioned the pride of ownership, and the convenience of being free of the FBO's control. This is all very true, but there is a price to be paid for ownership.

All maintenance will be your responsibility. You won't have a squawk book to write pilot/renter complaints into and expect the FBO to address them before the next flight. You will have to either repair them yourself or pay out of your own pocket to have them repaired.

Do you like the clean airplane rented from the FBO? If you own an airplane, you will have to keep it clean. Consider the size of an airplane. The top surface of the wings is better than 150 square feet, and that's a lot when you are doing the washing and polishing. I haven't even mentioned the windshields, upholstery, carpets, or oil-stained belly.

A Primer On Aircraft Financing

Financing any big ticket item costs money. The exact cost is usually well hidden within the fine print of a loan contract. You will have two figures in mind: the monthly payment and the total cost.

Monthly payments amortize (pay back) a loan. They include a portion of the principle and a portion of the interest of the entire loan. How much of each is determined by type of loan.

The interest rate is the price paid for use of another person's money. This applies whether you borrow from a bank, loan company, or individual. Two forms of interest are available: fixed and variable. Fixed means a single loan interest rate is stated in the contract and remains unchanged for the life of the contract. Variable rate interest may go up or down during the life of the loan contract, normally tracking the prime lending rate.

A variable rate loan could experience higher monthly payments due to a rise in the prime interest rate. When purchasing an airplane, or any other big ticket item, always plan for the worst when the loan is based upon a variable interest rate. A fixed rate loan is best because you know from month to month what the payment is.

A mixture of fixed and variable interest rates is the variable term loan which sets a never changing monthly payment for the life of the contract. However, the length of the contract can vary depending on the prime interest rate. If the rate rises, your interest portion of the repayment plan rises. In the long run you will owe more money, hence your loan payment plan will be extended, at the set monthly payment, for the number of months necessary to pay all the accrued interest.

Some loan contracts have a balloon payment tacked onto the end to keep monthly payments low. Let's say you have a $20,000 loan with low payments. During the life of the contract the sum total of the payments, less the interest, only amortized $5,000 of the principle. You must pay the remaining $15,000 as the last payment.

Another nasty surprise often found in loan contracts is the prepayment penalty clause. Generally, this means you will have to pay a premium to complete the loan contract at a date earlier than planned. The prepayment clause will call for such a stiff penalty for early payment that there will be no savings realized by early payoff. The latter could be expensive if the airplane is sold prior to completing the loan contract.

2

Making Decisions

BEFORE PURCHASING AN AIRPLANE give serious thought to usage. Be very objective and completely honest. Remember you are going to have this airplane for a long time and you want to be very satisfied with it.

Questions and Answers

Other books have been written and many stories told about purchasing used airplanes. They all boil down to a few simple questions that will help select the basic airplane you are going to need.

Planned Use

Is your flying for sport (evenings and weekends), transportation (business and family outings), or hauling (moving light cargo)?

Flying Skills

What are your real flying skills? Are you most comfortable with a low performance tricycle gear airplane? Or are you well qualified in a high performance retractable? Consider skills you presently have and skills you plan to acquire. Pilot skills should weigh heavily upon the selection of an airplane.

Passengers

How many people fly with you? Is most flying solo or perhaps with your wife or a flying buddy? Do you only occasionally take the entire family for a day of adventure? If renting a two-place plane, and it suits your needs, then stay in the two-place category. Some two-placers are quite high performance; don't think you will be limited by selecting a two-place airplane. When the infrequent need for a larger airplane arises, rent one.

Distance Traveled

How far do you generally fly? Are most of your flights fewer than 100 miles or frequently hundreds of miles? Be tough with the answers. Remember objectivity.

Speed

Closely related to the issue of distance traveled is the question of speed. How soon do you really need to get there? If you are going to fly for business a fast plane might be necessary. However, remember that speed usually equates to larger engines, more complex airplanes, and the resulting higher costs.

VFR/IFR

Avionics add to the value of a used airplane; they also add to the required maintenance. Black boxes are expensive to fix. If you need them, then by all means get them. If you are not instrument rated, or don't fly in bad weather, here is a good place to save money when acquiring and maintaining an airplane. Buy only what you need.

Airports

The airports that you will fly in and out of will influence the choice of airplanes. If flying from paved runways, then the airplane choice is wide open. However, if flying from rough grass strips or unimproved areas, select an airplane that will stand up to the use and abuse that unimproved airports will dish out.

Insight

After studying and answering these questions you should have the basic requirements of a prospective airplane in mind. If you have been completely honest, you are well on the way to purchasing an airplane that will suit your individual needs.

Of course, merely having a basic airplane in mind will not do for very long. There are many more factors to be considered before a final choice can be made.

Maintenance

Maintenance is one of aviation's biggest bugaboos. All airplanes require it, it's just that some require more than others. Basic automobile maintenance usually equates to fill it up, check the oil and water, then drive away. Airplanes are quite different: annual inspections (required by regulation), minor repairs, major repairs, and numerous additional details.

Maintenance should weigh heavily in decision making. The more complex an airplane, the more maintenance dollars you will spend. Consider the different maintenance requirements of the following choices:

- Airframe coverings may be metal or fabric. Fabric will need periodic replacement. Metal is for life.
- Landing gear is fixed or retractable. Retractable gear has many moving parts. These parts wear and will eventually need repair or replacement.
- Propellers are available as fixed-pitch or constant-speed. The latter might have as many as 200 parts. Which do you think will be the least expensive to maintain?
- Engines are often modified for performance reasons: turbo-charging. Modifications cost money to maintain and in most cases will reduce the TBO.

These four comparative examples illustrate that simple means less expensive. (I'll not use the word cheap because there is nothing cheap about airplane maintenance. All airplane maintenance is, in varying degrees, expensive.) When it comes to airplane equipment: If you don't have it, it can't break, and therefore it will cost nothing to maintain.

Expensive Forced Maintenance

Along with routine maintenance the AD (airworthiness directive) must be considered, as well as the SDR (service difficulty report).

Airworthiness Directives

Unfortunately, airplanes are not perfect in design or manufacture. They will, from time to time, require inspection/repairs/service as a result of unforeseen manufacturing problems. These problems generally affect a large number of a particular make/model. The required procedures set forth in ADs are described in FAR Part 39, and must be complied with.

The AD may be a simple one-time inspection, a periodic inspection (i.e., every 50 hours of operation), or a major modification to the airframe or engine. Some ADs are inexpensive, involving only minor inspections; others can be very expensive, involving extensive engine or airframe modifications or repairs.

ADs are not handled like automobile recalls. The aircraft manufacturer isn't normally responsible for the costs. Sometimes the manufacturers will offer the parts and/or labor free of charge, but don't count on it. Even though ADs correct deficient design or poor quality control of parts or workmanship, AD compliance is usually paid for by the owner. The manufacturer may even profit from selling the parts necessary to comply with the AD. (There is no large consumer voice involving aircraft manufacturer responsibility.)

Records of AD compliance become a part of the aircraft logbooks. When looking at an airplane, with purchase in mind, check for AD compliance in the applicable logbooks.

Mechanics and the FAA maintain AD files. A compliance check is part of the annual inspection. A brief list of ADs appears in Appendix A.

Service Difficulty Reports

SDRs are prepared by the FAA from malfunction or defect reports (MDRs) that are submitted by owners, pilots, and mechanics. SDRs are not the word of law like ADs, however, they should be referenced.

Some aircraft are so laden with ADs and SDRs that they fairly scream. Check out the proposed selection. Better to be discouraged now, at decision making time, than discouraged later when it's time to spend dollars for all the required service work.

AD and SDR information specific to a particular make/model aircraft is available through the Aircraft Owners and Pilots Association. (See AOPA information in Chapter 5.)

Insurability

Insurance companies are in business to make money by providing a service called *coverage*. Payment for this coverage is the insurance *premium*. Premiums are based upon two main factors: the pilot and the airplane.

The pilot factor is determined by the total number of hours flown, types of airplanes flown, ratings, and violation history.

The airplane factor is determined by past loss ratio history for that particular make and model. Availability of replacement parts in the event of a loss is considered. Availability is directly related to the total number of the make and model manufactured. Orphan airplanes—those long out of production—are expensive to insure and maintain because of parts problems.

Resale

What is the possibility of quick resale near the purchase price? It is very important, if you are concerned with resale, to consider current values and, in the event you need money in a hurry, how quickly the airplane will sell.

An orphan airplane is sometimes a very economical buy, but not usually a hot seller. If you purchase one, understand that when the time comes to sell it, you may have to sell cheap, or wait a long time to find a buyer. This is not to say I don't recommend orphans, just realize what you are getting into. If resale is a prime concern, then buy a Cessna or Piper basic four-place fixed-gear airplane.

Watch Out for Bargains

There are few bargains in the world and the airplane business is no exception to the rule. Any plane selling for a price that is seemingly lower than it should be probably has a serious flaw.

Even if you know of the flaw and feel it is not as bad as it sounds, get some professional advice before buying a bargain airplane.

Fixing even simple things on an airplane generally calls for the prime ingredient called money: lots of it. For example, the interior of a typical four-place airplane can cost more than $3,000 to be replaced; of course you could get the materials and do the work yourself for about $1,000. This is a good savings, until you find it takes the better part of the summer to get the job done right. The part of summer when you expected to take a flying vacation.

Are We Having Fun Yet?

If you are still being objective and honest with yourself, you are now ready to look at the types of aircraft currently available on the used market and evaluate them with respect to individual needs. Remember the final objective in the purchase of a used airplane is to fulfill personal desires with an airplane that is affordable to own and operate and not overtax your flying skills.

A Short Hangar Story

Some years back a friend of mine earned his private pilot's license, then bought an airplane. He learned to fly in a Cessna 150 but he bought a Cessna 180—a taildragger with a big engine that can be a fire-breathing dragon in inexperienced hands. The airplane dealer checked him out in the 180 and, after paying high insurance rates based upon his lack of proficiency in that type of airplane, he went out to play bush pilot.

It only took a couple of flights for his inexperience to catch up with him, and the plane took him for an unforgettable ride across the infield during a landing. It scared him so badly that the airplane sat unused for months, costing tie down fees, insurance premiums, and all the other things called fixed costs.

Finally I flew it a few times, then demonstrated and sold it. He later bought a Cessna 172 and I guess lived happily ever after.

The point I am trying to make is: Don't buy more airplane than you can handle, because if you can't handle it, you won't enjoy it, and you won't fly it.

3

Valuations

CERTAIN HIGH-DOLLAR ITEMS must be judged very carefully to place an accurate value on an airplane: airframe, engine(s), modifications, and avionics. The engine's life expectancy is the TBO, or time between overhauls. An airframe might experience fatigue or corrosion. Many airplanes have been modified for better performance or for a particular use. Modern avionics become outdated as electronics technology improves with the passing of each year.

Engines

Engines are the most expensive single item attached to an airplane. When it fails you will go no place and will need to spend heaps of money to get it fixed. Valuation of the engine on a used airplane is an important part of the overall value of an airplane.

Engine Buzzwords

TBO (time between overhaul). Engine manufacturer's recommended maximum engine life. It has no legal bearing on airplanes not used in commercial service: it's only an indicator. Many well-cared for engines last hundreds of hours beyond TBO, but not all.

Remanufacture. Disassembly, repair, alteration, inspection, cleaning and reassembly of an engine. This includes bringing all specifications back to factory-new limits. A factory remanufactured engine comes with a new logbook and zero time.

Overhaul. Disassembly, repair, inspection, cleaning, and reassembly of an engine. The work may be performed to new limits or to service limits.

Top overhaul. Rebuilding the head assemblies but not the entire engine. In other words, the case of the engine is not opened, only the cylinders are removed. A top overhaul can be utilized to bring oil burning and/or low compression engines within specifications. It is a method of stretching the life of an otherwise sound engine.

New limits. Dimensions and specifications used when constructing a new engine. Parts meeting these specifications will normally reach TBO with no further attention, except for routine maintenance.

Service limits. Dimensions and specifications below which use is forbidden. Many used parts will fit into this category, but they are unlikely to last the full TBO because they are partially worn.

Nitriding. Method of hardening cylinder barrels and crankshafts. The purpose is to reduce wear, thereby extending the useful life of the part.

Chrome plating. Process that brings the internal dimensions of a cylinder back to specifications. It produces a hard, machinable, and long-lasting surface. Break-in time for a chromed engine is longer than for normal engines. An advantage of chrome plating is resistance to destructive oxidation (rust) within combustion chambers.

Magnaflux/Magnaglow. Examinations that detect invisible defects in ferrous metals (cracks). Parts normally Magnafluxed/Magnaglowed are crankshafts, camshafts, piston pins, rocker arms, and the like.

Cylinder codes. Modified cylinders are coded with paint or banding. The color of the paint or band is a clue about the physical properties of the cylinder: orange indicates a chrome plate cylinder barrel; blue indicates a nitride cylinder barrel; green indicates cylinder barrel is .010 oversize; and yellow indicates .020 oversize.

Used Engines

Many airplane ads proudly state the hours on the engine, for instance 745 SMOH, which means 745 hours of use since the engine was overhauled. Not stated is useage or thoroughness of overhaul. Few standards exist.

Time and Value

The time (hours) since new or overhaul is an important factor when placing value on an airplane. The recommended TBO, less the hours currently on the engine, is the remaining time.

Three basic terms are usually used when referring to time on an airplane engine: low time, first third of TBO; mid time, second third of TBO; and high time, last third of TBO.

Naturally, other variables come into play when referring to TBO: Are the hours on the engine since new, remanufacture, or overhaul? What type of flying has the engine seen? Was it flown on a regular basis? What kind of maintenance did the engine get? The logbook should be of some help when answering any questions about maintenance (Fig. 3-1).

Airplanes that have not been flown on a regular basis, nor maintained in a like fashion, will never reach full TBO. Manufacturers refer to regular usage as 20 to 40 hours monthly.

However, few privately owned airplanes meet the upper limits of this requirement. Let's face it, most of us don't have the time or money required for

Value	Time	Status	Flying Type	TBO
Poor	1800	New	Training	2000
Good	1000	New	X-country	1800
Fair	800	New	Training	2000
Excell	500	New	X-country	2000
Vy Poor	1800	SMOH	Any type	2000
Fair	1000	SMOH	X-country	1800
Poor	1000	SMOH	Training	2000
Good	500	SMOH	X-country	2000

Fig. 3-1. Value of the engine by comparing the TIME/TBO with the type of flying.

such constant use. This 20 to 40 hours monthly equates to 240 to 480 hours yearly. That's a lot of flying.

When an engine isn't operated, acids and moisture in the oil will oxidize (rust) engine components. In addition, the lack of lubricant movement will cause the seals to dry out. Left long enough, the engine will seize and no longer be operable.

Abuse is just as hard on engines as no use. Hard climbs and fast descents cause abnormal heating and cooling conditions and are extremely destructive to air-cooled engines. Training aircraft often exhibit this trait due to intensive take-off and landing practice. Naturally, preventive maintenance—such as changing spark plugs and oil—should have been accomplished and logged throughout the engine's life (i.e., oil changes, plug changes, etc.). All maintenance must be logged, so say the FARs *(Federal Aviation Regulations)*.

Beware of the engine that has just a few hours since overhaul. Perhaps something is not right with the overhaul, or it was a very cheap job, just to make the plane more salable.

When it comes to overhauls, seek out the large shops that specialize in aircraft engine rebuilding. I'm not saying that the local FBO can't do a good job; I just feel that the large organizations specializing in this work have more experience and equipment. In addition, they have reputations to maintain and most will back you in the event of difficulties.

Engines are expensive to rebuild or overhaul. Here are typical costs for a complete overhaul (based on current average pricing): O-200 $5,000; O-300 $7,200; O-320 $6,000; O-360 $7,000; O-470 $8,000; IO-520 $10,000; and TIO-540 $14,000.

Airframes

General aviation has two airframes: all-metal and tube-and-fabric. With few exceptions, the latter are only found on classic airplanes. Most modern airplanes are all-metal construction.

The advantage of all-metal construction is easier outdoor storage and the fact that recovering is never necessary. The disadvantage is expensive repairs and outrageous painting costs (Fig. 3-2).

Tube and fabric airplanes are very expensive to recover, not as efficient in flight, and do not weather well outside.

Total hours in operation affects the value of an airframe. It stands to reason that when anything is exposed to the rigors of stress and strain, like airframes, sooner or later it will fail. Corrosion might become a problem and might be very expensive to repair.

If an airframe has been severely damaged the airplane's value might be reduced. Did repairs rebuild the plane like new or was it just make do? (To properly rebuild a severely damaged airplane, jigs assure the proper alignment of all parts.) Consider usage: Was it a trainer, crop duster, patrol, or rental airplane? If so, the hours are likely high and the usage rough.

Recognize there is no such thing in aviation as a little fixing up to remedy small problems. Upgrading an interior, paint, windows, and the like, is very expensive. Therefore, a plane that needs a little fix up is worth less money than a plane that needs no fix up.

Fig. 3-2. Painting an airplane is very expensive due to the hand labor involved.

Modifications

Many airplanes found on today's market are in need of modifications to update or otherwise improve them. Modifications can take many forms, however, and normally improve performance, attain greater economy of operation, or modernize the appearance of the plane. Most modifications require an STC (supplemental type certificate). Modifications cost hundreds or thousands of dollars.

Short Takeoff and Landing

Short takeoff and landing (STOL) conversions are perhaps king of all the modifications available to the airplane owner. The typical STOL modification changes the shape of the wing (usually a leading edge cuff), the addition of stall fences (to prevent air flow disruption from proceeding along the length of the wing), gap seals, and wingtips, and perhaps an increase in power. Results can be spectacular; they are also quite expensive.

Power

Power modification is the second most popular improvement made to airplanes and is often done in conjunction with STOL modifications. Engine replacement increases the useful load and flight performance figures of the aircraft. A power modification appears very costly but it is often no more expensive than a quality engine overhaul.

Wing Tips

Wing tips are changed to increase performance. Dr. Sighard Hoerner, Ph.D., designed a high-performance wingtip for the U.S. Navy that led to the development of improved general aviation wingtips. A properly designed wingtip can provide an increase of three to five mph in cruise speed and a small increase in climb performance, but most important are the improved low-speed handling characteristics: 10 to 20 percent reduction in takeoff roll, four to five mph lower stall speed, and improved slow-flight handling. Installation time might be as low as two to three hours. This is usually an inexpensive modification (Fig. 3-3).

Landing Gear

Taildragger conversions have become popular among owners of Cessna 150, 152, and 172 aircraft.

The nosewheel is removed, the main gear moved forward, and a tailwheel installed. Performance benefits of 8-10 mph increase in cruise, shorter takeoff distances, and better rough-field handling are claimed. I feel if a rough-field machine is necessary, then a proper STOL and increased power modification should also be made. This will cost a large amount of money, and the 150/152/172 owner would be well advised to consider the possibility of purchasing a more

Fig. 3-3. Wing tips can improve slow flight, landing, and takeoff characteristics.

appropriate aircraft for the job, such as a Super Cub, Cessna 180 or 185, or Maule.

Gap Seals

Gap seals are extensions of the lower wing surface from the rear spar to the leading edge of the flap and/or aileron. They cover several square feet of open space, allowing a smoother flow of air around the wing. This reduction of drag causes the aircraft to cruise from 1-3 mph faster and stall from 5-8 mph slower. Gap seals are often part of a STOL installation.

Auto Fuels

Considerable controversy surrounds the use of auto fuels (sometimes referred to as mogas) in certified aircraft engines. There are pros and cons for both sides, however I feel that it is up to the aircraft owner to make choices about the use of non-aviation fuels.

Economy is the center of mogas usage. Unleaded auto fuel is certainly less expensive than 100LL and it does appear to operate well in the older engines that require 80 octane fuel. This gives twofold savings: once at the pump and again at overhaul.

If you have a storage tank and pump, it might be advantageous to utilize auto fuel. It will be easier to locate a jobber willing to keep an auto fuel storage tank filled than it will be to find an avgas supplier willing to make small deliveries; this is particularly true at private airstrips.

Many FBOs are reluctant to make auto fuel available for reasons like product liability and less profit, however, this is slowly changing.

Engine manufacturers claim the use of auto fuel will void warranty service, but few airplanes using mogas have a new engine.

Prior to purchasing an airplane with an auto fuel STC or acquiring the STC for a plane, check with an insurance carrier and get their approval in writing.

For further information about legal use of auto fuels in an airplane contact:

Experimental Aircraft Association
Wittman Airfield
Oshkosh, WI 54903

Petersen Aviation, Inc.
Rt. 1 Box 18
Minden, NE 68959

Fuel Tanks

Larger or auxiliary fuel tanks are sometimes installed to increase operational range.

Avionics

New airplanes have instrument panels that resemble spaceship panels, certainly showing more than needed for simple flying. However, what appears complex is actually straightforward in operation and is designed to make flying and navigation easier.

Modern Equipment

Avionics today are full of capabilities: digital displays, computerized functions, small size. They are about as similar to past equipment as a portable computer is to a pad and pencil. Price-wise the new equipment represents bargains never before seen.

A good navcom cost approximately $1,800 15 years ago. This gave you 200 navigation channels and 360 communication channels. The radio was panel-mounted, and the VOR display (CDI) was mounted separately. Considering that as a rule of thumb most consumer goods today cost three times what they did 15 years ago, that navcom would cost $5,400 today.

Electronics have changed in the past years. Today the radio for $1,800 (and, in many cases, a good deal less) is a navcom with the same 200 navigation channels, a necessary increase to 720 communication channels, digital display, user-programmable memory channels, and a built-in CDI. It occupies a smaller area and uses far less power.

Don't let the price fool you. I've been watching the market moving toward the under-$1,000 complete high-quality navcom.

Avionics Buzzwords

It seems that everything about aviation is identified in abbreviations or buzzwords.

COMM or COM: a VHF transceiver for voice radio communications.
NAV: a VHF navigation receiver.
NAV/COMM: a combination of a comm and nav in one unit.
CDI: course deviation indicator.
LOC/GS: localizer/glide slope.
XPNDR: transponder (should include altitude reporting).
ADF: automatic direction finder.
DME: distance measuring equipment.
RNAV: random area navigation.
LORAN-C: a computer/receiver navigation system.
A-Panel: audio panel.
ELT: emergency locator transmitter.
MBR: marker beacon receiver.
HT: handheld transceiver.

VFR Flying

Equip a plane for VFR flying based upon where you fly: large airports or small uncontrolled fields. Equipment could limit you, particularly with today's TCA and ARSA requirements.

At the barest minimum, VFR operation requires a navcom, transponder, and ELT. You could do with only the ELT, but there is just no sense to it except flying around the patch.

Not too many years ago most cross-country flying was pilotage: reading charts and looking out the windows for checkpoints. Today's aviator has become accustomed to the advantages of modern navigation systems.

Take advantage of the modern navigation system and the safety it can provide with a VFR installation that includes a 720-channel navcom, transponder, ELT, and Loran-C. With this installation I can be comfortable and go pretty much wherever I desire.

IFR Flying

Flying IFR requires considerably more equipment that will represent a much higher cash investment. IFR operations usually require the following minimum equipment:

Dual navcom (720 channel)   Clock
MBR   ADF

LOC/GS   LORAN-C
Transponder   Audio Panel
ELT   DME

Several options are available to fill vacant spots on the instrument panel: some more expensive than others: some more practical than others; the two do not necessarily equate.

New Avionics

New equipment is state-of-the-art, offering the newest innovations, best reliability, and a warranty. An additional benefit of new equipment is new solid-state electronics units are physically smaller and draw considerably less electric power than tube-type predecessors. This is extremely important for the person seeking a full panel in a small plane.

Used Avionics

Used avionics can be purchased from dealers or individuals. *Trade-A-Plane* is a good source of used equipment. However, a few words of caution about used avionics: don't purchase anything with tubes in it or if it's more than six years old. If the manufacturer is out of business, don't buy it; parts could be a real problem.

Reconditioned Avionics

Several companies advertise reconditioned avionics at bargain, or at least low, prices. This equipment has been removed from service and completely checked out by an avionics shop. Parts that have failed, are near failure, or are likely to fail have been replaced.

However, you still get what you pay for: reconditioned is not new, not even remanufactured. It is used. Everything in the unit has been used, but not everything will be replaced during reconditioning. You will have some new parts and some old parts.

Reconditioned equipment purchases make sense for the budget-minded owner. Reconditioned radios do offer a fair-priced buy and usually carry a warranty. Few pieces of reconditioned equipment will exceed six or seven years age.

Computerized Navigation

Long range navigation, called Loran, has been around for many years. It is based upon low-frequency radio signals, rather than the VHF (very high frequency) signals normally associated with FAA navaids. Although not originally intended for general aviation, its use has become common place because of computer-based Loran-C.

Propagation properties of radio waves at the frequencies utilized by Loran are not limited by line-of-sight range. This gives distinct advantages over normal

VHF navaids like VORs. Unlike a VOR's limited range of 50 to 100 miles, Loran is usable many hundreds of miles from the actual transmitting station. This can be very practical for typical general aviation operations.

A Loran-C receiver can cost from less than $1,000 to more than $4,000. Installation can be several hundred additional dollars.

Some pilots view the instrument panel as a functional device, others see it as a statement made by the owner. In either case, care must be taken when filling up the panel. Don't install instrumentation merely for the sake of filling holes. Plan it well and make it functional and easy to use. Above all else, do it economically.

Final Valuation of a Plane

When you have looked at the engine, airframe, any modifications, and the avionics of an airplane, you should have a general feel for the overall worth of the airplane. Compare it to other airplanes available and compare their overall worth to your prospect.

A good rule of thumb for the selling price of an airplane is when the dollar value the seller places upon his valued possession is equaled by the top amount offered by the prospective purchaser for the same box of rocks.

4

Before You Purchase

SEARCHING FOR A GOOD USED AIRPLANE can be frustrating. A business might contract with an airplane broker and let him do all the leg work but most individuals elect to do the work themselves. After all, frustrating or not, that's part of airplane ownership.

The Search

Many models and price ranges are available, so the purchaser is encouraged to set a range of his expectations. This could be based upon features desired, options available, or most likely the cash available for such a purchase. (See Chapter 2 for information about decision making.)

Usually, one starts looking for a used airplane at his home field. If you know the FBO and feel comfortable with him, then perhaps this is a good way to search; tell him what you are looking for. Often an FBO will know about airplanes for sale, advertised and unadvertised. After all, he is an insider to the business.

If there is nothing of interest at your airport, then broaden the search. Check the bulletin boards at other nearby airports. Ask around while you're there, then walk around and look for airplanes with For Sale signs in the windows. You could even put an Airplane Wanted ad on the bulletin boards (Fig. 4-1).

Local newspapers sometimes have airplanes listed in the classified ads. However, in this day of specialization, several publications have become leaders in airplane advertising. Among them are:

Airworthy Publishing
210 Lorna Sq., Suite 123
Birmingham, AL 35216

Plane & Pilot News
7570 Peck Rd.
Ravenna, OH 44266

The Aircraft Bulletin
50 West 34th St., Suite 10A9
New York, NY 10001
(800) 243-7410

Trade-A-Plane
Crossville, TN 38555

Fig. 4-1. Could be you'll see something like this when walking around a small airport.

Other listings of used airplanes can be found in the various flight oriented magazines *AOPA Pilot*, *Flying*, and *Private Pilot*.

Alternate Sources

Three sources of used airplanes have not been mentioned because they all-too-often include airplanes that are not desirable for the individual purchaser to consider.

These sources include repossessions, law enforcement seizure auctions, and government surplus sales. All three have a common thread: you cannot test the airplane and can normally only make a quick inspection, if at all.

Repossession is the safest bet. You are purchasing an airplane that was flying in the civilian fleet. There will be no problems in titling or registering such a plane. Past maintenance may have been scanty, but should be recorded. After all, if an owner can't pay for it, he probably didn't take care of it either.

Remaining sources are far more complicated. The beginner is advised to steer well clear of these aircraft. That is, unless you have a good mechanic and the extra money necessary to make the airplane airworthy and licensable.

Aircraft sold at a seizure auction, or by a government agency, may have few,

few, if any, records. Airworthiness of the entire aircraft, or any part thereof, is in question. The latter being particularly true when purchasing a surplus military airplane.

The military often uses replacement parts that have not been certified for civilian use. This is not to say the parts are defective, only that they are not certified for civilian use. In all cases it is the responsibility of the owner to prove airworthiness.

Obtaining a clear title is not the problem because the selling agency will provide it. Usually, payment is expected in cash, and you must remove the airplane immediately or within a few days.

The following agencies sell used airplanes to the public:

Defense Surplus Sales Office
Dept. RK-24
P.O. Box 1370
Battle Creek, MI 49016

United States Marshal's Service
United States Customs Service
Drug Enforcement Agency
(Contact your respective local office.)

Reading the Ads

Most airplane ads use various familiar abbreviations. The abbreviations describe the individual airplane and tell how it is equipped. Ads have a telephone number, but seldom the location of the airplane. The clue is the area code.

Here's a sample ad:

68 C182, 2243TT,
763 SMOH, Oct ANN,
FGP, Dual NAV/COM,
GS, MB, ELT, Mode C
XPNDR, NDH.
$20,750 firm.
607-555-1234.

Translated: For sale, a 1968 Cessna 182 airplane with 2,243 total hours on the airframe and an engine with 763 hours since a major overhaul. The next annual inspection is due in October. It is equipped with a full gyro instrument panel, has two navigation and communication radios, a glideslope receiver and indicator, a marker beacon receiver, an emergency locator transmitter, Mode-C transponder, and best of all the airplane has no damage history. The price is $20,750, and the seller claims he will not bargain. (Most do, however.) Lastly is the telephone number.

A lot of information was packed inside those seven little lines. The abbreviations tell the story about the airplane. Following is a list of the more commonly used advertising abbreviations.

AD   airworthiness directive
ADF   automatic direction finder

AF	airframe
AF&E	airframe and engine
ALT	altimeter
ANN	annual inspection
ANNUAL	annual inspection
AP	autopilot
ASI	airspeed indicator
A&E	airframe and engine
A/P	autopilot
BAT	battery
B&W	black and white
CAT	carburetor air temperature
CHT	cylinder-head temperature
COMM	communications radio
CS	constant-speed propeller
C/S	constant-speed propeller
C/W	complied with
DBL	double
DG	directional gyro
DME	distance measuring equipment
FAC	factory
FBO	fixed base operator
FGP	full gyro panel
FWF	firewall forward
GAL	gallons
GPH	gallons per hour
GS	glideslope
HD	heavy-duty
HP	horsepower
HSI	horizontal situation indicator
HVY	heavy
IFR	instrument flight rules
ILS	instrument landing system
INS	instrument navigation system
INSP	inspection
INST	instrument
KTS	knots

L	left
LDG	landing
LE	left engine
LED	light-emitting diode
LH	left-hand
LIC	license
LOC	localizer
LTS	lights
L&R	left and right
MB	marker beacon
MBR	marker beacon receiver
MP	manifold pressure
MPH	miles per hour
MOD	modification
NAV	navigation
NAVCOM	navigation/communication radio
NDH	no damage history
OAT	outside air temperature
OX	oxygen
O2	oxygen
PMA	parts manufacture approval
PROP	propeller
PSI	pounds per square inch
R	right
RC	rate of climb
REMAN	remanufactured
REPALT	reporting altimeter
RH	right-hand
RMFD	remanufactured
RMFG	remanufactured
RNAV	random area navigation
ROC	rate of climb
SAFOH	since airframe overhaul
SCMOH	since (chrome/complete) major overhaul
SEL	single-engine land
SFACNEW	since factory new
SFN	since factory new
SFNE	since factory new engine
SFREM	since factory remanufacture

SFREMAN	since factory remanufacture
SFRMFG	since factory remanufacture
SMOH	since major overhaul
SNEW	since new
SPOH	since propeller overhaul
STC	supplemental type certificate
STOH	since top overhaul
STOL	shore takeoff and landing
TAS	true airspeed
TBO	time between overhauls
TLX	Telex
TNSP	transponder
TNSPNDR	transponder
TSN	time since new
TSO	technical service order
TT	total time
TTAF	total time airframe
TTA&E	total time airframe and engine
TTE	total time engine
TTSN	total time since new
TXP	transponder
T&B	turn and bank
VAC	vacuum
VFR	visual flight rules
VHF	very high frequency
VOR	visual omni range
XC	cross-country
XMTR	transmitter
XPDR	transponder
XPNDR	transponder
3LMB	three-light marker beacon

Don't forget the value of the area code in the telephone number because it indicates where the plane is located and that could be very important. After all, you may not want to travel a couple of thousand miles to look at it. Another thought is effect of climatic conditions on the airplane.

Climate affects airplanes considerably. Life along a sea coast can cause serious corrosion problems; sand of the Southwest will take its toll on the gyros, and the cold of the North can cause excessive engine wear. These problems can be avoided if the airplane was well cared for and treated properly.

United States Telephone Area Codes

201	NJ north	203	CT
202	Washington, DC	205	AL

206	WA west	503	OR
207	ME	504	LA east
208	ID	505	NM
209	CA Fresno	507	MN south
212	New York City	509	WA east
213	CA Los Angeles	512	TX south central
214	TX Dallas	513	OH southwest
215	PA east	515	IA central
216	OH northeast	516	NY Long Island
217	IL central	517	MI central
218	MN north	518	NY northeast
219	IN north		
		601	MS
301	MD	602	AZ
302	DE	603	NH
303	CO	605	SD
304	WV	606	KY east
305	FL southeast	607	NY south central
307	WY	608	WI southwest
308	NE west	609	NJ south
309	IL Peoria area	612	MN central
312	IL northeast	614	OH southeast
313	MI east	615	TN east
314	MO east	616	MI west
315	NY north central	617	MA east
316	KS south	618	IL south
317	IN central	619	CA southeast
318	LA west		
319	IA east		
		701	ND
401	RI	702	NV
402	NE east	703	VA north and west
404	GA north	704	NC west
405	OK west	707	CA Santa Rosa area
406	MT	712	IA west
408	CA San Jose area	713	TX Houston
409	TX southwest	714	CA southwest
412	PA southwest	715	WI north
413	MA west	716	NY west
414	WI east	717	PA central
415	CA San Francisco	718	NY southeast and NYC
417	MO southwest		
419	OH northwest	801	UT
		802	VT
501	AR	803	SC
502	KY west	804	VA southeast

805	CA west central	904	FL north
806	TX northwest	906	MI northwest
808	HI	907	AK
812	IN south	912	GA south
813	FL southwest	913	KS north
814	PA northwest and central	914	NY southeast
815	IL north central	915	TX southwest
816	MO northwest	916	CA northwest
817	TX north central	918	OK northeast
818	CA southwest	919	NC east
901	TN west		

The Telephone Inquiry

If you see an airplane listed in printed advertising, or on a bulletin board, you will need to make contact with the owner. Call on the telephone. Sounds simple enough, but first consider what you are going to ask.

Don't pretend to be an expert, but, don't be a tire kicker either. The owner wants to sell his airplane, not relive past experiences.

Ask the year, make, and model of the plane. You would be surprised at the number of mistakes I see in airplane ads that appear in the trade magazines and papers. This way you are sure you are both talking about the same airplane Sometimes an owner will have more than one airplane for sale. He might even be a broker.

Make notes as you ask:

☐ Total hours on the airframe.
☐ Make and type of engine.
☐ Hours on the engine since new.
☐ Hours since the last overhaul.
☐ What type of overhaul.
☐ Damage history.
☐ Asking price.
☐ Where it can be seen.

Sometimes an owner who is hot to sell will fly the airplane to you for inspection. Don't ask someone to do this unless you are serious and are able (have the money) to purchase it.

Pre-purchase Inspection

The object of a pre-purchase inspection of a used airplane is to preclude the purchase of a dog. No one wants to buy someone else's troubles. The pre-purchase inspection must be completed in an orderly, well planned manner. Take your time during this inspection, for these few minutes could well save you thousands of dollars later.

The very first item of inspection is the most-asked question of anyone selling anything: Why are you selling it? Fortunately, most people answer honestly. Often the owner is moving up to a larger airplane, and if so he will start to tell you all about his new prospective purchase. Listen to him, you can learn a lot about the owner by what he says. You can gain insight into his flying habits and how he treated the plane you are considering purchasing.

Perhaps he has other commitments: spouse says sell or he can no longer afford the plane. These can be to your advantage, as he is probably anxious to sell. One warning: If the seller is having financial difficulties, consider the quality of maintenance performed on the airplane.

Ask the seller if he knows of any problems or defects with the airplane. Again, he will probably be honest, but there could be things he doesn't know about.

Remember: Buyer beware! It's your money and your safety.

Definitions

Airworthy. The airplane must conform to the original type certificate, or those STCs (supplemental type certificates) issued for this particular airplane (by serial number). In addition, the airplane must be in safe operating condition relative to wear and deterioration.

Annual Inspection. All small airplanes must be inspected annually by an FAA-certified airframe and powerplant (A&P) mechanic who holds an IA (inspection authorization), by an FAA-certified repair station, or by the airplane's manufacturer. This is a complete inspection of the airframe, powerplant, and all sub-assemblies.

100-Hour Inspection. Is an inspection made every 100 hours of the same scope as the annual. It is required on all commercially operated small airplanes (rental, training, air taxi). This inspection may be performed by an A&P without an IA rating. An annual inspection will fulfill the 100-hour requirement, but the reverse is not true.

Preflight Inspection. A thorough inspection, by the pilot, of an aircraft prior to flight. The purpose is to spot obvious discrepancies by inspection of the exterior, interior, and engine of the airplane.

Preventive Maintenance. FAR Part 43 lists a number of airplane maintenance operations that are considered preventive in nature and may be performed by a certificated pilot, provided the airplane is not flown in commercial service. (These operations are described in Chapter 6.)

Repairs and Alterations. Two types of repairs and/or alterations are major and minor. Major repairs and alterations must be approved for a return to service by an A&P mechanic holding an IA authorization, a repair station, or by the FAA. Minor repairs and alterations may be returned to service by an A&P mechanic.

Performing an Inspection

The object of the inspection is to determine what is coming apart on the airplane from the effects of weather, stress, heat, vibration, and friction.

Weather can affect the airplane with many weapons. The arsenal includes, heat, sunlight, rain, snow, wind, temperature, humidity, and ultra-violet light.

Stress includes overloading of the structure causing deformation or outright structural failure, excessive landing weights, high speed maneuvers, turbulence, and hard landings.

Heat—other than heat caused by weather—is engine associated. Usually this affects rubber parts such as hoses and plastic fittings. It can also be associated with heat from a defective exhaust system.

Vibration is caused by the engine or by fluttering control surfaces. Generally it is the engine. Damage from vibration comes in the form of cracks in the aircraft structure or skin.

Friction can affect any moving part of the airplane. Frictional damage can be reduced by the use of lubricants and fixed only by complete repair.

The actual pre-purchase inspection consists of walk-around inspection, test flight, and mechanic's inspection.

Walk-Around

The walk-around is a very thorough pre-flight. It's divided into four simple, logical, steps.

Cabin

Assure that all required paperwork is with the airplane: airworthiness certificate, aircraft registration certificate, FCC radio station license, flight manual or operating limitations, and logbooks (airframe, engine, and propeller), with a current equipment list and weight and balance chart, which are required by the FARs.

While inside the airplane looking for the paperwork, notice the general condition of the interior; does it appear clean, or has it recently been scrubbed after a long period of inattention? Look in the corners, just like buying a used car. Care given the interior is a good indication of what care was given to the remainder of the airplane. If you have purchased used cars in the past, and have been successful, recall past experience for this phase of the inspection.

Look at the instrument panel; does it have what you want and need? Instruments in good condition? Knobs missing and glass faces broken (Fig. 4-2)? Is the equipment all original or updated? Are any updates neat in appearance and workable? Updating, particularly in avionics, is often done haphazardly with results that are neither pleasing to the eye nor workable for the pilot.

Look out the windows: clear, unyellowed, and uncrazed? Side windows are not expensive to replace and you can do it yourself. Windshields are another story and another much higher price.

Check the operation of the doors. They should close and lock with little effort. No outside light should be seen around door edges.

Check the seats for freedom of movement and adjustability. Check the seat tracks and the adjustment locks for damage. Check the carpet for wetness or

Fig. 4-2. If the cabin looks like this, run (don't walk) from it. There is no such thing in aviation as a little fixing for a few dollars.

moldy condition indicating long term exposure to water, possibly inducing corrosion. Open the rear fuselage compartment behind the seats and use a flashlight to look back towards the tail; seek corrosion, dirt, debris, indications of damage, frayed cables, loose fittings, and obviously repaired areas.

Be on the lookout for mouse houses, usually fluffy piles of insulation, fabric, or paper materials. The biggest problem with mouse houses is that mice have bad bathroom manners—they urinate in their beds. Mouse urine is one of the most caustic liquids known to aircraft mechanics because it eats through aluminum like acid. Watch out for it.

Finally, write down times shown on the tachometer and Hobbs meters, then reference them when checking the logbooks.

Airframe

Stand behind the airplane and look at all surfaces comparing one to another. Are they positioned as they should be or does one look out of place compared with the others? This could indicate past damage. Repeat this procedure from each side and from the front of the airplane.

Sight along each flying and control surface looking for dents, bends, or other indications of damage. Dents, wrinkles, or tears of the metal skin might indicate prior damage, or just careless handling. Each discrepancy must be examined very carefully. Total consideration of all dings and dents will reveal if the airplane has had an easy life or a rough life (Fig. 4-3). Wrinkles may indicate hidden structural damage from stress. A mechanic should check any instances of wrinkled skin. Damaged belly skins often indicate a wheels-up landing.

Is the paint in good condition, or is some of it on the ground under the airplane? Paint jobs are expensive, yet necessary for the protection of metal surfaces from corrosive elements, as well as please the eye of the beholder (Fig. 4-4).

Corrosion or rust on surfaces or control systems should be cause for alarm. Corrosion is to aluminum what rust is to iron. It's an oxidation and it is very destructive. Any corrosion or rust should be brought to the attention of a mechanic for judgment.

The landing gear should be checked for evidence of being sprung. Check the tires for signs of unusual wear that might indicate structural damage. Also look at the oleo strut(s) for signs of fluid leakage and proper extension.

Move all control surfaces and check each for damage; they should be free and smooth in movement, not be loose, subject to rattle, or exhibit sidewards movement; they should only move in their designed plane. When the controls

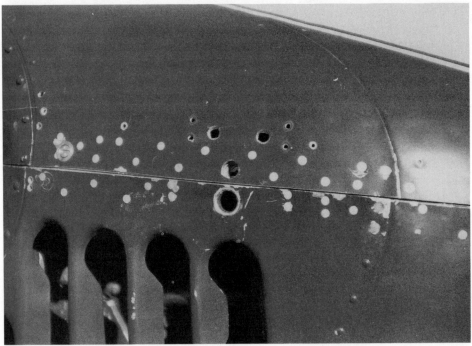

Fig. 4-3. Metal parts in poor condition, such as this cowl, should be avoided.

Fig. 4-4. Repairing peeling paint can break the bank.

are centered, the surfaces should also be centered. If they are not centered, a rigging problem may exist.

Remove the wing root fairings and check the condition of the wiring and hoses inside; look for mouse houses. Also check the wing attachment bolts. Check the antennas for proper mounting and any obvious damage.

Engine

Search for signs of oil leakage when checking the engine. Do this by looking at the engine, inside the cowl, and on the firewall. Oil will be dripping to the ground or onto the nosewheel if the leaks are bad enough. Assume that the seller has cleaned all the old oil drips away and remember that oil leaves stains; look for these stains (Fig. 4-5).

Check all the hoses and lines for signs of deterioration or chafing. Also check all the connections for tightness and signs of leakage. Examine the baffles for proper shape, alignment, and tightness. Baffles control the airflow for engine cooling and if they are improperly positioned the engine will be improperly

Fig. 4-5. Removing the engine cowling makes inspection easy.

cooled. The long-term result of poor baffling is damage to the engine. Check control linkages and cables for obvious damage and easy movement. Check the battery box and battery for corrosion.

Examine the exhaust pipes for rigidity, then reach inside and rub your finger along the inside wall. If your finger comes back perfectly clean, you can be assured that someone has washed the inside of the pipe(s). Washing is done to remove the oily deposits that form there when an engine is burning a lot of oil. Black oily goo indicates problems for a mechanic to pursue (Fig. 4-6).

The condition could be caused by a carburetor in need of adjustment or a large amount of oil blow-by, the latter indicating an engine in need of major expenditures for overhaul. A light gray dusty coating indicates proper operation. Also check for exhaust stains on the belly of the plane to the rear of the stacks (Fig. 4-7). This area has probably been washed, but look anyway. If you find black oily goo, then, as above, see a mechanic.

Inspect the propeller for damage such as nicks, cracks, or gauges. These often small defects cause stress areas on the prop. Any visible damage to a propeller must be checked by a mechanic. Also observe any movement that would indicate propeller looseness at the hub.

Fig. 4-6. Goo on the fingers like this means a mechanic should check the engine.

Fig. 4-7. A dark trail from the exhaust stack calls for a mechanic to check the engine.

Search for oil change or other maintenance stickers. Compare the times indicated on these stickers with those you wrote down from the tachometer and Hobbs meter. Copy the additional sticker information for later referral to logbooks.

Logbooks

If satisfied with what you've seen up to this point, then go back to the cabin and have a seat. Pull out the logbooks and start reading them. Look around the cockpit again.

Ensure that you're looking at the proper logs for this particular aircraft and verify that they are the original logs; sometimes logbooks get lost and replaced with new ones because of carelessness or theft. The latter is the reason that many owners keep photocopies of their logs in the aircraft and the originals in a safe place. The new logs may lack very important information or could be outright frauds. Fraud is a distinct possibility. Be on guard if the original logs are not available. A complete check of the airplane's FAA records will give most of the missing information. Verify serial numbers.

Look in the back of the airframe logbook for AD compliance. Check that it's up-to-date and that any required periodic inspections have been made. Now return to the most recent entry. This will generally be an annual or 100-hour inspection. The annual inspection will be a statement that reads:

March 27, 1988   Total Time: 2,815 hrs.
I certify that this aircraft has been inspected in accordance with an annual inspection and was determined to be in airworthy condition.
[signed]
[IA # 0000000]

From this point back to the first entry in the logbook you'll be looking for similar entries, always keeping track of the total time for continuity purposes and to indicate the regularity of usage (number of hours flown between inspections). Also, you will be looking for indications of major repairs and modifications. This will be flagged by the phrase, Form 337 filed. A copy of this form should be with the logs and will explain what work was accomplished. The work may be described in the logbook. Form 337 is filed with the FAA and copies are a part of the official record of each airplane. They are retrievable from the FAA. Review the current weight and balance sheet with the logbook.

The engine log will be quite similar to the airframe log and will contain information from the annual or 100-hour inspections. Total time will be noted and possibly an indication of time since any overhaul work, although you may have to do some math here. It's quite possible that this log and engine will not be original for the aircraft. As long as the facts are well-documented in the logs, there is no cause for alarm. After all, this would be the case if the original engine was replaced with a remanufactured product.

Check the engine's ADs for compliance and the appropriate entries in the log.

Pay particular attention to the numbers that indicate results of a differential compression check. These numbers will provide a good indication about the overall health of the engine. Each cylinder check is represented by a fraction, with the bottom number always 80. The 80 indicates the air pressure (pounds per square inch) utilized for the check which is the industry standard. The top number is the air pressure that the combustion chamber maintained while being tested; 80 would be perfect, but it is not attainable. The upper figure will always be less.

The reason for the lower number is air pressure loss that results from loose, worn, or broken rings, scored or cracked cylinder walls, or burned, stuck, or poorly seated valves. Mechanics can determine which is the cause and, of course, repair the damage.

Normal readings are usually a minimum of 70/80, and should be uniform (within two or three pounds) for all cylinders. A discrepancy between cylinders could indicate the need for a top overhaul of one or more cylinders. The FAA says that a loss in excess of 25 percent is cause for further investigation. That would be a reading of 60/80, which indicates a very tired engine in need of much work and much money.

If the engine has received a top or major overhaul, there will be a description of the work performed, a date, and the total time on the engine when the work was accomplished.

Read the information from the last oil change, which might contain a statement about debris found on the oil screen or in the oil filter. However, oil changes are often performed by owners, and may or may not be recorded in the log. If recorded, how often? I prefer every 25 hours but 50 is acceptable. Is there a record of oil analysis? If so, ask for it. Oil is cheap insurance for a long engine life.

Get your notebook out and cross-check those meter readings from the instrument panel and the information from the engine maintenance stickers.

The Test Flight

The test flight is a short flight to determine if the airplane feels right to you. It is not meant to be a "rip-snort'n, slam-bang, shake down ride."

I suggest that either the owner or a competent flight instructor accompany you on the test flight to eliminate problems of currency and ratings with the FAA and the owner's insurance company. (He does have insurance doesn't he?) It will also foster better relations with the owner.

Start the engine and pay particular attention to the gauges. Do they jump to life or are they sluggish? Watch the oil pressure gauge in particular. Did the pressure rise within a few seconds of start? Scrutinize the other gauges. Is everything "green?" Watch them during the ground run-up, then again during the takeoff and climb out. Do the numbers match those specified in the operational manual?

Test brake operation during taxi for smoothness and surety.

Operate all avionics. This might require flight to an airport that is equipped for IFR operations. A short cross-country jaunt would be an excellent chance to get familiar with the plane. Observe the gyro instruments for stability. Study the ventilation and heating system for proper operation. Make a few turns, some stalls, and fly level. Does the airplane perform as expected? Can it be trimmed for hands-off flight?

Return to the airport for a couple of landings. Notice proper brake operation and nosewheel shimmy.

Park and open the engine compartment to again look for oil leaks; examine the belly for indications of oil leakage and blow-by. A short flight should be enough to dirty things up again, if they were not dirty to begin with.

Mechanic's Inspection

If you are still satisfied with the airplane and want to pursue the matter further then have it inspected by an A&P or IA. The inspection will not be free, however it could save thousands. The average for a pre-purchase inspection is three to four hours labor at shop rates.

The mechanic will accomplish a search of ADs, a complete look at the logs, and an overall analysis of the airplane. An engine compression check and a bore-scope examination must be performed. The latter is the better means of determining real condition of the engine combustion chambers, looking into each cylinder and viewing the top of the piston, the valves, and the cylinder walls with a device called a borescope.

Points of Advice

Always use your personal mechanic for the pre-purchase inspection; someone you are paying to watch out for your interests, not someone who might have an interest in the sale of the plane, like an employee of the seller.

Get the plane checked even if the annual was just done, unless you know and trust the person who did the inspection.

You might be able to make a deal with the owner regarding the cost of the mechanic's inspection, particularly if an annual is due. It is not uncommon to see airplanes listed for sale with the phrase "annual at date of sale." I'm always leery of this because who knows how complete this annual will be? It is coming with the airplane, done by the seller, as part of the sale: Who is looking out for your interests? I know that the FARs are very explicit in their requirements, but I am not sure that all mechanics do equal work.

If an airplane seller refuses anything that has been mentioned in this chapter, then thank him for his time, walk away, and look elsewhere. Never let a seller control the situation. Your money, your safety, and possibly your very life are at stake. Airplanes are not hot sellers, and there is rarely a line forming to make a purchase. You are the buyer and have the final word.

5

As You Purchase

ASSUMING THAT YOU HAVE COMPLETELY INSPECTED the prospective purchase and found it acceptable at an agreeable price, you're ready to sit down and complete the paperwork that will lead to ownership.

A Trail of Paper

The first step in the paperwork of purchasing an airplane is to assure the craft has a clear title. This is accomplished by a title search.

The Title Search

A title search is accomplished by checking the airplane's individual records at the Mike Monroney Aeronautical Center in Oklahoma City, Oklahoma. These records include title information, chain of ownership, major repair and alteration (Form 337) information, and other data pertinent to a particular airplane. The FAA files this information by N-number.

The object of a title search is to assure that there are no liens or other hidden encumbrances against ownership of the airplane. In fact, it fulfills the same needs as a title search on real estate. The search may be conducted by you, your attorney, or other personal representative.

Most prospective airplane purchasers find it inconvenient to travel to Oklahoma City and search themselves, instead they contract with a third party specializing in this service. One party is AOPA (Aircraft Owners and Pilots Association).

AOPA can also search for liens against engines or propellers, provide a chain of title report, and offers inexpensive title insurance that will protect the purchaser against unrecorded liens, FAA recording mistakes, or other "clouds" on the title. Contact:

AOPA
421 Aviation Way
Frederick, MD 21701
(301) 695-2000

AOPA maintains an office in Oklahoma City where searches occur:

AOPA
Aircraft and Airmen Records Dept.
P.O. Box 19244
Southwest Station
Oklahoma City, OK 73144
(800) 654-4700

Last Look

Prior to full possession of the airplane make one last inspection before signing the documents. This will confirm that no new damage has occurred and that any items in question have been repaired.

Documents

The following documents must be presented with the airplane:
- [ ] Bill of Sale
- [ ] Airworthiness Certificate
- [ ] Airframe logbook
- [ ] Engine logbook
- [ ] Propeller logbook
- [ ] Equipment list (including weight and balance data)
- [ ] Flight manual

Forms to be Completed

AC Form 8050-2, Bill of Sale, is the standard means of recording the transfer of ownership (Fig. 5-1).

Form 8050-1, Aircraft Registration, is filed with the Bill of Sale, or its equivalent. If you are purchasing the airplane under a contract of conditional sale, then that contract must accompany the registration application in lieu of the AC Form 8050-2. The pink copy of the registration is retained by you and will remain in the airplane until the new registration is issued by the FAA (Fig. 5-2).

AC 8050-41, Release of Lien, must be filed by the seller if he still owes money on the airplane.

AC 8050-64, Assignment of Special Registration Number, will be issued upon written request (Fig. 5-3). All N-numbers consist of the prefix N, followed by one to five numbers, one to four numbers and a single-letter suffix, or one to three numbers and a two-letter suffix. A special registration number is similar to a personalized license plate for an automobile—sometimes referred to as a vanity plate.

FCC (Federal Communications Commission) Form 404, Application for Aircraft Radio Station License, must be completed if radio equipment is on board. The tear-off section will remain in the airplane as a temporary authorization until the new license is delivered (Figures 5-4A and 5-4B.).

UNITED STATES OF AMERICA
DEPARTMENT OF TRANSPORTATION ·FEDERAL AVIATION ADMINISTRATION

AIRCRAFT BILL OF SALE

FOR AND IN CONSIDERATION OF $ THE UNDERSIGNED OWNER(S) OF THE FULL LEGAL AND BENEFICIAL TITLE OF THE AIRCRAFT DESCRIBED AS FOLLOWS:

UNITED STATES REGISTRATION NUMBER N

AIRCRAFT MANUFACTURER & MODEL

AIRCRAFT SERIAL No.

DOES THIS   **DAY OF**   **19**

HEREBY SELL, GRANT, TRANSFER AND

DELIVER ALL RIGHTS, TITLE, AND INTERESTS

IN AND TO SUCH AIRCRAFT UNTO:

Do Not Write In This Block
FOR FAA USE ONLY

PURCHASER

NAME AND ADDRESS
(IF INDIVIDUAL(S), GIVE LAST NAME, FIRST NAME, AND MIDDLE INITIAL.)

DEALER CERTIFICATE NUMBER

AND TO   **EXECUTORS, ADMINISTRATORS, AND ASSIGNS TO HAVE AND TO HOLD SINGULARLY THE SAID AIRCRAFT FOREVER, AND WARRANTS THE TITLE THEREOF.**

IN TESTIMONY WHEREOF   **HAVE SET**   **HAND AND SEAL THIS**   **DAY OF**   **19**

NAME (S) OF SELLER (TYPED OR PRINTED)	SIGNATURE (S) (IN INK) (IF EXECUTED FOR CO-OWNERSHIP, ALL MUST SIGN.)	TITLE (TYPED OR PRINTED)

SELLER

ACKNOWLEDGMENT   (NOT REQUIRED FOR PURPOSES OF FAA RECORDING: HOWEVER, MAY BE REQUIRED BY LOCAL LAW FOR VALIDITY OF THE INSTRUMENT.)

ORIGINAL: TO FAA

AC FORM 8050-2 (8-76) (0052-629-0002)

Fig. 5-1. AC Form 8050-2.

FORM APPROVED
OMB No. 2120-0042

UNITED STATES OF AMERICA DEPARTMENT OF TRANSPORTATION
FEDERAL AVIATION ADMINISTRATION-MIKE MONRONEY AERONAUTICAL CENTER
AIRCRAFT REGISTRATION APPLICATION

CERT. ISSUE DATE

UNITED STATES REGISTRATION NUMBER **N**	
AIRCRAFT MANUFACTURER & MODEL	
AIRCRAFT SERIAL No.	FOR FAA USE ONLY

TYPE OF REGISTRATION (Check one box)

☐ 1. Individual ☐ 2. Partnership ☐ 3. Corporation ☐ 4. Co-owner ☐ 5. Gov't. ☐ 8. Non-citizen Corporation

NAME OF APPLICANT (Person(s) shown on evidence of ownership. If individual, give last name, first name, and middle initial.)

TELEPHONE NUMBER: (   )   –

ADDRESS (Permanent mailing address for first applicant listed.)

Number and street: _____

Rural Route: _____   P.O. Box:

CITY	STATE	ZIP CODE

☐ **CHECK HERE IF YOU ARE ONLY REPORTING A CHANGE OF ADDRESS**

ATTENTION! Read the following statement before signing this application. This portion MUST be completed.

A false or dishonest answer to any question in this application may be grounds for punishment by fine and / or imprisonment (U.S. Code, Title 18, Sec. 1001).

CERTIFICATION

I/WE CERTIFY:

(1) That the above aircraft is owned by the undersigned applicant, who is a citizen (including corporations) of the United States.

(For voting trust, give name of trustee: _____), or:

CHECK ONE AS APPROPRIATE:

a. ☐ A resident alien, with alien registration (Form 1-151 or Form 1-551) No. _____

b. ☐ A non-citizen corporation organized and doing business under the laws of (state) _____ and said aircraft is based and primarily used in the United States. Records or flight hours are available for inspection at _____

(2) That the aircraft is not registered under the laws of any foreign country; and
(3) That legal evidence of ownership is attached or has been filed with the Federal Aviation Administration.

NOTE: If executed for co-ownership all applicants must sign. Use reverse side if necessary.

TYPE OR PRINT NAME BELOW SIGNATURE

	SIGNATURE	TITLE	DATE
EACH PART OF THIS APPLICATION MUST BE SIGNED IN INK.	SIGNATURE	TITLE	DATE
	SIGNATURE	TITLE	DATE
	SIGNATURE	TITLE	DATE

NOTE: Pending receipt of the Certificate of Aircraft Registration, the aircraft may be operated for a period not in excess of 90 days, during which time the PINK copy of this application must be carried in the aircraft.

AC Form 8050-1 (8-84) (0052-00-628-9005)

Fig. 5-2. AC Form 8050-1 (keep the pink copy in the plane).

ASSIGNMENT OF SPECIAL REGISTRATION NUMBERS

		Special Registration Number
		N 7316

US Department of Transportation
Federal Aviation Administration

Aircraft Make and Model	BIG DEAL, BA-OH	Present Registration Number
Serial Number	00021	N 123BJ

Issue Date   July 31, 1985

MARION W. WILLIAMS
1000 Whitehouse Road
Oklahoma City, OK 73100

This is your authority to change the United States registration number on the above described aircraft to the special registration number shown.

Carry duplicate of this form in the aircraft together with the old registration certificate as interim authority to operate the aircraft pending receipt of revised certificate of registration. Obtain a revised certificate of airworthiness from your nearest Flight Standards field office.

The latest FAA Form 8130-6 on file is dated

The airworthiness classification and category

SIGN AND RETURN THE ORIGINAL of this form to the FAA Aircraft Registry, within 5 days after placing the special registration number on the aircraft. A revised certificate will then be issued. Unless this authority is used and this office so notified, the authority for use of the special number will expire on

CERTIFICATION I certify that the special registration number was placed on the aircraft described above.

Sign of Owner   *Marion W. Williams*

Title of Owner

Date Placed on Aircraft   August 1, 1985

RETURN FORM TO:
FAA Aircraft Registry
P.O. Box 25504
Oklahoma City, Oklahoma 73125

BELOW THIS POINT FOR FAA USE ONLY

☐ FP NAME
☐ NF
ADDRESS

FC   ZIP   EMP CODE   DATE

AC Form 8050-64 (11-82)

Fig. 5-3. AC Form 8050-64.

Federal Communications Commission
Gettysburg, PA 17326

APPLICATION FOR AIRCRAFT RADIO STATION LICENSE

Approved by OMB
3060-0040
Expires 3/31/89

- Read instructions above before completing application.   • Use typewriter or print clearly in ink.
- Sign and date application.   • Place First Class Postage on the reverse side of the card and mail.

1. FAA Registration or FCC Control Number.
(If FAA Registration is not required for your aircraft, explain in item 8.)   N

2. Is application for a fleet license? ☐ No ☐ Yes
If yes, give the number of aircraft in fleet, including planned expansion . . . .

3. Type of applicant (check one)
☐ I—Individual   ☐ C—Corporation
☐ P—Partnership   ☐ D—Individual with Business Name
☐ A—Association   ☐ G—Governmental entity

4. Applicant/Licensee Name (See Instructions)

5. Mailing Address (Number and Street, P.O. Box or Route No., City, State, ZIP Code)

6. Frequencies Requested (check appropriate box(es) in 6A and/or 6B.)

6A. DO NOT CHECK BOTH BOXES
☐ A—Private Aircraft ☐ C—Air Carrier

6B. ADDITIONAL INFORMATION IS REQUIRED IF YOU CHECK HERE (See Instructions)
☐ T—Flight Test HF   ☐ V—Flight Test VHF ☐ P—Portable ☐ O—Other (Specify)

7. Application is for:
☐ New Station ☐ Renewal
☐ Modification

8. Answer space for any required statements

9. READ CAREFULLY BEFORE SIGNING: 1. Applicant waives any claim to the use of any particular frequency regardless of prior use by license or otherwise. 2. Applicant will have unlimited access to the radio equipment and will control access to exclude unauthorized persons. 3. Neither applicant nor any member thereof is a foreign government or representative thereof. 4. Applicant certifies that all statements made in this application and attachments are true, complete, correct and made in good faith. 5. Applicant certifies that the signature is that of the individual, or partner, or officer or duly authorized employee of a corporation, or officer who is a member of an unincorporated association, or appropriate elected or appointed official on behalf of a governmental entity.

WILLFUL FALSE STATEMENTS MADE ON THIS FORM ARE PUNISHABLE BY FINE AND/OR IMPRISONMENT U.S. CODE TITLE 18. SECTION 1001

10. Signature

Date

FCC 404
March 1987

Fig. 5-4A. FCC Form 404 application (send this to the FCC).

**TEMPORARY AIRCRAFT RADIO STATION
OPERATING AUTHORITY**

Approved by OMB
3060-0040
Expires 3/31/89

Use this form if you want a temporary operating authority while your regular application, FCC Form 404, is being processed by the FCC. This authority authorizes the use of transmitters operating on the appropriate frequencies listed in Part 87 of the Commission's Rules.

- DO NOT use this form if you already have a valid aircraft station license.
- DO NOT use this form when renewing your aircraft license.
- DO NOT use this form if you are applying for a fleet license.
- DO NOT use this form if you do not have an FAA Registration Number.

ALL APPLICANTS MUST CERTIFY:

1. I am not a representative of a foreign government.
2. I have applied for an Aircraft Radio Station License by mailing a completed FCC Form 404 to the Federal Communications Commission, P.O. Box 1030, Gettysburg, PA 17326.
3. I have not been denied a license or had my license revoked by the FCC.

4. I am not the subject of any adverse legal action concerning the operation of a radio station.
5. I will ensure that the Aircraft Radio Station will be operated by an individual holding the proper class of license or permit required by the Commission's Rules.

WILLFUL FALSE STATEMENTS VOID THIS PERMIT AND ARE PUNISHABLE BY FINE AND/OR IMPRISONMENT.	
Name of Applicant (Print or Type)	Signature of Applicant
FAA Registration Number (Use as Temporary Call Sign)	Date FCC Form 404 Mailed

Your authority to operate your Aircraft Radio Station is subject to all applicable laws, treaties and regulations and is subject to the right of control of the Government of the United States. This authority is valid for 90 days from the date the FCC Form 404 is mailed.

YOU MUST POST THIS TEMPORARY OPERATING AUTHORITY ON BOARD YOUR AIRCRAFT

NOTICE TO INDIVIDUALS REQUIRED BY PRIVACY ACT OF 1974 AND THE PAPERWORK REDUCTION ACT OF 1980

Sections 301, 303 and 308 of the Communications Act of 1934, as amended, (licensing powers) authorize the FCC to request the information on this application. The purpose of the information is to determine your eligibility for a license. The information will be used by FCC staff to evaluate the application, to determine station location, to provide information for enforcement and rulemaking proceedings and to maintain a current inventory of licensees. No license can be granted unless all information requested is provided. Your response is required to obtain this authorization.

FCC 404-A
March 1987

DETACH HERE—DO NOT MAIL THIS PART

Fig. 5-4B. FCC Form 404 temporary authorization (retain this in your plane).

Assistance

Many forms must be completed and, although they are not complicated, you might want to seek assistance filling them out; check with your FBO or call another party, like AOPA.

AOPA, for a small fee, will provide closing services via telephone, then prepare and file the necessary forms to complete the transaction. This is particularly nice if the parties involved in the transaction are spread all over the country, which would be the case when purchasing an airplane long distance.

Another source of assistance in completing the necessary paperwork is the bank, particularly if the bank has a vested interest in your airplane—they hold the lien! Many banks will not accept a title search unless they requested it. The search may well be completed by the same organization you contracted, but don't worry, you'll get to pay for this one too. Everything banks do is charged to the customer in one way or another.

Who Really Owns The Airplane

Fraudulent airplane ownership is a rising problem. Although not as widespread a problem as those surrounding automobile ownership, each instance can result in aggravation, embarrassment, and the possible loss of funds.

An Old Tale

The simplest form of title fraud is best shown when you pay for an airplane and another person's name appears on the title, unbeknownst to you.

The story goes like this: A student pilot finds an airplane he wants and makes a deal with the owner. Funds change hands and a local flight instructor is asked to complete the paperwork. Fraud enters the picture when the instructor places his name on the FAA forms as the owner, takes the airplane, and is never seen again.

This old story has been flying around the hangar circuit for years, however it is something to think about. Other methods of fraud exist, both by omission and commission, that ought to be explained.

Links of Ownership

The chain of ownership follows paperwork filed with the FAA; no other paperwork is acknowledged. This means that if ownership was not changed with the FAA, then technically, ownership never changed.

Example: Mr. Smith sells his Piper Cub to Mr. Adams in 1983. Mr. Adams dies in 1988 leaving the airplane as part of the estate. The airplane is subsequently advertised for sale, and Mr. Kent decides to purchase it.

Mr. Kent runs a title check on the Cub and finds that the airplane is owned by Mr. Smith, not the estate of Mr. Adams. How could this happen? Simple! Mr. Adams never completed or filed the paperwork necessary to make the change with the FAA. Ownership will have to be cleared before Mr. Kent can purchase the airplane. Most likely he will need legal assistance.

Fixing Responsibility

A new specter in ownership fraud is fixing financial responsibility in the event of injury. The latter in the form of property damage or personal injury.

Example: You are upgrading to a larger airplane. You sell your trusty Ercoupe to Mr. Benson. The necessary papers are completed and presented with the airplane.

The next time you hear about the Ercoupe is when you are served papers in a lawsuit. It seems the airplane crashed and several people were injured on the ground. Mr. Benson never filed the paperwork with the FAA and you are still listed as the legal owner. The injured parties are seeking redress for their loss. Make copies of all papers related to the sale of an aircraft and save them for future reference. With proper copies and attorney's assistance you should survive any legal action. Consider a subsequent title search to verify transfer of ownership.

Outright Theft

Airplanes are often stolen then the registration numbers and general appearance of the aircraft are changed. An airplane broker with a place of business and good reputation sells the airplane. The broker is ignorant of the theft and sells the airplane to an unsuspecting buyer.

Example: Mr. Cody selects Piper N1234A from an airplane broker's inventory. He gets a title check and finds the owner is listed by the N-number and there are no "clouds" on the title. All appears in order and Mr. Cody makes the purchase.

Four months later the FBI shows up and interviews Mr. Cody. They explain that he is the victim of fraud; the real N1234A is in the Midwest. The airplane Mr. Cody purchased was stolen from Southern California, renumbered, and sold.

The Piper will be returned to its rightful owner; Mr. Cody will have no airplane, and will be out a considerable sum of money. He may have recourse against the broker, however it will be a costly battle.

Too Good

Some things are just too good to be true, however mortal humans sometimes cannot see this and will jump at such an offer.

Example: You are seated in the airport lounge one afternoon when a sharp looking Cessna 210 lands. The pilot enters and asks if anyone there is interested in purchasing his airplane. The price is unusually low and the plane looks good. You check the plane, fly it, and wind up purchasing it.

The pilot represents himself as the owner listed on the aircraft's papers. However, the real owner is in Florida for the winter and the airplane was stolen by the pilot from a small airport in the Northeast.

It is likely that the fraud won't be found until the airplane is reported stolen in the spring when the owner returns from Florida. The FBI will visit and take the airplane, leaving you with memories and an empty wallet.

How do you protect yourself? Ask for positive identification and make a call to the FBO where the pilot claimed he based the airplane. If the pilot gets upset, so what! You are protecting your interests. If something is wrong, back out of the deal. You might even wish to call the authorities and report this suspicious activity.

All Those Little Pieces

Some airplanes are rebuilds constructed from many parts around a data plate. This happens when an unscrupulous person purchases, or otherwise obtains, the logbooks and data (serial number) plates for a plane that has been wrecked. A plane to match the data plate is constructed from assorted parts, possibly from other wrecks.

Often the logbooks will not reflect the extent of repairs. Unfortunately, some planes reconstructed in this fashion will never fly properly, while others are downright dangerous to take into the air.

The average purchaser can easily be fooled by a reconstruction job, this is why he should have a mechanic inspect any airplane considered for purchase.

Self Defense

How do you protect yourself from title fraud? Where can you turn for assistance in making sure everything is as represented? Actually there is no single easy answer, however these suggestions may help avoid a sticky situation:

1. Purchase from a known individual or dealer.
2. Check serial numbers of the airframe, engine, and avionics against the logs and paperwork.
3. If you are not dealing with the owner directly, contact him/her on the telephone and ask him if it is indeed his airplane you are examining.
4. Do a title check and acquire title insurance.
5. If the deal appears too good to be true, it probably is!
6. When selling an airplane, do a title check 30 days after the sale to assure title transference to the new owner.

Insurance

Insure your airplane from the moment you sign on the dotted line. No one can afford to take risks.

Both basic types of aircraft insurance are discussed in Chapter 2: liability and hull.

Liability insurance protects you, or your heirs, in instances of claims against you resulting from your operation of an airplane: bodily injury or property damage. If someone is injured or killed as a result of your flying you will be sued, even if you are not at fault.

Hull insurance protects your investment from loss caused by nature, by fire, by theft, by vandalism, or while being operated. Lending institutions require hull insurance for their protection.

Save money by making the correct insurance choices based upon discussions with an insurance agent.

A Couple of Pits to Avoid

Beware of the term *exclusion*. Some policies use exclusions to avoid payoff in the event of a loss, for instance a requirement that all installed equipment be functioning properly during operation.

Example: A survivable accident occurs after an engine malfunction. During the post-crash investigation the insurance company discovers the VOR wasn't working properly. They refuse to pay for the loss because they require all installed equipment to be functioning properly during operation.

Another exclusion example—and all too often seen—says no payment will be made if any FARs have been violated. I am sure few accidents occur with no violation of the FARs.

Avoid policies that have exclusions, or other specific rules, setting maximum predetermined values for replacement parts. Such policies limit the amount paid for a specific part. You could be left holding the bag for the difference of the sum paid by the insurance company and the actual cost of the repair.

Always read the policy carefully and understand the exclusions. Ask questions, refuse the policy, do whatever is necessary to get what you want.

Limits

Beware of the policy that states: "$1 million total coverage with per seat limits of $100,000." If you own a two-place airplane your passenger limits are effectively reduced to only $100,000. After all, you only carry one other person in a two-placer.

Combined single limit is the recommended coverage, then you don't have to deal with per seat limits and you know actual coverage from the very start.

Check various aviation publications for telephone numbers of several aviation underwriters; many list toll-free telephone numbers. Check with more than one company because services, coverages, and rates do differ.

Examine personal health and life insurance policies. Be sure you are covered while flying a small airplane.

Getting the Airplane Home

In most cases you, the new owner, shall fly the airplane home where you will base it. However, in some instances the plane will be flown by the past owner or a dealer. Whatever the case may be, be sure the pilot is qualified to handle the airplane—legally and technically.

Legally means rated for the particular airplane with a current medical, a current biennial, and insurance coverage. Technically means that you can actually handle the airplane in a safe and proper manner.

In some instances the purchased aircraft might not be legal to fly due to damage or outdated inspection. If that is the case, contact the FAA office nearest where the aircraft is located. The office can arrange a Special Flight Permit, generally called a ferry permit, which allows an otherwise airworthy aircraft to be flown to a specified destination one time, one way. Before flying an aircraft on a ferry permit, check with the insurance company to ensure that you and your investment will be covered in the event of a loss.

Local Regulations

Many states and local jurisdictions register and tax aircraft. A few states even require a state pilot's license.

Appendix D is a list of various state aviation agencies. Contact the respective state agency to ensure compliance with any regulations.

6

After You Purchase

AN AIRPLANE OWNER MUST RECOGNIZE that proper care of an airplane directly influences the well-being of the financial investment and safety aspects of flight. Care includes: proper maintenance, storage, and cleaning. Fortunately most steps taken for financial reasons also aid the safety aspect; the opposite is also true.

Finding a Good FBO

When considering an FBO (fixed base operator) check with other owners and see what they think:
High-quality craftsmanship?
Reasonable prices?
Reasonably fast maintenance?
Approachable with problems?
Dealer for your airplane?
Flight instruction available?
Avionics service?
These are important points to consider, however the easiest and quickest means of sizing up an FBO is to examine the facility. Do the buildings look good and does the area offer proper physical security for an airplane?

Maintenance

All airplanes need maintenance, repairs, and inspections. Service work is expensive, although there are ways to save money, learn about your airplane, and become a better pilot for it.

Servicing Your Own Plane

Preventive maintenance is simple or minor preservation operations and the replacement of small standard parts not involving complex assembly operations, according to regulations.

FARs (Federal Aviation Regulations) specify that preventive maintenance may be performed by the pilot of an airplane not utilized in commercial service. All preventive maintenance work must be done in such a manner, and by use of materials of such quality, that the airframe, engine, propeller, or assembly worked on, will be at least equal to its original condition, according to regulations.

I strongly advise that before you undertake any of these allowable preventive maintenance procedures, discuss procedures with a licensed mechanic. The advice you receive may help you avoid making costly mistakes. You may have to pay a consultation fee, but it will be money well spent. Besides, the mechanic's time is money.

FAR Part 43, Appendix A lists the allowable preventive maintenance items. Only operations listed are considered preventive maintenance. The items applicable to powered airplanes are:

1. Removal, installation and repair of landing gear tires.
2. Replacing elastic shock absorber cords (bungees) on landing gear.
3. Servicing landing gear struts by adding oil, air, or both.
4. Servicing landing gear wheel bearings, such as cleaning and greasing.
5. Replacing defective safety wiring or cotter pins.
6. Lubrication not requiring disassembly other than removal of non-structural items such as cover plates, cowlings, and fairings.
7. Making simple fabric patches not requiring rib-stitching or the removal of structural parts or control surfaces.
8. Replenishing hydraulic fluid in the hydraulic reservoir.
9. Refinishing decorative coatings of the fuselage, wing, and tail-group surfaces (excluding balanced control surfaces), fairings, cowlings, landing gear, cabin, or cockpit interior when removal or disassembly of any primary structure or operating system is not required.
10. Applying preservative or protective material to components when no disassembly of any primary structure or operating system is involved and when such coating is not prohibited or is not contrary to good practices.
11. Repairing upholstery and decorative furnishings of the cabin or cockpit when it does not require disassembly of any primary structure or operating system or interfere with an operating system or affect the primary structure of the aircraft.
12. Making small, simple repairs to fairings, non-structural cover plates, cowlings and small patches, and reinforcements not changing the contour so as to interfere with the proper airflow.
13. Replacing side windows where that work does not interfere with the structure or any operating system, such as controls, electrical equipment, etc.
14. Replacing safety belts.
15. Replacing seats or seat parts with replacement parts approved for the air-

craft, not involving disassembly of any primary structure or operating system.

16. Trouble-shooting and repairing broken landing light wiring circuits.
17. Replacing bulbs, reflectors, and lenses of position and landing lights.
18. Replacing wheels and skis where no weight and balance computation is required.
19. Replacing any cowling not requiring removal of the propeller or disconnection of flight controls.
20. Replacing or cleaning spark plugs and setting of spark plug gap clearance.
21. Replacing any hose connection except hydraulic connections.
22. Replacing prefabricated fuel lines.
23. Cleaning fuel and oil strainers.
24. Replacing batteries and checking fluid level and specific gravity.
25. Replacement of non-structural standard fasteners incidental to operations.

Required Logbook Entries

Entries must be made in the appropriate logbook whenever preventive maintenance is performed. The aircraft cannot legally fly without logbook entry. A logbook entry must include description of work, date completed, name of the person doing the work, and approval for return to service (signature and certificate number) by the pilot approving the work.

Tools

A small quantity of quality tools should allow the owner to perform maintenance on an airplane:

☐ Multipurpose Swiss Army knife.
☐ 3/8" ratchet drive with a flex head as an option.
☐ 2, 4, 6" drive extensions.
☐ Sockets from 3/8" to 3/4" in 1/16" increments.
☐ 6" crescent wrench.
☐ 10" monkey wrench.
☐ 6 or 12-point closed (box) wrenches from 3/8" to 3/4".
☐ Set of open-end wrenches from 3/8" to 3/4".
☐ Pair of channel lock pliers (medium size).
☐ Phillips screwdriver set in the three common sizes.
☐ Flathead screwdriver set to include short (2") to long (8") sizes.
☐ Plastic electrician's tape.
☐ Container of assorted nuts and bolts.
☐ Spare set of spark plugs.
☐ A bag or box would be very handy to keep tools in order and protected.

The FAA encourages pilots and owners to carefully maintain airplanes. Properly performed preventive maintenance provides the pilot or owner a better understanding of the airplane, saves money, and offers a great sense of accomplishment.

If an FBO is concerned about preventive maintenance, Advisory Circular 150/5190-2A states, in part:

"Restrictions on Self-Service: Any unreasonable restriction imposed on the owners and operators of aircraft regarding the servicing of their own aircraft and equipment may be considered as a violation of agency policy. The owner of an aircraft should be permitted to fuel, wash, repair, paint, and otherwise take care of his own aircraft, provided there is no attempts to perform such services for others. Restrictions which have the effect of diverting activity of this type to a commercial enterprise amount to an exclusive right contrary to law."

With these words the FAA has allowed the owner of an aircraft to save his hard-earned dollars, and to become very familiar with his airplane, which no doubt contributes to safety.

Storage

Proper aircraft storage is more than mere parking in a hangar or at tiedown. Unfortunately, too many pilots pay little heed to the requirements of proper storage of their airplanes during periods of non-use.

Sad but true, most small airplanes are stored outdoors because hangar space is limited at most airports and space is expensive when located. It is not uncommon to find a two-to-five-year waiting list for hangar space. Outdoor storage is more common.

Tiedown

Basic airplane storage is a tiedown. I don't think there is a pilot anywhere not familiar with the basics of proper tiedown. After all, most trainer airplanes are tied down and the pre-flight and post-flight parts of each lesson included untying and tying the plane down (Fig. 6-1).

An airplane should be parked facing into the wind, if possible. This is not always possible because many airports have engineered tiedown systems with predetermined aircraft placement.

A proper tiedown must include secure anchors, normally loops made of concrete or steel placed in the ground. Each anchor must provide a minimum of 3,000 pounds (4,000 pounds for light twins) holding power. Three anchors are used for each airplane.

Some airports use an anchor and cable system for tiedowns. This consists of stout steel cables connecting properly installed anchors in two long parallel lines. The lines are approximately one airplane length apart. Airplanes are parked perpendicular to the cables, allowing the wings to be tied to one cable and the tail to the other cable. All planes are parked side-by-side, often times parked facing in alternate directions (Fig. 6-2).

Fig. 6-1. If you don't tie your airplane down this can happen.

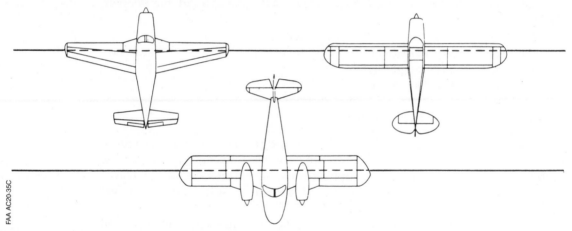

FAA AC20-35C

Fig. 6-2. Typical airport anchor and cable system.

Tiedown ropes must have a minimum 3,000 pounds tensile strength (4,000 pounds for twins). Nylon or Dacron ropes are recommended over natural fiber ropes such as manila; manila tends to shrink when wet and is prone to rot and mildew. Chains or steel rope can be used if care is taken to prevent damage at the tiedown points on the airplane.

Fasten tiedowns only to those points on the aircraft designed for the purpose. This means use the tiedown rings, not just any handy surface (Fig. 6-3).

Lock control surfaces with an internal control lock. Or fasten gust locks on the control surfaces to prevent movement during windy conditions. Decorate all external locks with colorful ribbons as a reminder to remove them before flight.

Cover the pitot tube and fuel vents to keep insects and debris out. Plug or cover nacelles or the cowling to discourage bird nests in the engine compartment.

FAA AC20-35C

Fig. 6-3. Use the proper tie points.

A Few Don'ts

Don't depend upon wooden stakes driven into the ground for tiedown anchors.

Don't use the wing struts for tiedown points.

Don't use cheap or lightweight rope for tiedowns.

Don't leave an airplane parked and not tied down.

Don't forget to lock the controls.

Heat and Sunlight Protection

Research shows us that the interior temperature of a parked aircraft can reach as much as 185°. This heat build-up will not only affect avionics, but will cause problems with instrument panels, upholstery, and a variety of other plastic things. This is the reason that many aircraft tied down outside have a cover over the windshield, either inside or outside (Fig. 6-4).

An inside cover's metallic-like reflective cover protects the interior and reduces heat by reflecting the sun's rays. The shields attach to the interior of the aircraft with Velcro fasteners.

Exterior covers will provide similar protection for the interior and provide additional exterior protection for refueling caps and fresh-air vents. They also cover expensive window surfaces for protection from blowing debris.

Hangars

Two types of indoor storage are the large hangar and the individual hangar. Individual is often referred to as a Tee-hangar for its general shape; I prefer the Tee hangar because it offers more security for the airplane. Security means one airplane stored in the hangar, therefore no one has access to the airplane without your knowledge. Also less exposure to airplane thieves and vandals.

The dreaded disease hangar rash (Fig. 6-5) might also be averted with storage in a private hangar. Hangar rash is associated with large hangars and occurs

Fig. 6-4. An exterior aircraft cover keeps out sunlight and protects window surfaces from airborne debris.

Fig. 6-5. Hangar rash comes from careless moving in tight quarters.

when planes are carelessly handled by non-caring ground personnel. In short, they get banged into one another, into walls, and equipment. The result is numerous small dings, dents, and scratches.

An often forgotten point of indoor storage is hours the airplane is accessible. The hangar will be locked when the FBO is closed, so you must make prior arrangements for a 4 a.m. liftoff, like parking it outside overnight.

Nonuse of the Airplane

Nothing is worse for an airplane than sitting on the ground unused. Of course this is true of all mechanical things, but particularly so for airplanes.

All too often I see airplanes for months on end never moving. Then one day the terror-of-the-air arrives at the airport, sticks his finger into the wind and says, "Let's go flying." He does a quick walk around of the plane, unties it, jumps in and starts it up. He then takes off into the wild blue yonder, all without a care about what has been happening to the airplane while it sat unattended.

Engines in aircraft that are flown occasionally tend to exhibit more cylinder wall corrosion than engines in aircraft that are flown regularly.

The recommended method of preventing cylinder wall corrosion and other corrosion is to fly the aircraft at least weekly; the engine warms to operating temperature, which vaporizes moisture and other by-products of combustion that can cause engine damage.

Proper storage and preservation techniques are a must, but not performed by many owners. As you shall see, these procedures take time and effort. Some people don't, for one reason or another, wish to expend themselves. Yet, without proper care, the airplane value will be reduced and flying safety impaired.

Aircraft storage recommendations are broken down: flyable storage (used infrequently), temporary storage (up to 90 days), and indefinite storage (more than 90 days).

Flyable Storage

Most modern aircraft are constructed of corrosion-resistant Alclad aluminum that will last indefinitely under normal conditions, if kept clean. However, Alclad aluminum is subject to oxidation (corrosion). The first indication of oxidation on an unpainted surface is formation of white deposits or spots. The corrosion can resemble white dust or take on a linty look. On painted surfaces, the paint becomes discolored or is blistered. Storage in a dry hangar is essential to good preservation and should be procured if possible.

Minimum care of the engine calls for a weekly propeller pull-through and, at a minimum, a flight once every 30 days. The propeller should be rotated by hand without starting the engine. For four- and six-cylinder non-geared engines, rotate the propeller six revolutions, then stop the propeller 45° to 90° from the original position. For six-cylinder geared engines, rotate the propeller four revolutions and stop the propeller 30° to 60° from the original position.

The monthly flight must have a minimum 30-minute duration to assure that the engine has reached normal oil and cylinder temperatures. Ground run-up is not an acceptable substitute for flight.

Temporary Storage

When an airplane will remain inoperative for a period not exceeding 90 days, considerable effort is necessary to protect it from neglect.

1. Fill the fuel tanks with the correct grade of fuel.
2. Clean and wax the aircraft.
3. Clean any grease and oil from the tires and coat them with a tire preservative.
4. Cover the nose wheel to protect it from oil drips.
5. Block up the fuselage to remove the weight from the tires. (Consult with an A&P for assistance.)
6. Cover all airframe openings to keep vermin, insects, and birds out.
7. Remove the top spark plug and spray preservative oil at room temperature through the upper spark plug hole of each cylinder with the piston approximately in bottom dead center position. Rotate the crankshaft as each pair of opposite cylinders is sprayed. Stop the crankshaft with no piston at top dead center. Re-install spark plugs. (Consult an A&P.)
8. Apply preservative to the engine interior by spraying approximately two ounces of preservative oil through the oil filler tube. (Consult an A&P.)
9. Seal all engine openings exposed to the atmosphere using suitable plugs, or moisture-resistant tape. Attach red streamers at each sealed location for removal prior to flight.

Indefinite Storage

An aircraft unused in excess of 90 days must be completely preserved. The following steps outline the basics of such preservation. It represents loads of work and considerable expense. However, to protect the airplane it is necessary. (Consider consultation with an A&P.)

1. Drain the engine oil and refill with MIL-C-6529 Type II oil. The aircraft should then be flown for 30 minutes, reaching, but not exceeding, normal oil and cylinder temperatures. Allow the engine to cool to ambient temperature.
2. Do everything for temporary storage except replacing the spark plugs.
3. Install dehydrator plugs in each of the top spark plug holes and make sure that each plug is blue in color when installed. Protect and support the spark plug leads.
4. If the engine is equipped with a pressure-type carburetor: Drain the carburetor by removing the drain and vapor vent plugs from the regulator

and fuel control unit. With the mixture control in Rich position, inject lubricating oil into the fuel inlet, at a pressure not to exceed 10 p.s.i. (pounds per square inch), until oil flows from the vapor vent opening. Allow excess oil to drain, plug the inlet, and tighten the drain and vapor vent plugs. Wire the throttle in the open position, place bags of desiccant in the intake, and seal the opening with moisture-resistant paper and tape, or a cover plate.

5. Place a bag of desiccant in the exhaust pipes and seal the openings with moisture-resistant tape.
6. Seal the cold-air inlet to the heater muff with moisture-resistant tape to exclude moisture and foreign objects.
7. Seal the engine breather by inserting a dehydrator plug in the breather hose and clamping in place.
8. Lubricate all airframe items.
9. Remove the battery and store it in a cool, dry place.
10. Place covers over the windshield and rear windows.
11. Engines, with propellers installed, that are preserved for storage in accordance with this section should have a tag affixed to the propeller in a conspicuous place with the following notation on the tag:

DO NOT TURN PROPELLER—ENGINE
PRESERVED; PRESERVATION DATE _____

Periodic examinations are necessary:

- Aircraft prepared for indefinite storage should have the cylinder dehydrator plugs visually inspected every 15 days. The plugs should be changed as soon as the color indicates unsafe conditions of storage. If the dehydrator plugs have changed color on one-half or more of the cylinders, all desiccant material on the engine should be replaced.
- The cylinder bores of all engines prepared for indefinite storage should be re-sprayed with a corrosion-preventive mixture every six months, or more frequently if a bore inspection indicates corrosion has started earlier than six months. Replace all desiccant packets and dehydrator plugs. Before spraying, the engine should be inspected for corrosion as follows: Inspect the interior of at least one cylinder on each engine through the spark plug hole. If the cylinder shows rust, spray the cylinder with corrosion preventive oil and turn the prop over six times, then re-spray all cylinders. Remove at least one rocker box cover from each engine and inspect the valve mechanism.

Return to Service

Prepare the airplane for a return to service:

1. Remove the aircraft from the blocks and check the tires for proper inflation.

2. Check the nose strut for proper inflation.
3. Remove all covers and plugs, and inspect the interior of the airframe for debris and foreign matter.
4. Clean and inspect the exterior of the aircraft.
5. Remove the cylinder dehydrator plugs, tape, and desiccant bags used to preserve the engine.
6. Drain the corrosion preventive mixture and fill with recommended lubricating oil.
7. If the carburetor has been preserved with oil, drain it by removing the drain and vapor vent plugs from the regulator and fuel control unit. With the mixture control in rich position, inject service-type gasoline into the fuel inlet, at a pressure not to exceed 10 p.s.i., until all of the oil is flushed from the carburetor. Re-install the carburetor plugs and attach the fuel line.
8. With the bottom plugs removed, rotate the propeller to clear excess preservative oil from the cylinders. Re-install the spark plugs and rotate the propeller by hand through compression strokes of all cylinders to check for possible liquid lock.
9. Install the battery.
10. Thoroughly clean and visually inspect the airplane.
11. Start the engine in the normal manner.
12. Test flight per airframe manufacturer's instructions.

Disclaimer. The aforementioned procedures are general recommendations applicable to many general aviation aircraft. For particulars on a specific airplane, check the service manual.

Lots of Work

As you can see, non-use of an airplane can be complicated and expensive. My best recommendation for an aircraft that will not be used for a period in excess of a couple of months is to sell it. You are not getting your money's worth from the airplane, and the lack of use will cost money in the long run.

Cleaning the Airplane

Normal upkeep of any airplane requires cleanliness. Cleaning means everything from wash and wax the exterior to proper care of the interior. Results will be a sharp looking airplane to be proud of.

Cleaning the Exterior

Exterior care of an airplane is not only important in the sense of appearance and value, but in safety as well. While cleaning the airplane you will notice small imperfections and minor damage, which can be corrected before they become big problems.

Complete washing with automotive-type cleaners will produce acceptable results and be less expensive than aircraft cleaners. Automotive wax will also provide adequate protection for painted or unpainted surfaces; wax means new space-age silicone preparations called sealers.

Inside Cleaning

The interior of an airplane is seen by all, including the pilot and his passengers. It is also used by all and is a problem to keep clean. My recommendation is a very thorough cleaning by use of standard automobile cleaning methods. Vacuum the interior because it is the only effective way to remove small debris.

Cleaning Aids

The following items are available at most grocery stores or automotive supply houses.

Spray Cleaner. Heavy-duty cleaner for the hard-to-remove stuff. Keep it away from the windshield, instruments, and painted surfaces.

Engine Cleaner. Degrease the engine area and oleo struts. It dissolves grease and can be washed off with water. When using it in the engine compartment, cover the magnetos and alternator with plastic bags to keep the cleaner and rinse water out. Engine cleaner is also good for cleaning the plane's belly. It is reasonably safe on painted surfaces if rinsed per instructions.

Spray Lubricant. General silicon spray lubricant stops squeaks and improves movement. It's good on cables, controls, seat runners, and doors. Keep it off windows.

Rubbing Compound. Clean away exhaust stains. Use carefully because you could remove stains *and* paint.

Touch-up paint. Many airplane colors are unavailable in small quantities for touch-up use. However, don't despair because any good automotive supply house (and some department stores) have inexpensive cans of spray paint to match almost any automotive color. Try to find one that closely matches your airplane's paint. Remember that a touch-up is just that, not a complete re-paint, and don't expect it to be more. Touching-up small blemishes and chips protects the airframe and perhaps improves the appearance slightly.

Spray furniture wax is invaluable for use on hard plastic surfaces like instrument panels and other vinyl objects.

Liquid resin rubber and vinyl cleaners and protectors are excellent for upholstery and other flexible surfaces. The only draw back is they leave very shiny and slippery surfaces. They will look and smell like new, however.

A good vacuum cleaner is a must for cleaning an airplane. Sweeping will not do the job.

Aircraft Theft

Theft of airplanes and equipment is something the owner must guard against at all times. Not just in the South where airplanes are stolen for drug running, but in all areas of the country. Equipment theft happens everywhere.

According to the IATB (International Aviation Theft Bureau) the most popular airplanes among thieves are the Cessna 172, 182, 210 and 310. The most active states for aircraft thefts are Florida, California, and Texas.

Theft Prevention

An owner can do several things to protect his investment from thieves. Among these are the use of various devices designed to prevent the operation of the ignition switch, throttle, controls, or a combination of them. On the exterior of the airplane special wheel locks or propeller locks may be installed.

No device will provide complete protection. The determined thief will counter the measures and steal the airplane. The idea is to make the airplane undesirable to the thief because it will take too much time to fly it away.

Equipment thefts have been on the upswing for several years, and no doubt will continue. This is a problem seen more near large urban areas. Contributing factors could be sophisticated aircraft, with better equipment, concentrated in a small area, or more thieves in a metropolitan area. Both factors probably go hand-in-hand.

Certain preventive measures will protect an airplane and its equipment:

1. Mark installed equipment (avionics) with a driver's or pilot's license number.
2. Park in well lighted areas. The dark corner of a deserted airport affords little protection for the airplane.
3. Use covers inside the windows to keep prying eyes out.
4. Use of a radio alert burglar alarm. These systems have been installed at a few airports with great success. Ask the FBO if it is available.
5. Photograph the instrument panel. This will show what equipment was installed, preventing any quibbling with the insurance company in the event of a loss.
6. Keep your log books in a secure place. There is no requirement they be kept in the airplane, only that they be made available for inspection upon request. Many owners keep copies in the plane.
7. Maintain a list of serial numbers and other data.

Equipment Theft

Two equipment theft scams are running that all owners should be aware of. The first is merely entering an airplane and removing avionics. The second involves theft of radio equipment and the thief replacing it with similar but stolen equipment. You could go on for months or years and never notice the swap. The latter can make equipment ownership tracing nearly impossible.

Another problem the typical owner is faced with today is the outright destruction of equipment that has been discouraged by anti-theft devices or marking. If they can't have it, they feel you shouldn't either.

How to Report Airplane Theft

In the event your airplane is stolen, you must report the loss to proper authorities as soon as possible. The less delay when reporting, the greater the chances of prompt recovery of the aircraft.

1. Immediately report the theft to the local law enforcement agency with jurisdiction over the airport. This will cause the aircraft's registration number to be entered into the NCIC (National Crime Information Center) computer data base. It will also cause a notice of the theft, called a look-out, to be flashed among local jurisdictions.
2. Request that the officer taking the report notify the nearest flight service station of the theft. This will alert the air traffic control system of the theft, as the information will be sent to all airports and centers.
3. Notify the International Aviation Theft Bureau:

   (301) 654-0500
   TELEX: 89-8468
   TWX: 710-824-0095

4. Notify your insurance company of the loss.

Part II

Used
Airplane Fleet

The following pages contain the photographs and specifications for most of the used airplanes you will find on today's market. There are a few makes and models that have not been included due to their scarcity. You will notice that with few exceptions, the airplanes included have an average value of $50,000.

Specifications and performance information is as accurate as possible, having come from the FAA, manufacturers, and owner organizations. However, keep in mind that each airplane is an individual example of the art, and may or may not meet the exact data presented. Additionally, many older airplanes have been modified to perform well beyond original performance data.

Complete performance data is not presented for every make and model. The reason is the typically small changes in the specifications and performance data from year to year; significant changes are noted.

7

Two-Place Airplanes

MOST PILOTS ARE QUITE FAMILIAR with two-place airplanes. After all, the majority of us learned to fly in a two-place airplane. Two-placers come in two basic styles: tandem seating (one person sits behind the other) and side by side version (both occupants sit beside each other, often quite snugly).

In most of these airplanes the key word is simplicity. They have small efficient engines, few moving parts, and minimal required maintenance, all totaling up to lower costs.

Some of the older two-placers are considered classic airplanes because they represent a bygone era. Examples would be the Piper J3, Aeronca 7AC, and the Taylorcraft BC-12D. But wait a minute, today's manufacturers are producing airplanes of those styles. In fact one, the Christen Husky, was introduced in 1987. And the Super Cub returned in the 1980s. Well, I guess you can see that these old classic airplanes are not so old after all. They represent good solid flying, and pilots still want that, even if the airplanes happen to be 40 years old.

Should the nostalgia bug bite, and you become interested in owning a classic airplane, read *A Pilot's Guide to Affordable Classics*, TAB # 2392.

Other two-placers are as modern as today, with many of the complexities found on larger airplanes: retractable landing gear, variable-pitch props, large engines, and more.

Several complex two-placers date from the 40s, such as the all-metal Swift, while others are as recent as the 80s. Two-placers don't have to be doggy trainers. They can give very high performance for speed and for aerobatics.

You will no doubt notice that many of these airplanes have the nose wheel "on the tail." This is called *conventional landing gear*. There was a time when all airplanes had conventional landing gear, now most have tricycle gear. Arguments rage about which is better, and I suppose the question will never be settled. The point I want to make is that anyone can be competent with either. So, never forsake an airplane just because it has conventional gear. You can learn to handle it.

Aeronca (Champion and Bellanca)

Aeronca airplanes were among the most popular trainers of the post war period. (I learned to fly in one, and that was considerably after World War II.) Although not many are seen today as trainers, they do make inexpensive sport planes.

All Aeronca two-place airplanes are of tube and fabric design; the airframe is made of a welded steel tube structure that is covered with fabric; wings are covered with "fabric." They were originally covered with Grade-A cotton cloth, while most examples today are covered with one of the new synthetic products.

Aeroncas are fun and easy to fly and are among the least expensive airplanes to operate. Although rather slow by today's standards, you can see what you're flying over. All Aeroncas have conventional landing gear, but don't let that scare you because they're honest little airplanes that display few bad habits.

Several planes in the "7" (Champ) series were based upon the WWII TA Defender and the L3 Liaison plane:

- 7AC had the A-65 Continental 65-hp engine. Although some were built with Franklin or Lycoming engines, most today have the Continental. The 7ACs—often referred to as Airknockers—were produced from 1945 through 1948. All were painted yellow, with red trim. According to historical records, Aeronca once produced 56 Champs in one day. The usual time to build one was 291 man-hours. The original price was $2,999.
- The 7CCM with the 90-hp Continental was introduced in 1948. The 7CCM had a slightly larger fin than the 7AC, and a few minor structural changes. The military configuration of this plane was the L-16B.
- The 7EC was the last try for Aeronca. Major changes were the Continental C-90-12F engine, electrical system, and metal propeller.

All told, more than 7,200 Champs were built before production was halted.

Aeronca also built the "11" series Chief with a wider body than the Champ. It seated two, side-by-side, and was powered by a Continental A-65 engine. An updated version, the 11CC Super Chief with a Continental C-85-8F and a metal propeller, was introduced in 1947.

As with so many of the post war era planes, a good design was hard to kill. Aeronca was one. In 1954 the Champion Aircraft Company of Osceola, Wisconsin, was formed. They reintroduced the Aeronca 7EC model as the Champion Traveler. The new 7EC was upholstered, carpeted, and had a propeller spinner.

A tricycle gear version, called the 7FC Tri-Traveler, was built for a short period of time. There is nothing unusual about these fine little planes, just an Airknocker with a nose wheel. Unfortunately, their popularity was never that of the Piper or Cessna competition.

A new Champ series started with the 7GC in 1959. These planes were produced with various engines. All display good short field capabilities.

- 7GC, 1959, Lycoming 140-hp engine.

- 7GCB, 1960-64, Lycoming 150-hp engine.
- 7GCBC, long-wing version of 7GCB (with flaps).

Citabria airplanes emerged in 1964. Citabria is "airbatic" spelled backwards. They have been very popular planes. Of course model numbers changed with engines.

- 7ECA, 1965-65, Continental 100-hp.
- 7ECA, 1966-71, Lycoming 115-hp.
- 7GCAA, 1965-77, Lycoming 150-hp.
- 7KCAB, 1967-77, Lycoming 150-hp engine fuel injected.

Bellanca—another old name in airplane manufacturing—merged with Champion in 1970. They continued producing the Champion line, then attempted to introduce a very low cost airplane, the 7ACA. It was built to sell for $4,995 and had a two-cylinder Franklin 60-hp engine. It was never popular, and few exist today.

The Decathlon 8KCAB series, with a newly designed wing and bigger engine, was introduced in 1971. The new wing featured near-symmetrical airfoil, shorter span, and wider cord than the Citabria wing. This, coupled with the 6G positive and 5G negative flight load limits, and the inverted engine system made the Decathlon perfect for advanced aerobatics. It was available in 150-hp or 180-hp.

The last entry from Bellanca was the 8GCBC Scout. It is a strong hearted work horse built for pipeline/power line patrol and ranching; several fish and game departments also fly them.

Fig. 7-1. Aeronca 7AC Champ or Air Knocker.

Make: Aeronca   Model: 7AC Champ
Year: 1945-48
Engine
    Make: Continental (Lycoming and Franklin alternates)
    Model: A-65
    Horsepower: 65
    TBO: 1800 hours

Speeds
    Maximum: 95 mph
    Cruise: 86 mph
    Stall: 38 mph
Fuel capacity: 13 gallons
Rate of climb: 370 fpm
Transitions
    Takeoff over 50-foot obstacle: NA
    Ground run: 630 feet
    Landing over 50-foot obstacle: NA
    Ground roll: 880 feet
Weights
    Gross: 1220 pounds
    Empty: 740 pounds
Seats: Two tandem
Dimensions
    Length: 21 feet 6 inches
    Height: 7 feet
    Span: 35 feet

Make: Aeronca   Model: 7CCM Champ
Year: 1947-50
Engine
    Make: Continental
    Model: C-90
    Horsepower: 90
    TBO: 1800 hours
Speeds
    Maximum: 103 mph
    Cruise: 90 mph
    Stall: 42 mph
Fuel capacity: 19 gallons
Rate of climb: 650 fpm
Transitions
    Takeoff over 50-foot obstacle: NA
    Ground run: 475 feet
    Landing over 50 foot obstacle: NA
    Ground roll: 850 feet
Weights
    Gross: 1300 pounds
    Empty: 810 pounds
Seats: Two tandem
Dimensions
    Length: 21 feet 6 inches
    Height: 7 feet
    Span: 35 feet

Fig. 7-2. Aeronca 11AC Chief.

Make: Aeronca   Model: 11AC Chief
Year: 1946-47
Engine
 Make: Continental
 Model: C-65
 Horsepower: 65
 TBO: 1800 hours
Speeds
 Maximum: 90 mph
 Cruise: 83 mph
 Stall: 38 mph
Fuel capacity: 15
Rate of climb: 360 fpm
Transitions
 Takeoff over 50-foot obstacle: NA
 Ground run: 580 feet
 Landing over 50-foot obstacle: NA
 Ground roll: 880 feet
Weights
 Gross: 1250 pounds
 Empty: 786 pounds
Seats: Two side by side
Dimensions
 Length: 20 feet 4 inches
 Height: 7 feet
 Span: 36 feet 1 inch

Make: Aeronca   Model: 11CC Super Chief
Year: 1947-79
Engine
 Make: Continental
 Model: C-85

Horsepower: 85
TBO: 1800 hours
Speeds
    Maximum: 102 mph
    Cruise: 95 mph
    Stall: 40 mph
Fuel capacity: 15
Rate of climb: 600 fpm
Transitions
    Takeoff over 50-foot obstacle: NA
    Ground run: 720 feet
    Landing over 50-foot obstacle: NA
    Ground roll: 880 feet
Weights
    Gross: 1350 pounds
    Empty: 820 pounds
Seats: Two side by side
Dimensions
    Length: 20 feet 7 inches
    Height: 7 feet
    Span: 36 feet 1 inch

Fig. 7-3. Champion Tri-Traveler.

Make: Champion   Model: 7-EC/FC (90) Traveler/Tri-Traveler
Year: 1955-62
Engine
    Make: Continental
    Model: C-90

Horsepower: 90
TBO: 1800 hours
Speeds
    Maximum: 135 mph
    Cruise: 105 mph
    Stall: 44 mph
Fuel capacity: 24 gallons
Rate of climb: 700 fpm
Transitions
    Takeoff over 50-foot obstacle: 980 feet
    Ground run: 630 feet
    Landing over 50-foot obstacle: 755 feet
    Ground roll: 400 feet
Weights
    Gross: 1450 pounds
    Empty: 860 pounds
Seats: Two tandem
Dimensions
    Length: 21 feet 6 inches
    Height: 7 feet 2 inches
    Span: 35 feet 2 inches

Make: Champion   Model: 7-EC/FC (150) Traveler/Tri-Traveler
Year: 1961-62
Engine
    Make: Continental
    Model: O-320
    Horsepower: 150
    TBO: 2000 hours
Speeds
    Maximum: 135 mph
    Cruise: 125 mph
    Stall: 44 mph
Fuel capacity: 24 gallons
Rate of climb: 900 fpm
Transitions
    Takeoff over 50-foot obstacle: 630 feet
    Ground run: 375 feet
    Landing over 50-foot obstacle: 755 feet
    Ground roll: 400 feet
Weights
    Gross: 1500 pounds
    Empty: 968 pounds
Seats: Two tandem
Dimensions
    Length: 21 feet 6 inches

Height: 7 feet 2 inches
Span: 35 feet 2 inches

Make: Champion   Model: 7-ECA (100) Citabria
Year: 1964-65
Engine
    Make: Continental
    Model: O-200
    Horsepower: 100
    TBO-1800 hours
Speeds
    Maximum: 117 mph
    Cruise: 112 mph
    Stall: 51 mph
Fuel capacity: 35 gallons
Rate of climb: 650 fpm
Transitions
    Takeoff over 50-foot obstacle: 890 feet
    Ground run: 480 feet
    Landing over 50-foot obstacle: 755 feet
    Ground roll: 400 feet
Weights
    Gross: 1650 pounds
    Empty: 980 pounds
Seats: Two tandem
Dimensions
    Length: 22 feet 7 inches
    Height: 6 feet 7 inches
    Span: 33 feet 5 inches

Fig. 7-4. Champion 7ECA.

Make: Champion   Model: 7-ECA (115) Citabria
Year: 1966-84
Engine
    Make: Lycoming
    Model: O-235
    Horsepower: 115
    TBO: 2000 hours
Speeds
    Maximum: 119 mph
    Cruise: 114 mph
    Stall: 51 mph
Fuel capacity: 35 gallons
Rate of climb: 725 fpm
Transitions
    Takeoff over 50-foot obstacle: 716 feet
    Ground run: 450 feet
    Landing over 50-foot obstacle: 775 feet
    Ground roll: 400 feet
Weights
    Gross: 1650 pounds
    Empty: 1060 pounds
Seats: Two tandem
Dimensions
    Length: 22 feet 7 inches
    Height: 6 feet 7 inches
    Span: 33 feet 5 inches

Make: Champion   Model: 7GC series
Year: 1960-84
Engine
    Make: Lycoming
    Model: O-320
    Horsepower: 150
    TBO: 2000 hours
Speeds
    Maximum: 130 mph
    Cruise: 128 mph
    Stall: 45 mph
Fuel capacity: NA
Rate of climb: 1145 fpm
Transitions
    Takeoff over 50-foot obstacle: 457 feet
    Ground run: 296 feet
    Landing over 50-foot obstacle: 690 feet
    Ground roll: 310 feet

Weights
    Gross: 1650 pounds
    Empty: 1150 pounds
Seats: Two tandem
Dimensions
    Length: 22 feet 8 inches
    Height: 6 feet 7 inches
    Span: 34 feet 3 inches

Fig. 7-5. Bellanca Fig. 8-KCAB Decathlon.

Make: Champion   Model: 7KCAB Citabria
Year: 1967-77
Engine
    Make: Lycoming
    Model: IO-320-E2A
    Horsepower: 150
    TBO: 2000 hours
Speeds
    Maximum: 133 mph
    Cruise: 125 mph
    Stall: 50 mph
Fuel capacity: 39 gallons
Rate of climb: 1120 fpm
Transitions
    Takeoff over 50-foot obstacle: 535 feet
    Ground run: 375 feet
    Landing over 50-foot obstacle: 755
    Ground roll: 400 feet

Weights
    Gross: 1650 pounds
    Empty: 1060 pounds
Seats: Two tandem
Dimensions
    Length: 22 feet 8 inches
    Height: 6 feet 7 inches
    Span: 33 feet 5 inches

Make: Bellanca   Model: 7-ACA Champ
Year: 1971-72
Engine
    Make: Franklin
    Model: 2A-120B
    Horsepower: 60
    TBO: 1500 hours
Speeds
    Maximum: 98 mph
    Cruise: 83 mph
    Stall: 39 mph
Fuel capacity: 13 gallons
Rate of climb: 400 fpm
Transitions
    Takeoff over 50-foot obstacle: 900 feet
    Ground run: 525 feet
    Landing over 50-foot obstacle: NA
    Ground roll: 300 feet
Weights
    Gross: 1220 pounds
    Empty: 750 pounds
Seats: Two tandem
Dimensions
    Length: 21 feet 9 inches
    Height: 7 feet
    Span: 35 feet 1 inch

Make: Bellanca   Model: 8-KCAB (150) Decathlon
Year: 1971-80
Engine
    Make: Lycoming
    Model: IO-320 (optional constant speed propeller)
    Horsepower: 150
    TBO: 2000 hours
Speeds
    Maximum: 147 mph
    Cruise: 137 mph

Stall: 54 mph
Fuel capacity: 40 gallons
Rate of climb: 1000 fpm
Transitions
    Takeoff over 50-foot obstacle: 1450 feet
    Ground run: 840 feet
    Landing over 50-foot obstacle: 1462 feet
    Ground roll: 668 feet
Weights
    Gross: 1800 pounds
    Empty: 1260 pounds
Seats: Two tandem
Dimensions
    Length: 22 feet 11 inches
    Height: 7 feet 8 inches
    Span: 32 feet

Make: Bellanca   Model: 8-KCAB (180) Decathlon
Year: 1977-84
Engine
    Make: Lycoming
    Model: AEIO-360-H1A
    Horsepower: 180
    TBO: 1400 hours
Speeds
    Maximum: 158 mph
    Cruise: 150 mph
    Stall: 54 mph
Fuel capacity: 40 gallons
Rate of climb: 1230 fpm
Transitions
    Takeoff over 50-foot obstacle: 1310 feet
    Ground run: 710 feet
    Landing over 50-foot obstacle: 1462 feet
    Ground roll: 668 feet
Weights
    Gross: 1800 pounds
    Empty: 1315 pounds
Seats: Two tandem
Dimensions
    Length: 22 feet 11 inches
    Height: 7 feet 8 inches
    Span: 32 feet

Fig. 7-6. Bellanca 8-GCBC Scout.

Make: Bellanca   Model: 8-GCBC Scout
Year: 1974-84
Engine
    Make: Lycoming
    Model: O-360-C2E (optional constant speed propeller)
    Horsepower: 180
    TBO: 2000 hours
Speeds
    Maximum: 135 mph
    Cruise: 122 mph
    Stall: 52 mph
Fuel capacity: 35 gallons
Rate of climb: 1080 fpm
Transitions
    Takeoff over 50-foot obstacle: 1090 feet
    Ground run: 510 feet
    Landing over 50-foot obstacle: 1245 feet
    Ground roll: 400 feet
Weights
    Gross: 2150 pounds
    Empty: 1315 pounds
Seats: Two tandem
Dimensions
    Length: 23 feet 10 inches
    Height: 8 feet 8 inches
    Span: 36 feet 2 inches

Beechcraft

Beech Aircraft Corp. is not known for two-seat airplanes but has produced two.

More recent is the Skipper, a low-wing, all-metal, tricycle-gear airplane. Naturally it's quite modern in appearance because it was introduced in 1979.

The Skipper has a modern design and appearance. A wing of honeycomb ribs and bonded skin has no rivets on the surface.

Declining general aviation sales in the early 1980s essentially forced the Skipper out of production. None were built in 1981 and a complete production halt soon followed.

The other member of the Beech two-place family is the T-34 Mentor. This tandem-seat, low-wing, all-metal airplane saw extensive service with the military as a trainer. Many pilots consider them as war birds, due to their extensive military history.

Most T-34s are flying with the Civil Air Patrol or military-sponsored flying clubs. Only a few have found their way into the civilian market and they command a premium price.

Beech Aircraft Corp.

Fig. 7-7. Beechcraft 77 Skipper.

Make: Beech   Model: 77 Skipper
Year: 1979-81
Engine
    Make: Lycoming
    Model: O-235-L2C
    Horsepower: 115
    TBO: 2000 hours
Speeds
    Maximum: 122 mph

Cruise: 112 mph
Stall: 54 mph
Fuel capacity: 29 gallons
Rate of climb: 720 fpm
Transitions
    Takeoff over 50-foot obstacle: 1280 feet
    Ground run: 780 feet
    Landing over 50-foot obstacle: 1313 feet
    Ground roll: 670 feet
Weights
    Gross: 1675 pounds
    Empty: 1103 pounds
Seats: Two side by side
Dimensions
    Length: 24 feet
    Height: 6 feet 11 inches
    Span: 30 feet

Fig. 7-8. Beechcraft T-34 Mentor.

Make: Beech   Model: T-34 Mentor
Year: 1948-58
Engine
    Make: Continental
    Model: O-470
    Horsepower: 225
    TBO: NA
Speeds
    Maximum: 189 mph
    Cruise: 173 mph

Stall: 54 mph
Fuel capacity: NA
Rate of climb: 1120 fpm
Transitions
    Takeoff over 50-foot obstacle: 1200 feet
    Ground run: NA
    Landing over 50-foot obstacle: 960 feet
    Ground roll: NA
Weights
    Gross: 2975 pounds
    Empty: 2246 pounds
Seats: Two tandem
Dimensions
    Length: 25 feet 11 inches
    Height: 9 feet 7 inches
    Span: 32 feet 10 inches

Christen

Christen Industries introduced a "blank-sheet-of-paper" airplane in 1987.

The Husky, a two-place airplane, resembles the Piper Super Cub. Perhaps this is correct because the airplane was a new design that was meant to fill the gap that opened when Piper stopped building Super Cubs. Airplanes like this are used extensively by border patrol, forestry services, conservation departments, pipeline and power line patrols, and ranchers.

No large number of Husky airplanes will appear on the used market for a long time, due to newness and low production numbers. However, they are new (not seen in today's general aviation market), and should be considered as an alternative to purchasing an aging Super Cub.

Christen Ind.

Fig. 7-9. Christen Husky.

Make: Christen   Model: A-1 Husky
Year: 1987-up
Engine
    Make: Lycoming
    Model: O-360-C1G
    Horsepower: 180
    TBO: 2000 hours
Speeds
    Maximum: 145 mph
    Cruise: 140 ph
    Stall: 42 mph
Fuel capacity: 52 gallons
Rate of climb: 1500 fpm

Transitions
    Takeoff over 50-foot obstacle: NA
    Ground run: 200 feet
    Landing over 50-foot obstacle: NA
    Ground roll: 350 feet
Weights
    Gross: 1800 pounds
    Empty: 1190 pounds
Seats: Two tandem
Dimensions
    Length: 22 feet 7 inches
    Height: 6 feet 7 inches
    Span: 35 feet 6 inches

Cessna

The first Cessna two-placer appeared in 1946 as the Model 120. The 120 was a metal-fuselage airplane with fabric-covered wings. Naturally, it was a taildragger. The seating, as in all the Cessna two-placers, was side-by-side. Control wheels graced the instrument panel.

The Model 140 that followed was a deluxe version of the 120 with an electrical system, flaps, and a plushier cabin.

Many 120s have been updated to look like 140s with the addition of extra side windows and electric systems.

The 140A was the only Cessna two-place airplane for almost a decade. It was all-metal and had a Continental C-90 engine. It's interesting to note that the 140A airplane sold new for $3,695 and now commands more than double that price. Production ceased in 1950 after more than 7,000 120s, 140s, and 140As were manufactured.

Cessna introduced a new two-place trainer airplane in 1959. Starting life as a tricycle gear version of the 140A, the Model 150 was destined to become the most popular training aircraft ever made. During the period from 1959 until 1977 the 150 saw many changes, the more important were:

Noteworthy improvements for the Cessna 150 were omni-vision (rear windows) in 1964, the swept tail in 1966, and the Aerobat model in 1970.

The Aerobat 150A—stressed to 6Gs positive and 3Gs negative—has been very popular for aerobatic training.

Cessna rolled out the 152 in 1978. Appearance wise, the 152 is nearly identical to the 150, but it has a Lycoming O-235 engine, which burns 100 low lead fuel.

A used Cessna 150 or 152 is possibly the best buy in today's used airplane market. If carefully selected and well cared for, you should not loose money when sold. Nor should you have problems selling it.

Cessna Aircraft Co.

Fig. 7-10. Cessna 140.

Make: Cessna   Model: 120 and 140
Year: 1946-50
Engine
     Make: Continental
     Model: C-90
     Horsepower: 90
     TBO: 1800 hours
Speeds
     Maximum: 125 mph
     Cruise: 115 mph
     Stall: 45 mph
Fuel capacity: 25 gallons
Rate of climb: 680 fpm
Transitions
     Takeoff over 50-foot obstacle: 1850 feet
     Ground run: 650 feet
     Landing over 50-foot obstacle: 1530 feet
     Ground roll: 460 feet
Weights
     Gross: 1500 pounds
     Empty: 850 pounds
Seats: Two side by side
Dimensions
     Length: 20 feet 9 inches
     Height: 6 feet 3 inches
     Span: 32 feet 8 inches

Fig. 7-11. Cessna 1959 150.

Make Cessna   Model: 150
Year: 1959-77
Engine
     Make: Continental
     Model: O-200
     Horsepower: 100
     TBO: 1800 hours

Fig. 7-12. Cessna 1972 150.

Fig. 7-13. Cessna 1976 150 Aerobat.

Speeds
    Maximum: 125 mph
    Cruise: 122 mph
    Stall: 48 mph
Fuel capacity: 26 gallons
Rate of climb: 670 fpm
Transitions
    Takeoff over 50-foot obstacle: 1385 feet
    Ground run: 735 feet
    Landing over 50-foot obstacle: 1075 feet
    Ground roll: 445 feet
Weights
    Gross: 1600 pounds
    Empty: 1060 pounds
Seats: Two side by side

Dimensions
    Length: 23 feet 9 inches
    Height: 8 feet 9 inches
    Span: 32 feet 8 inches

Fig. 7-14. Cessna 1983 152.

Make: Cessna   Model: 152
Year: 1978-85
Engine
    Make: Lycoming
    Model: O-235-L2C
    Horsepower: 110
    TBO: 2000 hours
Speeds
    Maximum: 127 mph
    Cruise: 123 mph
    Stall: 50 mph
Fuel capacity: 26 gallons
Rate of climb: 715 fpm
Transitions
    Takeoff over 50-foot obstacle: 1340 feet
    Ground run: 725 feet
    Landing over 50-foot obstacle: 1200 feet
    Ground roll: 475 feet
Weights
    Gross: 1670 pounds
    Empty: 1129 pounds
Seats: Two side by side
Dimensions
    Length: 24 feet 1 inches
    Height: 8 feet 6 inches
    Span: 33 feet 2 inches

Ercoupe

Ercoupes were designed to be the most foolproof airplanes ever built. Originally they only had a control wheel for all directional maneuver. The control wheel operated the ailerons and rudder via control interconnections and even steered the nose wheel. No coordination was required to make aerial turns. In addition to the coordination effect, the controls were limited in the amount of travel, thereby avoiding stall entries. The original Ercoupe was supposed to be spin proof, a fact that led to issuance of "limited" pilot licenses in the late 40s when spin training was required.

Many modifications are available for the Ercoupe control system, such as rudder pedals. Rudder pedals eventually became an option.

The first Ercoupes had metal fuselages and fabric-covered wings; later models were all-metal. Ercoupes have tricycle landing gear. One popular feature is the fighter-like canopy that may be opened during flight.

Crosswind landings are unique. The trailing beam main gear takes the shock of the crabbed landing, then makes any directional correction. This is not as novel as you might think; the Boeing 707 lands the same way, unable to drop a wing during crosswind landings due to low engine-to-ground clearance.

Early Ercoupe model numbers indicated engine horsepower: 415C, 65 hp: 415D, 75 hp: 415E/G, 85 hp.

Ercoupe was the original name, but numerous companies have been associated with the airplane.

Forney Aircraft Company of Fort Collins, Colorado, became the owner of the production rights in 1956. Forney produced the F1, which was powered by a Continental C-90-12 engine, until 1960.

Alon Inc., of McPhearson, Kansas, purchased the Ercoupe production rights in the middle 1960s after Forney gave up. They introduced the A-2 as a 90-hp aircraft with optional rudder pedals and sliding canopy for $7,825.

Alon gave up in 1967 and sold the production rights to Mooney Aircraft of Kerrville, Texas. Mooney produced the A-2 as the A-2A. Mooney completely redesigned the Ercoupe in 1968 and called it the M-10 Cadet. It didn't sell well and was quickly discontinued.

Interestingly, the Ercoupe was designed to be very safe. Stalls were very minimal, and spins were impossible. A placard reads: This Airplane Characteristically Incapable of Spinning. When Mooney introduced the Cadet, stalls and spins were also introduced. The Ercoupe's twin-tail gave way to the Mooney vertical tail.

Last remnants of the Ercoupe went the way of so many other good things in life when production ceased in 1970, probably for all time.

More than 5,000 Ercoupes were manufactured (including Forney, Alon, and Mooney). A large number of these fine little planes are still flying, no doubt due to their small thirst for fuel, low prices, and low taxation of pilot skills.

A mechanic who is familiar with Ercoupes should examine an airplane prior to purchase. Some airplanes are close to 40 years old and corrosion might be present.

Fig. 7-15. Ercoupe 415.

Make: Ercoupe   Model: 415
Year: 1946-49
Engine
    Make: Continental
    Model: C-75-12(F)
    Horsepower: 75
    TBO: 1800 hours
Speeds
    Maximum: 125 mph
    Cruise: 114 mph
    Stall: 56 mph
Fuel capacity: 24 gallons
Rate of climb: 550 fpm
Transitions
    Takeoff over 50-foot obstacle: 2250 feet
    Ground run: 560 feet
    Landing over 50-foot obstacle: 1750 feet
    Ground roll: 350 feet
Weights
    Gross: 1400 pounds
    Empty: 815 pounds
Seats: Two side by side
Dimensions
    Length: 20 feet 9 inches
    Height: 5 feet 11 inches
    Span: 30 feet

Make: Forney   Model: F1
Year: 1957-60

Engine
    Make: Continental
    Model: C-90-12F
    Horsepower: 90
    TBO: 1800 hours
Speeds
    Maximum: 130 mph
    Cruise: 120 mph
    Stall: 56 mph
Fuel capacity: 24 gallons
Rate of climb: 600 fpm
Transitions
    Takeoff over 50-foot obstacle: 2100 feet
    Ground run: 500 feet
    Landing over 50-foot obstacle: 1750 feet
    Ground roll: 600
Weights
    Gross: 1400 pounds
    Empty: 890 pounds
Seats: Two side by side
Dimensions
    Length: 20 feet 9 inches
    Height: 5 feet 11 inches
    Span: 30 feet

Air Pix

Fig. 7-16. Alon A2.

Make: Alon   Model: A-2 and Mooney A2-A
Year: 1965-68
Engine
    Make: Continental
    Model: C-90-16F
    Horsepower: 90
    TBO: 1800 hours

Speeds
    Maximum: 128 mph
    Cruise: 124 mph
    Stall: 56 mph
Fuel capacity: 24 gallons
Rate of climb: 640 fpm
Transitions
    Takeoff over 50-foot obstacle: 2100 feet
    Ground run: 540 feet
    Landing over 50-foot obstacle: 1750 feet
    Ground roll: 650 feet
Weights
    Gross: 1450 pounds
    Empty: 930 pounds
Seats: Two side by side
Dimensions
    Length: 20 feet 2 inches
    Height: 5 feet 11 inches
    Span: 30 feet

Fig. 7-17. Mooney M-10 Cadet.

Make: Mooney   Model: M-10 Cadet
Year: 1969-70
Engine
    Make: Continental
    Model: C-90
    Horsepower: 90
    TBO: 1800 hours
Speeds
    Maximum: 118 mph
    Cruise: 110 mph
    Stall: 46 mph

Fuel capacity: 24 gallons
Rate of climb: 835 fpm
Transitions
    Takeoff over 50-foot obstacle: 1953 feet
    Ground run: 534 feet
    Landing over 50-foot obstacle: 1015 feet
    Ground roll: 431 feet
Weights
    Gross: 1450 pounds
    Empty: 950 pounds
Seats: Two side by side
Dimensions
    Length: 20 feet 8 inches
    Height: 7 feet 8 inches
    Span: 30 feet

Gulfstream (Grumman)

Jim Bede is a name often associated with small airplane design and over the years he has tried some novel approaches to airplane construction. His two-place airplane first flew as the AA-1, manufactured by American Aviation.

Wings were produced by bonding the metal skins to the frame with special adhesive—no rivets. Unfortunately there have been problems with the bonding, so some airplanes might have rivets in the wings for strength.

The Gulfstream airplanes are hot and unforgiving of pilot inattention. They land hot and need much room for takeoff.

The AA-1, AA-1B, Trainer, and TR-2 have the same airframe and basic engine combination: Lycoming O-235-C2C 108-hp engine from 1969-1976, O-235-L2C 115-hp for AA-1C, T-Cat, and Lynx.

You might see these airplanes advertised as Gulfstream American, Grumman American, or American Aviation.

Fig. 7-18. Gulfstream American AA-1.

Make: Gulfstream   Model: AA-1, AA-1B, TR-2 Trainer
Year: 1969-76
Engine
    Make: Lycoming
    Model: O-235-C2C
    Horsepower: 108
    TBO: 2000 hours
Speeds
    Maximum: 138 mph

Cruise: 124 mph
Stall: 60 mph
Fuel capacity: 24 gallons
Rate of climb: 710 fpm
Transitions
    Takeoff over 50-foot obstacle: 1590 feet
    Ground run: 890 feet
    Landing over 50-foot obstacle: 1100 feet
    Ground roll: 410 feet
Weights
    Gross: 1500 pounds
    Empty: 1000 pounds
Seats: Two side by side
Dimensions
    Length: 19 feet 3 inches
    Height: 6 feet 9 inches
    Span: 24 feet 5 inches

Make: Gulfstream   Model: AA-1C T-Cat/Lynx
Year: 1977-78
Engine
    Make: Lycoming
    Model: O-235-L2C
    Horsepower: 115
    TBO: 2000 hours
Speeds
    Maximum: 145 mph
    Cruise: 135 mph
    Stall: 60 mph
Fuel capacity: 22 gallons
Rate of climb: 700 fpm
Transitions
    Takeoff over 50-foot obstacle: 1590 feet
    Ground run: 890 feet
    Landing over 50-foot obstacle: 1125 feet
    Ground roll: 425 feet
Weights
    Gross: 1600 pounds
    Empty: 1066 pounds
Seats: Two side by side
Dimensions
    Length: 19 feet 3 inches
    Height: 7 feet 6 inches
    Span: 24 feet 5 inches

Luscombe

Luscombe two-seat airplanes feature stick controls and have notable reputations. First, the Luscombe has one of the strongest airframe and wing structures ever manufactured. Secondly, they are thought to have poor ground handling characteristics.

The first is true, the second is no doubt a story spread by those who don't really know. Luscombes can be touchy on landings due to the narrow-track landing gear. However, if the pilot stays on his toes he'll have no problems. (Actually, the same applies to all conventional-gear airplanes.)

Luscombes were produced from 1946 through 1949 by the Luscombe Airplane Corp. of Dallas, Texas. In the early 50s, Texas Engineering and Manufacturing Company (TEMCO) built the Luscombe 8F version. In 1955 Silvaire Aircraft Corp. was formed in Fort Collins, Colorado. Silvaire produced only the 8F. All production stopped in 1960 with 6,057 Series-8 Luscombes manufactured.

Like most other makes of airplanes, the various models indicated the engine horsepower: 8A, Continental 65 hp engine; 8B, Lycoming 65 hp engine; 8C/D, Continental 75 hp engine; 8E, Continental 85 hp engine; and 8F, Continental 90 hp engine.

Due to superior handling qualities, a Luscombe purchaser is cautioned to carefully inspect for damage caused by over stress from aerobatics.

Fig. 7-19. Luscombe 1946 8A.

Make: Luscombe   Model: 8A
Year: 1946-49
Engine
    Make: Continental
    Model: A-65
    Horsepower: 65
    TBO: 1800 hours

Speeds
   Maximum: 112 mph
   Cruise: 102 mph
   Stall: 48 mph
Fuel capacity: 14 gallons
Rate of climb: 550 fpm
Transitions
   Takeoff over 50-foot obstacle: 1950 feet
   Ground run: 1050 feet
   Landing over 50-foot obstacle: 1540 feet
   Ground roll: 450 feet
Weights
   Gross: 1260 pounds
   Empty: 665 pounds
Seats: Two side by side
Dimensions
   Length: 19 feet 8 inches
   Height: 6 feet 1 inches
   Span: 34 feet 7 inches

Make: Luscombe   Model: 8E
Year: 1946-47
Engine
   Make: Continental
   Model: C-85
   Horsepower: 85
   TBO: 1800 hours
Speeds
   Maximum: 122 mph
   Cruise: 112 mph
   Stall: 48 mph
Fuel capacity: 25 gallons
Rate of climb: 800 fpm
Transitions
   Takeoff over 50-foot obstacle: 1875 feet
   Ground run: 650 feet
   Landing over 50-foot obstacle: 1540 feet
   Ground roll: 450 feet
Weights
   Gross: 1400 pounds
   Empty: 810 pounds
Seats: Two side by side
Dimensions
   Length: 19 feet 8 inches
   Height: 6 feet 1 inches
   Span: 34 feet 7 inches

Fig. 7-20. Luscombe 8F.

Make: Luscombe   Model: 8F
Year: 1948-60
Engine
     Make: Continental
     Model: C-90
     Horsepower: 90
     TBO: 1800 hours
Speeds
     Maximum: 128 mph
     Cruise: 120 mph
     Stall: 48 mph
Fuel capacity: 25 gallons
Rate of climb: 900 fpm
Transitions
     Takeoff over 50-foot obstacle: 1850 feet
     Ground run: 550 feet
     Landing over 50-foot obstacle: 1540 feet
     Ground roll: 450 feet
Weights
     Gross: 1400 pounds
     Empty: 870 pounds
Seats: Two side by side
Dimensions
     Length: 20 feet
     Height: 6 feet 3 inches
     Span: 35 feet

Piper

No other name is more often associated with small airplanes than Piper. Many people refer to every small airplane as a Piper Cub.

Most famous is the J3. It was introduced in 1939 and was manufactured until World War II and again after the war. Production rates rose to a point of one every 10 minutes. Production ended in 1947 after building 14,125.

The J4 Cub Coupe, built before the war, used many J3 parts, which kept costs of design and production to a minimum. None were built after the war.

A J5 Cub Cruiser was introduced prior to the war; it seated three persons and shared many J3 parts. The pilot sat in a single bucket seat up front with a bench seat for two in the rear. After the war, the J5-C and PA-12 appeared. All are under powered by today's standards and none will fly three adults on a real hot day unless the original engine has been replaced with something larger.

The "J" in the early Piper model numbers indicated Walter C. Jamouneau, Piper's chief engineer. Later the PA designator was utilized to indicate Piper Aircraft.

In 1947 the PA-11 Cub Special replaced the J3. The 65-hp or 95-hp engine was completely enclosed by a cowling. The PA-11 can be soloed from the front seat, unlike the J3.

The PA-15 was introduced as the Vagabond in 1948. It was about as basic an airplane as you can imagine. The PA-15 had a Lycoming O-145 engine, rated at 65-hp, and seated two side-by-side. The main landing gear was solid, with the only shock-absorbing action from finesse of the pilot during landings.

Soon the PA-17, also called the Vagabond, came out. It was a better PA-15 with such niceties as bungee-type landing gear, floor mats, and the Continental A-65 engine, which is supposed to have considerably more pep than the Lycoming O-145.

The Super Cub, PA-18, is an airplane with roots traced back to the J3. Although built with a completely redesigned airframe, the PA-18 does outwardly look like a J3. It's a fun plane to fly, but most are work airplanes: photography, mapping, fish spotting, spraying, glider towing, and bush flying.

Production started in 1949 and more than 9,000 Super Cubs were built with a variety of engines from 90- to 150-hp.

The last two-place Piper airplane with tube-and-fabric design was the PA-22-108 colt. It was really a two-seat, flapless version of the Tri-Pacer, powered with a 108-hp Lycoming engine. The Colt was meant to be used as a trainer, however, most are used for fun flying.

Piper did build a modern trainer, the PA-38 Tomahawk. It's an all metal, low wing, tricycle gear airplane. Unfortunately it has been the victim of numerous ADs. Early models can be purchased for bargain prices. Later versions were improved.

Fig. 7-21. Piper J3 Cub.

Make: Piper   Model: J3 Cub
Year: 1939-47
Engine
    Make: Continental
    Model: A-65
    Horsepower: 65
    TBO: 1800 hours
Speeds
    Maximum: 87mph
    Cruise: 75 mph
    Stall: 38 mph
Fuel capacity: 9 gallons
Rate of climb: 450 fpm
Transitions
    Takeoff over 50-foot obstacle: 730 feet
    Ground run: 370 feet
    Landing over 50-foot obstacle: 470 feet
    Ground roll: 290 feet
Weights
    Gross: 1220 pounds
    Empty: 680 pounds
Seats: Two tandems
Dimensions
    Length: 22 feet 4 inches
    Height: 6 feet 8 inches
    Span: 35 feet 2 inches

Fig. 7-22. Piper J4 Cub Coupe.

Make: Piper   Model: J4 Cub Coupe
Year: 1939-41
Engine
     Make: Continental
     Model: A-65
     Horsepower: 65
     TBO: 1800 hours
Speeds
     Maximum: 95 mph
     Cruise: 80 mph
     Stall: 42 mph
Fuel capacity: 25 gallons
Rate of climb: 450 fpm
Transitions
     Takeoff over 50-foot obstacle: 750 feet
     Ground run: 370 feet
     Landing over 50-foot obstacle: 480 feet
     Ground roll: 300 feet
Weights
     Gross: 1301 pounds
     Empty: 650 pounds
Seats: Two side by side
Dimensions
     Length: 22 feet 6 inches
     Height: 6 feet 10 inches
     Span: 36 feet 2 inches

Make: Piper   Model: J5
Year: 1941

Engine
    Make: Continental
    Model: A-75
    Horsepower: 75
    TBO: 1800 hours
Speeds
    Maximum: 95 mph
    Cruise: 80 mph
    Stall: 43 mph
Fuel capacity: 25 gallons
Rate of climb: 400 fpm
Transitions
    Takeoff over 50-foot obstacle: 1250 feet
    Ground run: 750 feet
    Landing over 50-foot obstacle: 900 feet
    Ground roll: 400 feet
Weights
    Gross: 1450 pounds
    Empty: 820 pounds
Seats: Three
Dimensions
    Length: 22 feet 6 inches
    Height: 6 feet 10 inches
    Span: 35 feet 6 inches

Make: Piper   Model: J5C
Year: 1946
Engine
    Make: Lycoming
    Model: O-235-2
    Horsepower: 100
    TBO: 2000 hours
Speeds
    Maximum: 110 mph
    Cruise: 95 mph
    Stall: 45 mph
Fuel capacity: 20 gallons
Rate of climb: 650 fpm
Transitions
    Takeoff over 50-foot obstacle: 1050 feet
    Ground run: 650 feet
    Landing over 50-foot obstacle: 950 feet
    Ground roll: 450 feet
Weights
    Gross: 1550 pounds
    Empty: 860 pounds

Seats: Three
Dimensions
    Length: 22 feet 6 inches
    Height: 6 feet 10 inches
    Span: 35 feet 6 inches

Make: Piper   Model: PA-11 Cub Special (65)
Year: 1947-49
Engine
    Make: Continental
    Model: A-65
    Horsepower: 65
    TBO: 1800 hours
Speeds
    Maximum: 100 mph
    Cruise: 87 mph
    Stall: 38 mph
Fuel capacity: 18 gallons
Rate of climb: 550 fpm
Transitions
    Takeoff over 50-foot obstacle: 730 feet
    Ground run: 370 feet
    Landing over 50-foot obstacle: 470 feet
    Ground roll: 290 feet
Weights
    Gross: 1220 pounds
    Empty: 730 pounds
Seats: Two tandem
Dimensions
    Length: 22 feet 4 inches
    Height: 6 feet 8 inches
    Span: 35 feet 2 inches

Make: Piper   Model: PA-11 Cub Special (90)
Year: 1948-49
Engine
    Make: Continental
    Model: C-90
    Horsepower: 90
    TBO: 1800 hours
Speeds
    Maximum: 112 mph
    Cruise: 100 mph
    Stall: 40 mph
Fuel capacity: 18 gallons
Rate of climb: 900 fpm

Transitions
    Takeoff over 50-foot obstacle: 475 feet
    Ground run: 250 feet
    Landing over 50-foot obstacle: 550 feet
    Ground roll: 290 feet
Weights
    Gross: 1220 pounds
    Empty: 750 pounds
Seats: Two tandem
Dimensions
    Length: 22 feet 4 inches
    Height: 6 feet 8 inches
    Span: 35 feet 2 inches

Fig. 7-23. Piper PA-12 Cruiser.

Make: Piper   Model: PA-12
Year: 1946-47
Engine
    Make: Lycoming
    Model: O-235
    Horsepower: 100 (some have 108 hp)
    TBO: 2000 hours
Speeds
    Maximum: 115 mph
    Cruise: 105 mph
    Stall: 49 mph
Fuel capacity: 30 gallons
Rate of climb: 650 fpm
Transitions
    Takeoff over 50-foot obstacle: 720 feet
    Ground run: 410 feet
    Landing over 50-foot obstacle: 470 feet
    Ground roll: 360 feet

Weights
   Gross: 1500 pounds
   Empty: 855 pounds
Seats: Three
Dimensions
   Length: 23 feet 1 inches
   Height: 6 feet 9 inches
   Span: 35 feet 6 inches

Fig. 7-24. Piper PA-17 Vagabond.

Make: Piper   Model: PA-15/17 Vagabond
Year: 1948-50
Engine
   Make: Continental (Lycoming on PA-15)
   Model: A-65
   Horsepower: 65
   TBO: 1800 hours
Speeds
   Maximum: 100 mph
   Cruise: 90 mph
   Stall: 45 mph
Fuel capacity: 12 gallons
Rate of climb: 510 fpm
Transitions
   Takeoff over 50-foot obstacle: 1572 feet
   Ground run: 800 feet
   Landing over 50-foot obstacle: 1280 feet
   Ground roll: 450 feet
Weights
   Gross: 1100 pounds
   Empty: 620 pounds
Seats: Two side by side

Dimensions
    Length: 18 feet 7 inches
    Height: 6 feet
    Span: 29 feet 3 inches

Fig. 7-25. Piper PA-18 Super Cub.

Make: Piper   Model: PA-18 Super Cub (90)
Year: 1950-61
Engine
    Make: Continental
    Model: C-90
    Horsepower: 90
    TBO: 1800 hours
Speeds
    Maximum: 112 mph
    Cruise: 100 mph
    Stall: 42 mph
Fuel capacity: 18 gallons
Rate of climb: 700 fpm
Transitions
    Takeoff over 50-foot obstacle: 1150 feet
    Ground run: 400 feet
    Landing over 50-foot obstacle: 800 feet
    Ground roll: 385 feet
Weights
    Gross: 1500 pounds
    Empty: 800 pounds
Seats: Two tandem
Dimensions
    Length: 22 feet 5 inches
    Height: 6 feet 6 inches
    Span: 35 feet 3 inches

Make: Piper   Model: PA-18 Super Cub (125)
Year: 1951-52
Engine
    Make: Lycoming
    Model: O-290-D
    Horsepower: 125
    TBO: 2000 hours
Speeds
    Maximum: 125 mph
    Cruise: 112 mph
    Stall: 41 mph
Fuel capacity: NA
Rate of climb: 940 fpm
Transitions
    Takeoff over 50-foot obstacle: 650 feet
    Ground run: 420 feet
    Landing over 50-foot obstacle: 725 feet
    Ground roll: 350 feet
Weights
    Gross: 1500 pounds
    Empty: 845 pounds
Seats: Two tandem
Dimensions
    Length: 22 feet 5 inches
    Height: 6 feet 6 inches
    Span: 35 feet 3 inches

Make: Piper   Model: PA-18 Super Cub (150)
Year: 1955-83
Engine
    Make: Lycoming
    Model: O-320-A2A
    Horsepower: 150
    TBO: 2000 hours (1200 without modifications)
Speeds
    Maximum: 130 mph
    Cruise: 115 mph
    Stall: 43 mph
Fuel capacity: NA
Rate of climb: 960 fpm
Transitions
    Takeoff over 50-foot obstacle: 500 feet
    Ground run: 200 feet
    Landing over 50-foot obstacle: 725 feet
    Ground roll: 350 feet

Weights
    Gross: 1750 pounds
    Empty: 930 pounds
Seats: Two tandem
Dimensions
    Length: 22 feet 5 inches
    Height: 6 feet 6 inches
    Span: 35 feet 3 inches

Fig. 7-26. Piper PA-22 Colt.

Make: Piper   Model: PA-22-108 Colt
Year: 1961-63
Engine
    Make: Lycoming
    Model: O-235-C1B
    Horsepower: 108
    TBO: 2000 hours
Speeds
    Maximum: 120 mph
    Cruise: 108 mph
    Stall: 54 mph
Fuel capacity: 36 gallons
Rate of climb: 610 fpm
Transitions
    Takeoff over 50-foot obstacle: 1500 feet
    Ground run: 950 feet
    Landing over 50-foot obstacle: 1250 feet
    Ground roll: 500 feet
Weights
    Gross: 1650 pounds

Empty: 940 pounds
Seats: Two side by side
Dimensions
    Length: 20 feet
    Height: 6 feet 3 inches
    Span: 30 feet

Fig. 7-27. Piper PA-38 Tomahawk.

Make: Piper   Model: PA-38 Tomahawk
Year: 1978-82
Engine
    Make: Lycoming
    Model: O-235-L2C
    Horsepower: 112
    TBO: 2000 hours
Speeds
    Maximum: 125 mph
    Cruise: 122 mph
    Stall: 54 mph
Fuel capacity: 30 gallons
Rate of climb: 720 fpm
Transitions
    Takeoff over 50-foot obstacle: 1340 feet
    Ground run: 810 feet
    Landing over 50-foot obstacle: 1520 feet
    Ground roll: 710 feet
Weights
    Gross: 1670 pounds
    Empty: 1128 pounds
Seats: Two side by side
Dimensions
    Length: 23 feet 1 inch
    Height: 9 feet 1 inch
    Span: 34 feet

Swift

The Swift airplane was far ahead of other airplanes, built of all metal. It has retractable conventional landing gear and seats two. Originally built with a 125 hp engine, many have been modified by adding larger engines. I have seen several with 225 hp. They are real hot rods, and take plenty of pilot skill to safely handle.

Fig. 7-28. Swift GC-B1.

Make: Swift   Model: GC1B
Year: 1946-50
Engine
    Make: Continental
    Model: C-125
    Horsepower: 125
    TBO: 1800 hours
Speeds
    Maximum: 150 mph
    Cruise: 140 mph
    Stall: 50 mph
Fuel capacity: 30 gallons
Rate of climb: 1000 fpm
Transitions
    Takeoff over 50-foot obstacle: 1185 feet
    Ground run: 830 feet
    Landing over 50-foot obstacle: 880 feet
    Ground roll: 650 feet
Weights
    Gross: 1710 pounds
    Empty: 1125 pounds
Seats: Two side by side
Dimensions
    Length: 20 feet 9 inches
    Height: 6 feet 1 inch
    Span: 29 feet 3 inch

Taylorcraft

Taylorcraft airplanes started as part of Piper Aircraft. Originally C. Gilbert Taylor was in business with William Piper, however, there was a parting of the ways and Mr. Taylor set about on his own. Although built at the same time as the Piper Cub series, the Taylor airplanes never enjoyed Cub-like popularity.

Taylorcraft's BC-12 was introduced in 1941 but it saw a short production run due to the start of WWII.

After the war, Taylorcraft—like all the other aircraft companies—restarted production. The new plane was the BC-12D, an updated version of the pre war BC-12. The BC-12D is a tube-and-fabric, side-by-side seat airplane powered by a Continental 65-hp engine. Despite more wind resistance than the Piper J3, the Taylorcraft can out pace the Cub by better than 20 mph. The cockpit had dual control wheels, but brakes only on the pilot's side. About 3,000 BC-12Ds were built before production stopped in 1950.

By late 1950 Taylorcraft Aviation Corp., of Alliance, Ohio, was a thing of the past, and a new company, Taylorcraft Inc., began in Conway, Pennsylvania. This company introduced the Taylorcraft Model 19.

The Model 19 Sportsman was powered with an 85-hp Continental engine. About 200 airplanes were built before Taylorcraft Aviation folded in 1957. Until 1965 Univair, of Aurora, Colorado, built parts for the Taylorcrafts; no planes were built.

Production was restarted in 1965 at Alliance, Ohio. The airplane was called the Taylorcraft F-19 and was powered with a Continental O-200 engine. Other than slight updating, little had changed from the BC-12D airplanes. It really is difficult to improve upon something that is as good, and time-proven, as the postwar T-craft airplanes.

In 1980 the Continental engine was dropped in favor of the 118-hp Lycoming, which called for a new model number, the F-21. In 1985 the company moved to the old Piper plant at Lock Haven, Pennsylvania.

A Taylorcraft in good condition is about the most efficient (cheap) airplane you can fly because they burn a little over four gallons of fuel per hour.

Fig. 7-29. Taylorcraft BC-12D.

Make: Taylorcraft   Model: BC-12D
Year: 1946-47
Engine
    Make: Continental
    Model: A-65-8A
    Horsepower: 65
    TBO: 1800 hours
Speeds
    Maximum: 100 mph
    Cruise: 95 mph
    Stall: 38 mph
Fuel capacity: 18 gallons
Rate of climb: 500 fpm
Transitions
    Takeoff over 50-foot obstacle: 700 feet
    Ground run: 350 feet
    Landing over 50-foot obstacle: 450 feet
    Ground roll: 300 feet
Weights
    Gross: 1200 pounds
    Empty: 730 pounds
Seats: Two side by side
Dimensions
    Length: 21 feet 9 inches
    Height: 6 feet 10 inches
    Span: 36 feet

Make: Taylorcraft   Model: F-19
Year: 1974-79
Engine
    Make: Continental
    Model: O-200
    Horsepower: 100
    TBO: 1800 hours
Speeds
    Maximum: 127 mph
    Cruise: 115 mph
    Stall: 43 mph
Fuel capacity: 24 gallons
Rate of climb: 775 fpm
Transitions
    Takeoff over 50-foot obstacle: 350 feet
    Ground run: 200 feet
    Landing over 50-foot obstacle: 350 feet
    Ground roll: 275 feet

Weights
      Gross: 1500 pounds
      Empty: 900 pounds
Seats: Two side by side
Dimensions
      Length: 22 feet 1 inch
      Height: 6 feet 10 inch
      Span: 36 feet

Taylorcraft

Fig. 7-30. Taylorcraft F-21.

Make: Taylorcraft   Model: F-21 and F-21A/B
Year: 1980-88
Engine
      Make: Lycoming
      Model: O-235-L2C
      Horsepower: 118
      TBO: 2000 hours
Speeds
      Maximum: 125 mph
      Cruise: 120 mph
      Stall: 43 mph
Fuel capacity: 24 gallons
Rate of climb: 875 fpm
Transitions
      Takeoff over 50-foot obstacle: 350 feet
      Ground run: 275 feet

Landing over 50-foot obstacle: 350 feet
Ground roll: 275 feet
Weights
Gross: 1500 pounds
Empty: 990 pounds
Seats: Two side by side
Dimensions
Length: 22 feet 3 inches
Height: 6 feet 6 inches
Span: 36 feet

Varga

The Varga is an all-metal, military looking airplane that closely resembles the Beech T-34 Mentor. It was first built by Morrisey, then Shinn, before becoming the Varga. It has tricycle landing gear and tandem "green-house" seating. A few were produced as tail draggers. Two models, 150-hp and 180-hp, were built.

Air Pix

Fig. 7-31. Varga 2150.

Make: Varga   Model: 2150 Kachina
Year: 1977-80
Engine
    Make: Lycoming
    Model: O-320-A2C
    Horsepower: 150
    TBO: 2000 hours
Speeds
    Maximum: 135 mph
    Cruise: 120 mph
    Stall: 52 mph
Fuel capacity: 33 gallons
Rate of climb: 910 fpm
Transitions
    Takeoff over 50-foot obstacle: NA
    Ground run: 440 feet
    Landing over 50-foot obstacle: NA
    Ground roll: 450 feet
Weights
    Gross: 1817 pounds

        Empty: 1125 pounds
Seats: Two tandem
Dimensions
        Length: 21 feet 3 inches
        Height: 7 feet
        Span: 30 feet

Make: Varga   Model: 2180
Year: 1981-82
Engine
        Make: Lycoming
        Model: O-360-A4AD
        Horsepower: 180
        TBO: 2000 hours
Speeds
        Maximum: 150 mph
        Cruise: 133 mph
        Stall: 52 mph
Fuel capacity: 33 gallons
Rate of climb: 1310 fpm
Transitions
        Takeoff over 50-foot obstacle: NA
        Ground run: 400 feet
        Landing over 50-foot obstacle: NA
        Ground roll: 450 feet
Weights
        Gross: 1817 pounds
        Empty: 1175 pounds
Seats: Two tandem
Dimensions
        Length: 21 feet 3 inches
        Height: 7 feet
        Span: 30 feet

8

Four-Place Easy Fliers

THE FOUR-PLACE "EASY FLIER" airplane is by far the most airplane for the money. Over the years many have been produced by different companies, but there are only two basic designs: high-wing and low-wing.

There are few complexities about this group of airplanes. All have fixed landing gear, and most have fixed-pitch propellers. A few have constant-speed props as options. All have engines of less than 200 hp.

These airplanes, with few moving assemblies like retractable landing gear and constant-speed propellers, are usually inexpensive to maintain and don't over tax the abilities of the pilot.

Four-place easy fliers provide adequate transportation for personal and business needs. They are, as a group, easily found, easily sold, and easily equipped to fulfill most flying requirements. The majority of these planes are of all-metal construction and have tricycle landing gear.

A few classics belong in this category too and might be fabric covered (Stinsons, Tri-Pacers, Pacers).

Aero Commander

The Aero Commander Darter started life as the Volaire, and was made in Aliquippa, Pennsylvania. Only a few were made before Aero Commander, a division of Rockwell International, bought the design.

The airplane is very similar to the Cessna 172, is all metal, and has similar performance data. It was aimed at the Cessna 172 market, but failed and was soon removed from production.

Volaires were under powered with only 135-hp; Model 100 Darters have a 150-hp engine.

The biggest drawback I can see with these planes is availability of parts. Brake handles instead of toe brakes can be awkward.

Aero Commander built a larger version of the 100, called the Lark. It was powered with a 180-hp engine. Like the low-power version, it did not prove to be popular. Aero Commanders can also be found under Aero Commander, Rockwell, or Volaire in classified advertisements.

Fig. 8-1. Aero Commander 100 Darter.

Make: Aero Commander   Model: 100 Darter
Year: 1965-69
Engine
    Make: Lycoming
    Model: O-320-A2B (O-290 if Volaire version)
    Horsepower: 150 (135 if O-290 engine)
    TBO: 2000 hours (1200 without modifications)
Speeds
    Maximum: 133 mph
    Cruise: 128 mph
    Stall: 55 mph
Fuel capacity: 44 gallons
Rate of climb: 785 fpm
Transitions
    Takeoff over 50-foot obstacle: 1550 feet
    Ground run: 870 feet
    Landing over 50-foot obstacle: 1215 feet
    Ground roll: 650 feet
Weights
    Gross: 2250 pounds
    Empty: 1280 pounds
Seats: Four
Dimensions
    Length: 22 feet 6 inches
    Height: 9 feet 4 inches
    Span: 35 feet

Fig. 8-2. Aero Commander 100 Lark.

Make: Aero Commander   Model: 100 Lark
Year: 1968-71
Engine
    Make: Lycoming
    Model: O-360-A2F
    Horsepower: 180
    TBO: 2000 hours
Speeds
    Maximum: 138 mph
    Cruise: 132 mph
    Stall: 60 mph
Fuel capacity: 44 gallons
Rate of climb: 750 fpm
Transitions
    Takeoff over 50-foot obstacle: 1575 feet
    Ground run: 875 feet
    Landing over 50-foot obstacle: 1280 feet
    Ground roll: 675 feet
Weights
    Gross: 2450 pounds
    Empty: 1450 pounds
Seats: Four
Dimensions
    Length: 24 feet 9 inches
    Height: 10 feet 1 inch
    Span: 35 feet

Beechcraft

The typical Beechcraft four-place "easy flier" is of low-wing design and all-metal construction.

Landing gear is extremely strong and the articulating strut provides very smooth landings. They are usually well equipped with avionics, but values remain low due to a general lack of popularity.

Assorted engines have been utilized in these airplanes: 1963, Lycoming 169-hp; 1964, Continental 165-hp fuel-injected; and 1968, Lycoming 180-hp.

Model 23s carry several names: 1963, Model 23 Musketeer; 1964-65, Model A23 II Musketeer; 1966-67, Model A23 IIIA Custom; 1968-69, Model B23 Custom; 1970-71, Model C23 Custom; and 1972-83, Model C23 Sundowner. The model 23-24 was introduced in 1966 as the Super III with a 200-hp Lycoming fuel-injected engine.

Beech started production of the A23-19 Sport in 1966. It was considered a two- or four-place airplane, which meant with four persons on board you did not carry full fuel, due to gross weight. An optional aerobatic version was available.

Make: Beechcraft   Model: 23 Musketeer
Year: 1963
Engine
    Make: Lycoming
    Model: O-320-D2B
    Horsepower: 160
    TBO: 2000 hours (1200 without modifications)
Speeds
    Maximum: 144 mph
    Cruise: 135 mph
    Stall: 62 mph
Fuel capacity: 60 gallons
Rate of climb: 710 fpm
Transitions
    Takeoff over 50-foot obstacle: 1320 feet
    Ground run: 925 feet
    Landing over 50-foot obstacle: 1260 feet
    Ground roll: 640 feet
Weights
    Gross: 2300 pounds
    Empty: 1300 pounds
Seats: Four
Dimensions
    Length: 25 feet
    Height: 8 feet 3 inches
    Span: 32 feet 9 inches

Make: Beechcraft   Model: A23 II and IIIA Musketeer
Year: 1964-68

Engine
    Make: Continental
    Model: IO-346-A
    Horsepower: 165
    TBO: 1500 hours
Speeds
    Maximum: 146 mph
    Cruise: 138 mph
    Stall: 58 mph
Fuel capacity: 60 gallons
Rate of climb: 728 fpm
Transitions
    Takeoff over 50-foot obstacle: 1460 feet
    Ground run: 990 feet
    Landing over 50-foot obstacle: 1260 feet
    Ground roll: 640 feet
Weights
    Gross: 2350 pounds
    Empty: 1375 pounds
Seats: Four
Dimensions
    Length: 25 feet
    Height: 8 feet 3 inches
    Span: 32 feet 9 inches

Fig. 8-3. Beechcraft B-23 Musketeer.

Make: Beechcraft   Model: 23 B and C Custom
Year: 1968-71
Engine
    Make: Lycoming

Model: O-360-A4K
Horsepower: 180
TBO: 2000 hours
Speeds
    Maximum: 151 mph
    Cruise: 143 mph
    Stall: 60 mph
Fuel capacity: 60 gallons
Rate of climb: 820 fpm
Transitions
    Takeoff over 50-foot obstacle: 1380 feet
    Ground run: 950 feet
    Landing over 50-foot obstacle: 1275 feet
    Ground roll: 640 feet
Weights
    Gross: 2450 pounds
    Empty: 1416 pounds
Seats: Four
Dimensions
    Length: 25 feet
    Height: 8 feet 3 inches
    Span: 32 feet 9 inches

Fig. 8-4. Beechcraft C-23 Sundowner.

Make: Beechcraft   Model: C23 Sundowner
Year: 1972-83
Engine
    Make: Lycoming
    Model: O-360-A4G
    Horsepower: 180
    TBO: 2000 hours

Speeds
    Maximum: 147 mph
    Cruise: 133 mph
    Stall: 59 mph
Fuel capacity: 57 gallons
Rate of climb: 792 fpm
Transitions
    Takeoff over 50-foot obstacle: 1955 feet
    Ground run: 1130 feet
    Landing over 50-foot obstacle: 1484 feet
    Ground roll: 700 feet
Weights
    Gross: 2450 pounds
    Empty: 1494 pounds
Seats: Four
Dimensions
    Length: 25 feet 9 inches
    Height: 8 feet 3 inches
    Span: 32 feet 9 inches

Make: Beechcraft   Model: A23-24 Super III
Year: 1966-69
Engine
    Make: Lycoming
    Model: O-360-A2B
    Horsepower: 200
    TBO: 1800 hours (1200 without modifications)
Speeds
    Maximum: 158 mph
    Cruise: 150 mph
    Stall: 61 mph
Fuel capacity: 60 gallons
Rate of climb: 880 fpm
Transitions
    Takeoff over 50-foot obstacle: 1380 feet
    Ground run: 950 feet
    Landing over 50-foot obstacle: 1300 feet
    Ground roll: 660 feet
Weights
    Gross: 2550 pounds
    Empty: 1410 pounds
Seats: Four
Dimensions
    Length: 25 feet
    Height: 8 feet 3 inches
    Span: 32 feet 9 inches

Fig. 8-5. Beechcraft 23-19 Sport.

Make: Beechcraft   Model: 23-19/19A Sport and Sport III
Year: 1966-67
Engine
    Make: Lycoming
    Model: O-329-E2C
    Horsepower: 150
    TBO: 2000 hours
Speeds
    Maximum: 140 mph
    Cruise: 131 mph
    Stall: 56 mph
Fuel capacity: 60 gallons
Rate of climb: 700 fpm
Transitions
    Takeoff over 50-foot obstacle: 1320 feet
    Ground run: 885 feet
    Landing over 50-foot obstacle: 1220 feet
    Ground roll: 590 feet
Weights
    Gross: 2250 pounds
    Empty: 1374 pounds
Seats: Four (will not carry full fuel and four adult passengers)
Dimensions
    Length: 25 feet 1 inch
    Height: 8 feet 2 inches
    Span: 32 feet 7 inches

Make: Beechcraft   Model: B-19 Sport
Year: 1968-78
Engine
    Make: Lycoming
    Model: O-320-E2C
    Horsepower: 150
    TBO: 2000 hours
Speeds
    Maximum: 127 mph
    Cruise: 123 mph
    Stall: 57 mph
Fuel capacity: 57 gallons
Rate of climb: 680 fpm
Transitions
    Takeoff over 50-foot obstacle: 1635 feet
    Ground run: 1030 feet
    Landing over 50-foot obstacle: 1690 feet
    Ground roll: 825 feet
Weights
    Gross: 2150 pounds
    Empty: 1414 pounds
Seats: Four
Dimensions
    Length: 25 feet 9 inches
    Height: 8 feet 3 inches
    Span: 32 feet 9 inches

Cessna

The modern Cessna line of four-place airplanes started in 1948 with the model 170, which had a metal fuselage and a fabric-covered wing with conventional landing gear; B models are all-metal.

No doubt you can see the resemblance between the 170 and the 172—the 172 is a 170 with a nosewheel. The advent of the nosewheel rang the death knell for the 170 and in 1956 170 production stopped. Production of 172s continued into the 80s when all of general aviation faltered.

A good 170 will take you just about anywhere and do it economically. They are considered classics, based upon their years of production. In practice they are as modern as today.

The 172 has seen many refinements since entering production in 1956: 1960, swept-back tail; 1963, omni-vision; 1964, electric flaps; 1968, Lycoming O-320-E2D engine; 1970, conical wing tips; 1971, tubular landing gear; 1977, the O-320-H2AD low lead 160 hp engine; and 1981, Lycoming O-320-D2J engine.

The 172 is also known as the Skyhawk or Skyhawk 100, depending upon factory installed equipment. In 1977 the R172 Hawk XP was introduced with an IO-360-KB 195-hp fuel-injected Continental engine.

Cessna brought out the 175 Skylark in 1958 with a GO-300 Continental. It never achieved the popularity of the 172 due to chronic engine problems. The 175's GO-300 engine is geared and develops higher horsepower by operating at higher rpms, which leads to early wear problems. After all, common sense tells you that any engine running at 3,000 rpms will wear out faster than operating at 2,500 rpms. Additionally, the gear box needs regular maintenance.

Certain 175s that have had the GO-300 engine replaced with an O-320 or O-360 can represent good buys because they are stigmatized by the 175 model number.

Cessna 177 Cardinals appeared in 1968. The first 177s were under powered with a 150-hp Lycoming engine; 1969 models, and later, had 180-hp engines. A new airfoil in 1970 tried to improve low speed handling. Some models have constant-speed propellers. Cardinals remained in production until 1978.

Fig. 8-6. Cessna 1956 170B.

Make: Cessna   Model 170 (all)
Year: 1948-56
Engine
    Make: Continental
    Model: C-145-2
    Horsepower: 145
    TBO: 1800 hours
Speeds
    Maximum: 135 mph
    Cruise: 120 mph
    Stall: 52 mph
Fuel capacity: 42 gallons
Rate of climb: 660 fpm
Transitions
    Takeoff over 50-foot obstacle: 1820 feet
    Ground run: 700 feet
    Landing over 50-foot obstacle: 1145 feet
    Ground roll: 500 feet
Weights
    Gross: 2200 pounds
    Empty: 1260 pounds
Seats: Four
Dimensions
    Length: 25 feet
    Height: 6 feet 5 inches
    Span: 36 feet

Cessna Aircraft Co.

Fig. 8-7. Cessna 1956 172.

Make Cessna   Model: 172 Skyhawk
Year: 1956-67
Engine
    Make: Continental

Model: O-300 A (D after 1960)
Horsepower: 145
TBO: 1800 hours
Speeds
Maximum: 138 mph
Cruise: 130 mph
Stall: 49 mph
Fuel capacity: 42 gallons
Rate of climb: 645 fpm
Transitions
Takeoff over 50-foot obstacle: 1525 feet
Ground run: 865 feet
Landing over 50-foot obstacle: 1250 feet
Ground roll: 520 feet
Weights
Gross: 2300 pounds
Empty: 1260 pounds
Seats: Four
Dimensions
Length: 26 feet 6 inches
Height: 8 feet 11 inches
Span: 36 feet 2 inches

Fig. 8-8. Cessna 1968 Skyhawk.

Make: Cessna   Model: 172 Skyhawk
Year: 1968-76
Engine
Make: Lycoming
Model: O-320-E2D

Horsepower: 150
TBO: 2000 hours
Speeds
    Maximum: 139 mph
    Cruise: 131 mph
    Stall: 49 mph
Fuel capacity: 42 gallons
Rate of climb: 645 fpm
Transitions
    Takeoff over 50-foot obstacle: 1525 feet
    Ground run: 865 feet
    Landing over 50-foot obstacle: 1250 feet
    Ground roll: 520 feet
Weights
    Gross: 2300 pounds
    Empty: 1265 pounds
Seats: Four
Dimensions
    Length: 26 feet 6 inches
    Height: 8 feet 11 inches
    Span: 36 feet 2 inches

Make: Cessna   Model: 172 Skyhawk
Year: 1977-80
Engine
    Make: Lycoming
    Model: O-320-H2AD
    Horsepower: 160
    TBO: 2000 hours
Speeds
    Maximum: 141 mph
    Cruise: 138 mph
    Stall: 51 mph
Fuel capacity: 43 gallons
Rate of climb: 700 fpm
Transitions
    Takeoff over 50-foot obstacle: 1825 feet
    Ground run: 890 feet
    Landing over 50-foot obstacle: 1280 feet
    Ground roll: 540 feet
Weights
    Gross: 2400 pounds
    Empty: 1414 pounds
Seats: Four
Dimensions
    Length: 26 feet 6 inches

Height: 8 feet 11 inches
Span: 36 feet 2 inches

Fig. 8-9. Cessna 1978 Hawk XP II.

Make: Cessna   Model: 172 Skyhawk XP
Year: 1977-81
Engine
    Make: Continental
    Model: IO-360-K (KB after 1977)
    Horsepower: 195
    TBO: 1500 hours (2000 on KB)
Speeds
    Maximum: 153 mph
    Cruise: 150 mph
    Stall: 54 mph
Fuel capacity: 52 gallons
Rate of climb: 870 fpm
Transitions
    Takeoff over 50-foot obstacle: 1360 feet
    Ground run: 800 feet
    Landing over 50-foot obstacle: 1345 feet
    Ground roll: 635 feet
Weights
    Gross: 2550 pounds
    Empty: 1546 pounds
Seats: Four
Dimensions
    Length: 26 feet 6 inches
    Height: 8 feet 11 inches
    Span: 36 feet 2 inches

Fig. 8-10. Cessna 1959 Skylark 175.

Make: Cessna   Model: 175 Skylark and Powermatic
Year: 1958-62
Engine
    Make: Continental
    Model: GO-300 E
    Horsepower: 175
    TBO: 1200 hours
Speeds
    Maximum: 139 mph
    Cruise: 131 mph
    Stall: 50 mph
Fuel capacity: 52 gallons
Rate of climb: 850 fpm
Transitions
    Takeoff over 50-foot obstacle: 1340 feet
    Ground run: 735 feet
    Landing over 50-foot obstacle: 1155 feet
    Ground roll: 590 feet
Weights
    Gross: 2300 pounds
    Empty: 1330 pounds
Seats: Four
Dimensions
    Length: 25 feet
    Height: 8 feet 5 inches
    Span: 36 feet

Fig. 8-11. Cessna Cardinal 177.

Make: Cessna   Model: 177 Cardinal (150)
Year: 1968
Engine
    Make: Lycoming
    Model: O-320-E2D
    Horsepower: 150
    TBO: 2000 hours
Speeds
    Maximum: 144 mph
    Cruise: 134 mph
    Stall: 53 mph
Fuel capacity: 49 gallons
Rate of climb: 670 fpm
Transitions
    Takeoff over 50-foot obstacle: 1575 feet
    Ground run: 845 feet
    Landing over 50-foot obstacle: 1135 feet
    Ground roll: 400 feet
Weights
    Gross: 2350 pounds
    Empty: 1415 pounds
Seats: Four
Dimensions
    Length: 27 feet 3 inches
    Height: 8 feet 7 inches
    Span: 35 feet 7 inches

Make: Cessna   Model: 177 Cardinal (180)
Year: 1969-78
Engine
    Make: Lycoming
    Model: O-360-A1F6 (A1F6D after 1975)
    Horsepower: 180
    TBO: 2000 hours (1800 on A1F6D without mod)
Speeds
    Maximum: 150 mph
    Cruise: 139 mph
    Stall: 53 mph
Fuel capacity: 50 gallons
Rate of climb: 840 fpm
Transitions
    Takeoff over 50-foot obstacle: 1400 feet
    Ground run: 750 feet
    Landing over 50-foot obstacle: 1220 feet
    Ground roll: 600 feet
Weights
    Gross: 2500 pounds
    Empty: 1430 pounds
Seats: Four
Dimensions
    Length: 27 feet 3 inches
    Height: 8 feet 7 inches
    Span: 35 feet 7 inches

Gulfstream American

Gulfstream built two airplanes in the four-place "easy flier" category. The AA5 and AA5A Traveler or Cheetah have a 150-hp engine and the AA5B Tiger has a 180-hp engine. Production ceased in 1979.

Gulfstream airplanes are unusual because they have space-age wing construction. No rivets hold the skins in place; adhesive holds the skin to the honeycombed wing ribs.

Gulfstreams have a sliding canopy. Step over the sidewall of the cabin and step onto the seat. It can be inconvenient for ladies and provides a complete cabin wash down in rain.

Fig. 8-12. Gulfstream AA5 Cheetah.

Make: Gulfstream   Model: AA5/AA5A Traveler/Cheetah
Year: 1972-79
Engine
    Make: Lycoming
    Model: O-320-E2G
    Horsepower: 150
    TBO: 2000 hours
Speeds
    Maximum: 150 mph
    Cruise: 140 mph
    Stall: 58 mph
Fuel capacity: 38 gallons
Rate of climb: 660 fpm
Transitions

Takeoff over 50-foot obstacle: 1600 feet
Ground run: 880 feet
Landing over 50-foot obstacle: 1100 feet
Ground roll: 380 feet
Weights
Gross: 2200 pounds
Empty: 1200 pounds
Seats: Four
Dimensions
Length: 22 feet
Height: 8 feet
Span: 32 feet 6 inches

Fig. 8-13. Gulfstream AA5 Tiger.

Make: Gulfstream   Model: AA5B Tiger
Year: 1975-79
Engine
Make: Lycoming
Model: O-360-A4K
Horsepower: 180
TBO: 2000 hours
Speeds
Maximum: 170 mph
Cruise: 160 mph

Stall: 61 mph
Fuel capacity: 51 gallons
Rate of climb: 850 fpm
Transitions
    Takeoff over 50-foot obstacle: 1550 feet
    Ground run: 865 feet
    Landing over 50-foot obstacle: 1120 feet
    Ground roll: 410 feet
Weights
    Gross: 2400 pounds
    Empty: 1285 pounds
Seats: Four
Dimensions
    Length: 22 feet
    Height: 8 feet
    Span: 31 feet 6 inches

Luscombe

The Luscombe Sedan is all-metal with conventional landing gear. Few were built and they are infrequently seen on the used market. Sedans had a rear window, something Cessna discovered 20 years later. Luscombe Sedans are unusually easy to handle due to very wide gear stance.

Air Pix

Fig. 8-14. Luscombe 11 Sedan.

Make: Luscombe   Model: 11 Sedan
Year: 1948-50
Engine
    Make: Continental
    Model: C-165
    Horsepower: 165
    TBO: 1800 hours
Speeds
    Maximum: 140 mph
    Cruise: 130 mph
    Stall: 55 mph
Fuel capacity: 42 gallons
Rate of climb: 900 fpm
Transitions
    Takeoff over 50-foot obstacle: 1540 feet
    Ground run: 800 feet
    Landing over 50-foot obstacle: 1310 feet
    Ground roll: 500 feet
Weights
    Gross: 2280 pounds
    Empty: 1280 pounds
Seats: Four
Dimensions
    Length: 23 feet 6 inches
    Height: 6 feet 10 inches
    Span: 38 feet

Maule

The Maule M-4 was conceived as a homebuilt called the Bee Dee M4. Rather than market it as a homebuilt, designer B.D. Maule decided to produce the airplane himself.

Constructed of a tubular fuselage covered with Fiberglass and with all-metal wings, these planes exhibit excellent short-field capabilities, yet have good cruise speeds. They are fine examples of matching engine power to wing design.

Several models of the Maule are available, mostly outgrowths of the M-4, but with much more power. (See Chapter 10.)

Fig. 8-15. Maule M-4.

Make: Maule   Model: M-4 Jeteson
Year: 1962-67
Engine
    Make: Continental
    Model: O-300-A
    Horsepower: 145
    TBO: 1800 hours
Speeds
    Maximum: 180 mph
    Cruise: 150 mph
    Stall: 40 mph
Fuel capacity: 42 gallons
Rate of climb: 700 fpm
Transitions
    Takeoff over 50-foot obstacle: 900 feet
    Ground run: 700 feet
    Landing over 50-foot obstacle: 600 feet
    Ground roll: 450 feet
Weights
    Gross: 2100 pounds
    Empty: 1100 pounds
Seats: Four
Dimensions
    Length: 22 feet
    Height: 6 feet 2 inches
    Span: 29 feet 8 inches

Piper

Piper started production of four-place airplanes with the Family Cruiser PA-14; it was small and underpowered; only 237 were manufactured; it was replaced with the PA-16 Clipper, a slightly larger plane.

In 1950 the PA-20 Pacer series appeared. Like the PA-14s and 16s, the original PA-20s were tube and fabric construction and had conventional landing gear. They had small engines and did not display eye dazzling performance numbers.

Evolution of the Pacer resulted in the Tri-Pacer, billed as an anyone can fly it airplane because of tricycle landing gear. It became a success and soon the Tri-Pacer's sales far outstripped the Pacer. General aviation customers were demanding easier-to-handle airplanes and they found what they wanted in the Tri-Pacer.

PA-22s, as Tri-Pacers are officially known, were built with several different engines. Power varied from 125- to 160-hp.

Piper introduced the PA-28 series in 1961. Unlike previous Piper products, this new airplane was of all-metal construction and had low wings. The PA-28 series is the backbone for all of Piper's all-metal single-engine products.

Initially the PA-28 was produced as the Model 140, powered with a 150-hp Lycoming engine. An optional version PA-28 160 with a 160-hp engine was also available.

The Cherokee 140 was introduced in 1964 as a two-to-four place trainer. Initially delivered with a 140-hp engine, the 150-hp Lycoming was available for increased load carrying. The Model 140 is also called the Cruiser or Fliteliner. It was produced from 1964 to 1977.

The PA-28 180 was built from 1963 until 1975 and is a true four-place airplane. Later called the Challenger or Archer, it had a 180-hp engine.

Piper in 1974 changed wing design of the entire PA-28 series. Often called the Warrior wing, it resulted in increased load carrying abilities and very gentle stall characteristics. The new wing was added to the Challenger and Archer fuselage (slightly larger) and designated the Model 151. It had a 150 hp engine and was built from 1974 through 1977. It was replaced by the Model 161 with a 160-hp low lead engine in late 1977.

The PA-28 181 was introduced in 1976 as the Archer II with a 180-hp Lycoming engine.

Make: Piper   Model: PA-14 Cruiser
Year: 1948-49
Engine
    Make: Lycoming
    Model: O-235-C1
    Horsepower: 115
    TBO: 2000 hours
Speeds
    Maximum: 123 mph
    Cruise: 110 mph
    Stall: 46 mph

Fuel capacity: 38 gallons
Rate of climb: 540 fpm
Transitions
    Takeoff over 50-foot obstacle: 1770 feet
    Ground run: 720 feet
    Landing over 50-foot obstacle: 1410 feet
    Ground roll: 470 feet
Weights
    Gross: 1850 pounds
    Empty: 1020 pounds
Seats: Four
Dimensions
    Length: 23 feet 2 inches
    Height: 6 feet 7 inches
    Span: 35 feet 6 inches

Fig. 8-16. Piper PA-16.

Make: Piper   Model: PA-16 Clipper
Year: 1949
Engine
    Make: Lycoming
    Model: O-235-C1
    Horsepower: 115
    TBO: 2000 hours
Speeds
    Maximum: 125 mph
    Cruise: 112 mph
    Stall: 50 mph

Fuel capacity: 36 gallons
Rate of climb: 580 fpm
Transitions
    Takeoff over 50-foot obstacle: 1910 feet
    Ground run: 720 feet
    Landing over 50-foot obstacle: 1440 feet
    Ground roll: 600 feet
Weights
    Gross: 1650 pounds
    Empty: 850 pounds
Seats: Four
Dimensions
    Length: 20 feet 1 inch
    Height: 6 feet 2 inches
    Span: 29 feet 3 inches

Fig. 8-17. Piper PA-20 Pacer.

Make: Piper   Model: PA-20 Pacer
Year: 1951-52
Engine
    Make: Lycoming
    Model: O-290-D
    Horsepower: 125
    TBO: 2000 hours
Speeds
    Maximum: 134 mph
    Cruise: 119 mph
    Stall: 47 mph
Fuel capacity: 36 gallons
Rate of climb: 550 fpm
Transitions
    Takeoff over 50-foot obstacle: 1725 feet
    Ground run: 1210 feet
    Landing over 50-foot obstacle: 1280 feet
    Ground roll: 780 feet

Weights
    Gross: 1800 pounds
    Empty: 970 pounds
Seats: Four
Dimensions
    Length: 20 feet 4 inches
    Height: 6 feet 1 inch
    Span: 29 feet 3 inches

Make: Piper   Model: PA-20 Pacer
Year: 1952-54
Engine
    Make: Lycoming
    Model: O-290-D2 (optional constant speed propeller)
    Horsepower: 135
    TBO: 1500 hours
Speeds
    Maximum: 139 mph
    Cruise: 125 mph
    Stall: 48 mph
Fuel capacity: 36 gallons
Rate of climb: 620 fpm
Transitions
    Takeoff over 50-foot obstacle: 1600 feet
    Ground run: 1120 feet
    Landing over 50-foot obstacle: 1280 feet
    Ground roll: 780 feet
Weights
    Gross: 1920 pounds
    Empty: 1020 pounds
Seats: Four
Dimensions
    Length: 20 feet 4 inches
    Height: 6 feet 1 inch
    Span: 29 feet 3 inches

Make: Piper   Model: PA-22 Tri-Pacer
Year: 1951-52
Engine
    Make: Lycoming
    Model: O-290-D
    Horsepower: 125
    TBO: 2000 hours
Speeds
    Maximum: 134 mph
    Cruise: 130 mph
    Stall: 48 mph

Fig. 8-18. Piper PA-22 Tri-Pacer.

Fuel capacity: 36 gallons
Rate of climb: 550 fpm
Transitions
    Takeoff over 50-foot obstacle: 1600 feet
    Ground run: 1120 feet
    Landing over 50-foot obstacle: 1280 feet
    Ground roll: 650 feet
Weights
    Gross: 1850 pounds
    Empty: 1060 pounds
Seats: Four
Dimensions
    Length: 20 feet 4 inches
    Height: 8 feet 3 inches
    Span: 29 feet 3 inches

Make: Piper   Model: PA-22 Tri-Pacer
Year: 1952-54
Engine
    Make: Lycoming
    Model: O-290-D2
    Horsepower: 135
    TBO: 1500 hours
Speeds
    Maximum: 137 mph
    Cruise: 132 mph
    Stall: 48 mph
Fuel capacity: 36 gallons
Rate of climb: 620 fpm

Transitions
    Takeoff over 50-foot obstacle: 1550 feet
    Ground run: 1080 feet
    Landing over 50-foot obstacle: 1280 feet
    Ground roll: 650 feet
Weights
    Gross: 1850 pounds
    Empty: 1060 pounds
Seats: Four
Dimensions
    Length: 20 feet 4 inches
    Height: 8 feet 3 inches
    Span: 29 feet 3 inches

Make: Piper   Model: PA-22 Tri-Pacer
Year: 1955-60
Engine
    Make: Lycoming
    Model: O-320-A1A
    Horsepower: 150
    TBO: 2000 hours (1200 without modifications)
Speeds
    Maximum: 139 mph
    Cruise: 132 mph
    Stall: 49 mph
Fuel capacity: 36 gallons
Rate of climb: 725 fpm
Transitions
    Takeoff over 50-foot obstacle: 1500 feet
    Ground run: 1050 feet
    Landing over 50-foot obstacle: 1280 feet
    Ground roll: 650 feet
Weights
    Gross: 2000 pounds
    Empty: 1100 pounds
Seats: Four
Dimensions
    Length: 20 feet 4 inches
    Height: 8 feet 3 inches
    Span: 29 feet 3 inches

Make: Piper   Model: PA-22 Tri-Pacer
Year: 1958-60
Engine
    Make: Lycoming
    Model: O-320-B2A

Horsepower: 160
TBO: 2000 hours (1200 without modifications)
Speeds
    Maximum: 141 mph
    Cruise: 133 mph
    Stall: 48 mph
Fuel capacity: 36 gallons
Rate of climb: 800 fpm
Transitions
    Takeoff over 50-foot obstacle: 1480 feet
    Ground run: 1035 feet
    Landing over 50-foot obstacle: 1280 feet
    Ground roll: 650 feet
Weights
    Gross: 2000 pounds
    Empty: 1110 pounds
Seats: Four
Dimensions
    Length: 20 feet 5 inches
    Height: 8 feet 3 inches
    Span: 29 feet 3 inches

Fig. 8-19. Piper PA-28 140 Cruiser.

Make: Piper   Model: PA-28 140
Year: 1964-77
Engine
    Make: Lycoming
    Model: O-320-E2A
    Horsepower: 150
    TBO: 2000 hours (1200 without modifications)

Speeds
    Maximum: 139 mph
    Cruise: 130 mph
    Stall: 53 mph
Fuel capacity: 36 gallons
Rate of climb: 660 fpm
Transitions
    Takeoff over 50-foot obstacle: 1750 feet
    Ground run: 800 feet
    Landing over 50-foot obstacle: 1890 feet
    Ground roll: 535 feet
Weights
    Gross: 2150 pounds
    Empty: 1205 pounds
Seats: Four
Dimensions
    Length: 23 feet 3 inches
    Height: 7 feet 3 inches
    Span: 30 feet

Make: Piper   Model: PA-28 Cherokee
Year: 1962-67
Engine
    Make: Lycoming
    Model: O-320-B2B
    Horsepower: 160
    TBO: 2000 hours (1200 without modifications)
Speeds
    Maximum: 141 mph
    Cruise: 132 mph
    Stall: 55 mph
Fuel capacity: 36 gallons
Rate of climb: 700 fpm
Transitions
    Takeoff over 50-foot obstacle: 1700 feet
    Ground run: 775 feet
    Landing over 50-foot obstacle: 1890 feet
    Ground roll: 550 feet
Weights
    Gross: 2200 pounds
    Empty: 1210 pounds
Seats: Four
Dimensions
    Length: 23 feet 3 inches
    Height: 7 feet 3 inches
    Span: 30 feet

Fig. 8-20. Piper PA-28 180 Challenger.

Make: Piper   Model: PA-28 Challenger/Archer
Year: 1963-75
Engine
    Make: Lycoming
    Model: O-360-A3A
    Horsepower: 180
    TBO: 2000 hours (1200 without modifications)
Speeds
    Maximum: 150 mph
    Cruise: 141 mph
    Stall: 57 mph
Fuel capacity: 50 gallons
Rate of climb: 720 fpm
Transitions
    Takeoff over 50-foot obstacle: 1620 feet
    Ground run: 725 feet
    Landing over 50-foot obstacle: 1150 feet
    Ground roll: 600 feet
Weights
    Gross: 2400 pounds
    Empty: 1225 pounds
Seats: Four
Dimensions
    Length: 23 feet 3 inches
    Height: 7 feet 3 inches
    Span: 30 feet

Make: Piper   Model: PA-28-151 Warrior
Year: 1974-77
Engine
    Make: Lycoming
    Model: O-320-E3D

Horsepower: 150
TBO: 2000 hours
Speeds
Maximum: 134 mph
Cruise: 126 mph
Stall: 58 mph
Fuel capacity: 48 gallons
Rate of climb: 649 fpm
Transitions
Takeoff over 50-foot obstacle: 1760 feet
Ground run: 1065 feet
Landing over 50-foot obstacle: 1115 feet
Ground roll: 595 feet
Weights
Gross: 2325 pounds
Empty: 1301 pounds
Seats: Four
Dimensions
Length: 23 feet 8 inches
Height: 7 feet 3 inches
Span: 35 feet

Fig. 8-21. Piper PA-28 161 Warrior II.

Make: Piper   Model: PA-28-161 Warrior II
Year: 1977-up
Engine
    Make: Lycoming
    Model: O-320-D3G
    Horsepower: 160
    TBO: 2000 hours
Speeds
    Maximum: 145 mph
    Cruise: 140 mph
    Stall: 57 mph
Fuel capacity: NA
Rate of climb: 710 fpm
Transitions
    Takeoff over 50-foot obstacle: 1490 feet
    Ground run: 975 feet
    Landing over 50-foot obstacle: 1115 feet
    Ground roll: 595 feet
Weights
    Gross: 2325 pounds
    Empty: 1353 pounds
Seats: Four
Dimensions
    Length: 23 feet 8 inches
    Height: 7 feet 3 inches
    Span: 35 feet

Piper Aircraft Corp.

Fig. 8-22. Piper PA-28 181 Archer II.

Make: Piper   Model: PA-28-181 Archer II
Year: 1976-up
Engine
    Make: Lycoming
    Model: O-360-A4M
    Horsepower: 180
    TBO: 2000 hours
Speeds
    Maximum: 154 mph
    Cruise: 148 mph
    Stall: 61 mph
Fuel capacity: 48 gallons
Rate of climb: 735 fpm
Transitions
    Takeoff over 50-foot obstacle: 1625 feet
    Ground run: 870 feet
    Landing over 50-foot obstacle: 1390 feet
    Ground roll: 925 feet
Weights
    Gross: 2550 pounds
    Empty: 1413 pounds
Seats: Four
Dimensions
    Length: 23 feet 8 inches
    Height: 7 feet 3 inches
    Span: 35 feet

Stinson

Stinsons were built of tube and fabric. Many have been metalized—covered with metal panels in place of fabric, all have conventional landing gear.

Franklin engines—heavy case and light case—were used on these airplanes. Only the heavy case engine is acceptable because the light case did not stand up well to use and abuse.

The 108-1 models had 150-hp engines and Model 108-2 and -3 had 165-hp engines. Many have been modified by the addition of Lycoming or Continental engines ranging from 200- to 250-hp. Stinsons make good seaplanes.

Piper bought out Stinson in 1948 and produced a few Model 108s before production was halted. Any Stinson with a serial number above 4231 is a Piper airplane.

Make: Stinson   Model: 108-1 Voyager
Year: 1946-47
Engine
    Make: Franklin
    Model: 6A4-150-B23
    Horsepower: 150
    TBO: 1200
Speeds
    Maximum: 130 mph
    Cruise: 117 mph
    Stall: 57 mph
Fuel capacity: 50 gallons
Rate of climb: 700 fpm
Transitions
    Takeoff over 50-foot obstacle: 1750 feet
    Ground run: 945 feet
    Landing over 50-foot obstacle: 1400 feet
    Ground roll: 940 feet
Weights
    Gross: 2230 pounds
    Empty: 1206 pounds
Seats: Four
Dimensions
    Length: 24 feet
    Height: 7 feet
    Span: 33 feet 11 inches

Fig. 8-23. Stinson 108.

Make: Stinson   Model: 108-2/3 Voyager and Station Wagon
Year: 1947-48
Engine
    Make: Franklin
    Model: 6A4-165-B3
    Horsepower: 165
    TBO: 1200
Speeds
    Maximum: 133 mph
    Cruise: 125 mph
    Stall: 61 mph
Fuel capacity: 50 gallons
Rate of climb: 750 fpm
Transitions
    Takeoff over 50-foot obstacle: 1400 feet
    Ground run: 980 feet
    Landing over 50-foot obstacle: 1680 feet
    Ground roll: 940 feet
Weights
    Gross: 2400 pounds
    Empty: 1300 pounds
Seats: Four
Dimensions
    Length: 24 feet
    Height: 7 feet
    Span: 33 feet 11 inches

9

Complex Airplanes

COMPLEX AIRPLANES REPRESENT the pinnacle of single-engine aircraft design and capabilities. They are real people movers and are used extensively by businessmen who require fast and reliable transportation.

Complex airplane cruise speeds are higher, ranges are longer, and load capacities are greater than simpler four-place airplanes. They have more features like retractable landing gear and constant-speed propellers. Many complex airplanes offer up to six-place seating.

Purchase and maintenance expenses of these airplanes are considerably higher than for the simpler four-place planes. However, if you can justify this airplane class, then expenses will not be out of line.

Most of these airplanes are IFR-equipped. Perhaps this is an indication of business usage, where reliable transportation is a requirement rather than a pleasure.

Airplane ownership might offer tax advantages for a business. Ownership can also present difficult tax problems to surmount. Consult an accountant for financial advice if you are going to use an airplane for business.

Aero Commander

Aero Commander produced two series of complex single-engine airplanes: Meyers and 112/114.

The Meyers 200 is a sleek, low wing, very fast airplane. The cabin is smaller than the older Beechcraft Bonanzas but not too cramped for the average family.

It was first produced with a 260-hp engine, then after 1964 a 285-hp engine. Production ceased in 1967.

Model 112s came out in 1972 and were powered with a 200-hp fuel-injected engine. The manufacturer claimed that the cabin was the most spacious in its class. The 112TC Alpine with a turbo-charged 210-hp engine debuted in 1976. The same airplane, except powered with a 260-hp fuel-injected engine, is called the Model 114 Gran Turismo. It was built from 1976 to 1979.

Search for them under Meyers, Aero Commander, Rockwell, and Gulfstream in classified ads.

Fig. 9-1. Aero Commander 200 Meyers.

Make: Aero Commander   Model: 200 A/B Meyers
Year: 1959-64
Engine
    Make: Continental
    Model: IO-470-D
    Horsepower: 260
    TBO: 1500 hours
Speeds
    Maximum: 216 mph
    Cruise: 195 mph
    Stall: 62 mph
Fuel capacity: 40 gallons
Rate of climb: 1245 fpm
Transitions
    Takeoff over 50-foot obstacle: 1260 feet
    Ground run: 1010 feet
    Landing over 50-foot obstacle: 1150 feet
    Ground roll: 850 feet
Weights
    Gross: 3000 pounds
    Empty: 1975 pounds
Seats: Four
Dimensions
    Length: 24 feet 4 inches
    Height: 8 feet 6 inches
    Span: 30 feet 5 inches

Make: Aero Commander   Model: 200 A/B Meyers
Year: 1965-67

Engine
    Make: Continental
    Model: IO-520 A
    Horsepower: 285
    TBO: 1700 hours
Speeds
    Maximum: 215 mph
    Cruise: 210 mph
    Stall: 64 mph
Fuel capacity: 40 gallons
Rate of climb: 1450 fpm
Transitions
    Takeoff over 50-foot obstacle: 1150 feet
    Ground run: 900 feet
    Landing over 50-foot obstacle: 1150 feet
    Ground roll: 850 feet
Weights
    Gross: 3000 pounds
    Empty: 1990 pounds
Seats: Four
Dimensions
    Length: 24 feet 4 inches
    Height: 8 feet 6 inches
    Span: 30 feet 5 inches

Fig. 9-2. Rockwell 112.

Make: Rockwell   Model: 112
Year: 1972-77
Engine
    Make: Lycoming
    Model: IO-360-C1B6
    Horsepower: 200
    TBO: 1800 hours
Speeds
    Maximum: 175 mph
    Cruise: 165 mph
    Stall: 61 mph
Fuel capacity: 60 gallons
Rate of climb: 1000 fpm
Transitions
    Takeoff over 50-foot obstacle: 1460 feet
    Ground run: 880 feet
    Landing over 50-foot obstacle: 1310 feet
    Ground roll: 680 feet
Weights
    Gross: 2550 pounds
    Empty: 1530 pounds
Seats: Four
Dimensions
    Length: 24 feet 11 inches
    Height: 8 feet 5 inches
    Span: 32 feet 9 inches

Make: Rockwell   Model: 112 Alpine
Year: 1976-79
Engine
    Make: Lycoming
    Model: TO-360-C1B6D
    Horsepower: 210
    TBO: 1400 hours
Speeds
    Maximum: 196 mph
    Cruise: 187 mph
    Stall: 61 mph
Fuel capacity: 60 gallons
Rate of climb: 900 fpm
Transitions
    Takeoff over 50-foot obstacle: 1750 feet
    Ground run: 930 feet
    Landing over 50-foot obstacle: 1250 feet
    Ground roll: 680 feet

Weights
    Gross: 2950 pounds
    Empty: 2035 pounds
Seats: Four
Dimensions
    Length: 24 feet 11 inches
    Height: 8 feet 5 inches
    Span: 32 feet 9 inches

Make: Rockwell   Model: 114 Gran Turismo
Year: 1976-79
Engine
    Make: Lycoming
    Model: IO-540-T3B5D
    Horsepower: 260
    TBO: 2000 hours
Speeds
    Maximum: 191 mph
    Cruise: 181 mph
    Stall: 63 mph
Fuel capacity: 68 gallons
Rate of climb: 1030 fpm
Transitions
    Takeoff over 50-foot obstacle: 2150 feet
    Ground run: NA
    Landing over 50-foot obstacle: 1200 feet
    Ground roll: NA
Weights
    Gross: 3260 pounds
    Empty: 2070 pounds
Seats: Four
Dimensions
    Length: 24 feet 11 inches
    Height: 8 feet 5 inches
    Span: 32 feet 9 inches

Beechcraft

The name Beechcraft goes back further, historically, than most other manufacturers found in this book. Many early Beech airplanes are not appropriate for this book. However, one large single-engine plane Beech built is not only historic, it is also a capable people mover.

The Staggerwing Beech was built in a bygone era. It was fast, powerful, and very roomy. The cabin was larger than any airplane in the same class today. Its engine was radial and although expensive to maintain, it makes the right sound. (You'll know it when you hear it and never forget it.)

Staggerwings were built from the 1930s through the 1940s, they are classics in the truest sense of the word. Of tube and fabric construction, many Staggerwings had retractable landing gear. They are very expensive to purchase, and even more expensive to operate and maintain.

The V-tailed Model 35 Bonanza has probably captured the imagination of more pilots, and non-pilots, over the years than any other light plane. The basic style has been utilized for over 35 years.

The first Model 35 had a 185-hp engine, a wooden prop, and seated four people. Many improvements and refinements have been made down through the years, but a Bonanza is still a Bonanza. The Model 35 remained in production through the early 1980s. The final models were powered with a 285-hp engine and seated six.

It's difficult to find an early Model-35 in stock condition. Most have been updated appearance wise, avionics wise, and, of course, power wise.

The Model 33 Debonair was introduced in 1960. It was a four-seat conventional tail airplane powered with a 225-hp engine. An optional 285-hp version became available in 1966. The Debonair was dropped in 1968, however the Model 33 continues as a Bonanza.

Beechcraft introduced the Sierra in 1970 as the model 24R. It had a 200-hp engine, constant-speed prop, and retractable landing gear. The Sierra was top of the line built for Beech Aero Centers, which were set up to sell and rent the lower end of Beechcraft products.

Make: Beechcraft   Model: D17S Staggerwing (unofficial name)
Year: 1937-48
Engine
    Make: Pratt & Whitney
    Model: R-985
    Horsepower: 450
    TBO: NA
Speeds
    Maximum: 212 mph
    Cruise: 202 mph
    Stall: 60 mph
Fuel capacity: 124 gallons
Rate of climb: 1500 fpm

Fig. 9-3. Beechcraft 17 Staggerwing.

Transitions
    Takeoff over 50-foot obstacle: 1130 feet
    Ground run: 610 feet
    Landing over 50-foot obstacle: 980 feet
    Ground roll: 750 feet
Weights
    Gross: 4250 pounds
    Empty: 2540 pounds
Seats: Four
Dimensions
    Length: 26 feet 10 inches
    Height: 8 feet
    Span: 32 feet

Make: Beechcraft   Model: 24R Sierra
Year: 1970-83
Engine
    Make: Lycoming
    Model: IO-360-A1B6
    Horsepower: 200
    TBO: 1800 hours
Speeds
    Maximum: 170 mph

Fig. 9-4. Beechcraft 24R Sierra.

Cruise: 162 mph
Stall: 66 mph
Fuel capacity: 59 gallons
Rate of climb: 862 fpm
Transitions
    Takeoff over 50-foot obstacle: 1980 feet
    Ground run: 1260 feet
    Landing over 50-foot obstacle: 1670 feet
    Ground roll: 752 feet
Weights
    Gross: 2750 pounds
    Empty: 1610 pounds
Seats: Four
Dimensions
    Length: 25 feet 9 inches
    Height: 8 feet 3 inches
    Span: 32 feet 9 inches

Make: Beechcraft   Model: 33 Debonair/Bonanza
Year: 1960-70
Engine
    Make: Continental
    Model: IO-470-J
    Horsepower: 225
    TBO: 1500 hours
Speeds
    Maximum: 195 mph
    Cruise: 185 mph
    Stall: 60 mph
Fuel capacity: 50 gallons
Rate of climb: 960 fpm

Transitions
    Takeoff over 50-foot obstacle: 1235 feet
    Ground run: 940 feet
    Landing over 50-foot obstacle: 1282 feet
    Ground roll: 635 feet
Weights
    Gross: 3000 pounds
    Empty: 1745 pounds
Seats: Four-Five
Dimensions
    Length: 25 feet 6 inches
    Height: 8 feet 3 inches
    Span: 32 feet 10 inches

Fig. 9-5. Beechcraft F33A Bonanza.

Make: Beechcraft   Model: 33 Debonair/Bonanza
Year: 1966-up
Engine
    Make: Continental
    Model: IO-520-BA
    Horsepower: 285
    TBO: 1700 hours
Speeds
    Maximum: 208 mph
    Cruise: 200 mph
    Stall: 63 mph
Fuel capacity: 50 gallons

Rate of climb: 1136 fpm
Transitions
    Takeoff over 50-foot obstacle: 1873 feet
    Ground run: 1091 feet
    Landing over 50-foot obstacle: 1500 feet
    Ground roll: 795 feet
Weights
    Gross: 3400 pounds
    Empty: 1965 pounds
Seats: Five-Six
Dimensions
    Length: 25 feet 6 inches
    Height: 8 feet 3 inches
    Span: 33 feet 5 inches

Beech Aircraft Corp.

Fig. 9-6. Beechcraft 35 Bonanza.

Make: Beechcraft   Model: 35-A35 Bonanza
Year: 1947-49
Engine
    Make: Continental
    Model: E-185-1
    Horsepower: 185 (205 and 225 optional)
    TBO: 1500 hours
Speeds
    Maximum: 184 mph
    Cruise: 172 mph
    Stall: 55 mph
Fuel capacity: 39 gallons
Rate of climb: 950 fpm
Transitions
    Takeoff over 50-foot obstacle: 1440 feet
    Ground run: 1200 feet

Landing over 50-foot obstacle: 925 feet
Ground roll: 580 feet
Weights
    Gross: 2550 pounds
    Empty: 1458 pounds
Seats: Four
Dimensions
    Length: 25 feet 1 inch
    Height: 6 feet 6 inches
    Span: 32 feet 9 inches

Make: Beechcraft   Model: B35 Bonanza
Year: 1950
Engine
    Make: Continental
    Model: E-185-8
    Horsepower: 196
    TBO: 1500 hours
Speeds
    Maximum: 184 mph
    Cruise: 170 mph
    Stall: 56 mph
Fuel capacity: 39 gallons
Rate of climb: 890 fpm
Transitions
    Takeoff over 50-foot obstacle: 1515 feet
    Ground run: 1275 feet
    Landing over 50-foot obstacle: 950 feet
    Ground roll: 625 feet
Weights
    Gross: 2650 pounds
    Empty: 1575 pounds
Seats: Four
Dimensions
    Length: 25 feet 1 inch
    Height: 6 feet 6 inches
    Span: 32 feet 9 inches

Make: Beechcraft   Model: C35/D35 Bonanza
Year: 1951-53
Engine
    Make: Continental
    Model: E-185-11
    Horsepower: 205
    TBO: 1500 hours

Speeds
    Maximum: 190 mph
    Cruise: 175 mph
    Stall: 55 mph
Fuel capacity: 39 gallons
Rate of climb: 1100 fpm
Transitions
    Takeoff over 50-foot obstacle: 1500 feet
    Ground run: 1250 feet
    Landing over 50-foot obstacle: 975 feet
    Ground roll: 625 feet
Weights
    Gross: 2700 pounds
    Empty: 1650 pounds
Seats: Four
Dimensions
    Length: 25 feet 1 inch
    Height: 6 feet 6 inches
    Span: 32 feet 9 inches

Make: Beechcraft   Model: E35/G35 Bonanza
Year: 1954-56
Engine
    Make: Continental
    Model: E-225-8
    Horsepower: 225
    TBO: 1500 hours
Speeds
    Maximum: 194 mph
    Cruise: 184 mph
    Stall: 55 mph
Fuel capacity: 39 gallons
Rate of climb: 1300 fpm
Transitions
    Takeoff over 50-foot obstacle: 1270 feet
    Ground run: 1060 feet
    Landing over 50-foot obstacle: 1025 feet
    Ground roll: 680 feet
Weights
    Gross: 2775 pounds
    Empty: 1722 pounds
Seats: Four
Dimensions
    Length: 25 feet 1 inch
    Height: 6 feet 6 inches
    Span: 32 feet 9 inches

Make: Beechcraft   Model: H35 Bonanza
Year: 1957
Engine
    Make: Continental
    Model: O-470-G
    Horsepower: 240
    TBO: 1500 hours
Speeds
    Maximum: 206 mph
    Cruise: 196 mph
    Stall: 57 mph
Fuel capacity: 39 gallons
Rate of climb: 1250 fpm
Transitions
    Takeoff over 50-foot obstacle: 1260 feet
    Ground run: 1050 feet
    Landing over 50-foot obstacle: 1050 feet
    Ground roll: 710 feet
Weights
    Gross: 2900 pounds
    Empty: 1833 pounds
Seats: Four
Dimensions
    Length: 25 feet 1 inch
    Height: 6 feet 6 inches
    Span: 32 feet 9 inches

Make: Beechcraft   Model: J35/M35 Bonanza
Year: 1958-60
Engine
    Make: Continental
    Model: O-470-C
    Horsepower: 250
    TBO: 1500 hours
Speeds
    Maximum: 210 mph
    Cruise: 195 mph
    Stall: 57 mph
Fuel capacity: 39 gallons
Rate of climb: 1250 fpm
Transitions
    Takeoff over 50-foot obstacle: 1185 feet
    Ground run: 950 feet
    Landing over 50-foot obstacle: 1050 feet
    Ground roll: 710 feet

Weights
    Gross: 2900 pounds
    Empty: 1820 pounds
Seats: Four
Dimensions
    Length: 25 feet 1 inch
    Height: 6 feet 6 inches
    Span: 32 feet 9 inches

Beech Aircraft Corp.

Fig. 9-7. Beechcraft N35 Bonanza.

Make: Beechcraft   Model: N35/P35 Bonanza
Year: 1961-63
Engine
    Make: Continental
    Model: IO-470-N
    Horsepower: 260
    TBO: 1500 hours
Speeds
    Maximum: 205 mph
    Cruise: 190 mph
    Stall: 60 mph
Fuel capacity: 49 gallons
Rate of climb: 1150 fpm
Transitions
    Takeoff over 50-foot obstacle: 1260 feet
    Ground run: 1050 feet
    Landing over 50-foot obstacle: 1100 feet
    Ground roll: 650 feet
Weights
    Gross: 3125 pounds

Empty: 1855 pounds
Seats: Five
Dimensions
    Length: 25 feet 1 inch
    Height: 6 feet 6 inches
    Span: 32 feet 9 inches

Fig. 9-8. Beechcraft V35B Bonanza.

Make: Beechcraft   Model: S35/V35 Bonanza
Year: 1964-84
Engine
    Make: Continental
    Model: IO-520-B
    Horsepower: 285
    TBO: 1700 hours
Speeds
    Maximum: 210 mph
    Cruise: 203 mph
    Stall: 63 mph
Fuel capacity: 50 gallons
Rate of climb: 1136 fpm
Transitions
    Takeoff over 50-foot obstacle: 1320 feet
    Ground run: 965 feet
    Landing over 50-foot obstacle: 1177 feet
    Ground roll: 647 feet
Weights
    Gross: 3400 pounds
    Empty: 1970 pounds
Seats: Five-Six

Dimensions
    Length: 25 feet 1 inch
    Height: 6 feet 6 inches
    Span: 32 feet 9 inches

Make: Beechcraft   Model: V35 Turbo Bonanza
Year: 1966-70
Engine
    Make: Continental
    Model: TSIO-520-D
    Horsepower: 285
    TBO: 1400 hours
Speeds
    Maximum: 240 mph
    Cruise: 224 mph
    Stall: 63 mph
Fuel capacity: 50 gallons
Rate of climb: 1225 fpm
Transitions
    Takeoff over 50-foot obstacle: 1320 feet
    Ground run: 950 feet
    Landing over 50-foot obstacle: 1177 feet
    Ground roll: 647 feet
Weights
    Gross: 3400 pounds
    Empty: 2027 pounds
Seats: Six
Dimensions
    Length: 25 feet 1 inch
    Height: 6 feet 6 inches
    Span: 32 feet 9 inches

Beech Aircraft Corp.

Fig. 9-9. Beechcraft A36 Bonanza.

Make: Beechcraft   Model: 36/A36 Bonanza
Year: 1968-83
Engine
    Make: Continental
    Model: IO-520-BB
    Horsepower: 285
    TBO: 1700 hours
Speeds
    Maximum: 206 mph
    Cruise: 193 mph
    Stall: 60 mph
Fuel capacity: 74 gallons
Rate of climb: 1030 fpm
Transitions
    Takeoff over 50-foot obstacle: 2040 feet
    Ground run: 1140 feet
    Landing over 50-foot obstacle: 1450 feet
    Ground roll: 840 feet
Weights
    Gross: 3600 pounds
    Empty: 2295 pounds
Seats: Six
Dimensions
    Length: 27 feet 6 inches
    Height: 8 feet 5 inches
    Span: 33 feet 6 inches

Bellanca

Bellanca airplanes have been good performers throughout the years, but there aren't so many of them around like other makes. Bellanca has been in and out of business several times, however this is no mark against the airplanes. Northern Aircraft Company, Downer Aircraft, Inter-Aire, Bellanca Sales, and Miller Flying Service have been associated with manufacturing at one time or another.

The Bellanca fuselage is fabric-covered and wings are wooden. It is said to be the strongest wing in the industry; later Bellancas, the Vikings, are aerobatic.

Bellanca tails had three surfaces prior to 1964, similar to Lockheed Constellations. Later models had standard tails with a single vertical surface.

Make: Bellanca   Model: 14-19 Cruisemaster
Year: 1950-51
Engine
    Make: Lycoming
    Model: O-435-A
    Horsepower: 190
    TBO: 1200 hours
Speeds
    Maximum: 200 mph
    Cruise: 180 mph
    Stall: 44 mph
Fuel capacity: 40 gallons
Rate of climb: 1250 fpm
Transitions
    Takeoff over 50-foot obstacle: 1270 feet
    Ground run: 850 feet
    Landing over 50-foot obstacle: 1025 feet
    Ground roll: 450 feet
Weights
    Gross: 2600 pounds
    Empty: 1575 pounds
Seats: Four
Dimensions
    Length: 23 feet
    Height: 6 feet 2 inches
    Span: 34 feet 2 inches

Make: Bellanca   Model: 14-19-2 Cruisemaster
Year: 1957-59
Engine
    Make: Continental
    Model: O-470-K
    Horsepower: 230
    TBO: 1500 hours

Speeds
    Maximum: 206 mph
    Cruise: 196 mph
    Stall: 46 mph
Fuel capacity: 40 gallons
Rate of climb: 1500 fpm
Transitions
    Takeoff over 50-foot obstacle: 1025 feet
    Ground run: 760 feet
    Landing over 50-foot obstacle: 1150 feet
    Ground roll: 470 feet
Weights
    Gross: 2700 pounds
    Empty: 1640 pounds
Seats: Four
Dimensions
    Length: 23 feet
    Height: 6 feet 2 inches
    Span: 34 feet 2 inches

Fig. 9-10. Bellanca.

Make: Bellanca   Model: 14-19-3 (A-C)
Year: 1959-68
Engine
    Make: Continental
    Model: IO-470-F
    Horsepower: 260
    TBO: 1500 hours
Speeds
    Maximum: 208 mph

Cruise: 203 mph
Stall: 62 mph
Fuel capacity: 40 gallons
Rate of climb: 1500 fpm
Transitions
    Takeoff over 50-foot obstacle: 1000 feet
    Ground run: 340 feet
    Landing over 50-foot obstacle: 800 feet
    Ground roll: 400 feet
Weights
    Gross: 3000 pounds
    Empty: 1850 pounds
Seats: Four
Dimensions
    Length: 23 feet 6 inches
    Height: 6 feet 5 inches
    Span: 34 feet 2 inches

Make: Bellanca   Model: 17-30 Viking
Year: 1967-70
Engine
    Make: Continental
    Model: IO-520-K1A
    Horsepower: 300
    TBO: 1700
Speeds
    Maximum: 192 mph
    Cruise: 188 mph
    Stall: 62 mph
Fuel capacity: 58 gallons
Rate of climb: 1840 fpm
Transitions
    Takeoff over 50-foot obstacle: 908 feet
    Ground run: 450 feet
    Landing over 50-foot obstacle: 1050 feet
    Ground roll: 575 feet
Weights
    Gross: 3200 pounds
    Empty: 1900 pounds
Seats: Four
Dimensions
    Length: 23 feet 7 inches
    Height: 7 feet 4 inches
    Span: 34 feet 2 inches

Fig. 9-11. Bellanca Viking.

Make: Bellanca   Model: 17-30A/31
Year: 1970-78
Engine
    Make: Continental
    Model: IO-520-K1A
    Horsepower: 300
    TBO: 1700
Speeds
    Maximum: 208 mph
    Cruise: 202 mph
    Stall: 70 mph
Fuel capacity: 68 gallons
Rate of climb: 1210 fpm
Transitions
    Takeoff over 50-foot obstacle: 1420 feet
    Ground run: NA
    Landing over 50-foot obstacle: 1340 feet
    Ground roll: NA
Weights
    Gross: 3325 pounds
    Empty: 2185 pounds
Seats: Four

Dimensions
    Length: 26 feet 4 inches
    Height: 7 feet 4 inches
    Span: 34 feet 2 inches

Make: Bellanca   Model: 17-31T
Year: 1969-79
Engine
    Make: Continental
    Model: IO-520-K1A (Rayjay Turbo charging)
    Horsepower: 300
    TBO: 1700
Speeds
    Maximum: 222 mph
    Cruise: 215 mph
    Stall: 62 mph
Fuel capacity: 72 gallons
Rate of climb: 1800 fpm
Transitions
    Takeoff over 50-foot obstacle: 890 feet
    Ground run: 460 feet
    Landing over 50-foot obstacle: 1100 feet
    Ground roll: 575 feet
Weights
    Gross: 3200 pounds
    Empty: 2010 pounds
Seats: Four
Dimensions
    Length: 23 feet 7 inches
    Height: 7 feet 4 inches
    Span: 34 feet 2 inches

Cessna

Together with the Beechcraft Staggerwing, another airplane that is complex and suitable for this chapter yet with historical interest is the Cessna 190.

The 190 and 195 airplanes were produced later than the radial-engine Staggerwings. The Cessnas also have radial engines and the "right sound."

The Cessna 182 evolved from the conventional geared 180. The 182 is a real work horse, able to carry passengers in comfort, with baggage. It doesn't have retractable landing gear but it is a complex airplane because of gross weight and the 230-hp engine.

Changes to the 182 might help identification of the various year models: 1960, swept tail; 1962, rear window; 1972, tubular landing gear; and 1977, 100 octane engine.

In 1960 the Model 210 Centurion entered production as a four-seat plane with a 260-hp engine and retractable gear; engine increased to 285 hp in 1964.

Cessna Aircraft Co.

Fig. 9-12. Cessna 1949 195.

Make: Cessna   Model: 190/195
Year: 1947-54
Engine
    Make: Jacobs
    Model: R-755 (Continental R-670 240 horsepower in the 190)
    Horsepower: 245 to 300
    TBO: 1000 hours
Speeds
    Maximum: 176 mph
    Cruise: 170 mph
    Stall: 64 mph
Fuel capacity: 80 gallons
Rate of climb: 1050 feet
Transitions
    Takeoff over 50-foot obstacle: 1670 feet
    Ground run: NA

Landing over 50-foot obstacle: 1495 feet
Ground roll: NA
Weights
    Gross: 3350 pounds
    Empty: 2030 pounds
Seats: Five
Dimensions
    Length: 27 feet 3 inches
    Height: 7 feet 2 inches
    Span: 36 feet 2 inches

Cessna Aircraft Co.

Fig. 9-13. Cessna 1956 182.

Make: Cessna   Model: 182 Skylane
Year: 1956-86
Engine
    Make: Continental
    Model: O-470 (O-470-U after 1976)
    Horsepower: 230
    TBO: 1500 hours
Speeds
    Maximum: 165 mph
    Cruise: 157 mph
    Stall: 57 mph
Fuel capacity: 56 gallons
Rate of climb: 890 fpm
Transitions
    Takeoff over 50-foot obstacle: 1350 feet
    Ground run: 705 feet
    Landing over 50-foot obstacle: 1350 feet
    Ground roll: 590 feet

Weights
    Gross: 2950 pounds
    Empty: 1595 pounds
Seats: Four
Dimensions
    Length: 28 feet 2 inches
    Height: 9 feet 2 inches
    Span: 35 feet 10 inches

Make: Cessna   Model: 210
Year: 1960-63
Engine
    Make: Continental
    Model: IO-470-E
    Horsepower: 260
    TBO: 1500 hours
Speeds
    Maximum: 198 mph
    Cruise: 189 mph
    Stall: 60 mph
Fuel capacity: 84 gallons
Rate of climb: 1270 fpm
Transitions
    Takeoff over 50-foot obstacle: 1210 feet
    Ground run: 695 feet
    Landing over 50-foot obstacle: 1110 feet
    Ground roll: 725 feet
Weights
    Gross: 3000 pounds
    Empty: 1780 pounds
Seats: Four
Dimensions
    Length: 27 feet 9 inches
    Height: 9 feet 9 inches
    Span: 36 feet 7 inches

Fig. 9-14. Cessna 1972 210 Centurion.

Make: Cessna   Model: 210 Centurion
Year: 1964-73
Engine
    Make: Continental
    Model: IO-520-A
    Horsepower: 285
    TBO: 1700 hours
Speeds
    Maximum: 200 mph
    Cruise: 188 mph
    Stall: 65 mph
Fuel capacity: 84 gallons
Rate of climb: 860 fpm
Transitions
    Takeoff over 50-foot obstacle: 1900 feet
    Ground run: 1100 feet
    Landing over 50-foot obstacle: 1500 feet
    Ground roll: 765 feet
Weights
    Gross: 3800 pounds
    Empty: 2134 pounds
Seats: Six
Dimensions
    Length: 27 feet 9 inches
    Height: 9 feet 9 inches
    Span: 36 feet 7 inches

Make: Cessna   Model: 210 Turbo Centurion
Year: 1974-76
Engine
    Make: Continental
    Model: TSIO-520
    Horsepower: 300
    TBO: 1400 hours
Speeds
    Maximum: 200 mph
    Cruise: 196 mph
    Stall: 65 mph
Fuel capacity: 84 gallons
Rate of climb: 1060 fpm
Transitions
    Takeoff over 50-foot obstacle: 2050 feet
    Ground run: 1215 feet
    Landing over 50-foot obstacle: 1585 feet
    Ground roll: 815 feet

Weights
    Gross: 3850 pounds
    Empty: 2220 pounds
Seats: Six
Dimensions
    Length: 28 feet 2 inches
    Height: 9 feet 8 inches
    Span: 36 feet 9 inches

Fig. 9-15. Cessna 1983 172 Cutlass RG.

Make: Cessna   Model: 172-RG
Year: 1980-85
Engine
    Make: Lycoming
    Model: O-360-F1A6
    Horsepower: 180
    TBO: 2000 hours
Speeds
    Maximum: 167 mph
    Cruise: 161 mph
    Stall: 58 mph
Fuel capacity: 66 gallons
Rate of climb: 800 fpm
Transitions
    Takeoff over 50-foot obstacle: 1775 feet
    Ground run: 1060 feet
    Landing over 50-foot obstacle: 1340 feet
    Ground roll: 625 feet
Weights
    Gross: 2650 pounds
    Empty: 1555 pounds
Seats: Four

Dimensions
    Length: 27 feet 5 inches
    Height: 8 feet 10 inches
    Span: 35 feet 10 inches

Fig. 9-16. Cessna 177 Cardinal RG.

Make: Cessna   Model: 177-RG Cardinal
Year: 1971-78
Engine
    Make: Lycoming
    Model: IO-360-A1B6D
    Horsepower: 200
    TBO: 1800 hours (1400 without modifications)
Speeds
    Maximum: 180 mph
    Cruise: 171 mph
    Stall: 57 mph
Fuel capacity: 60 gallons
Rate of climb: 925 fpm
Transitions
    Takeoff over 50-foot obstacle: 1585 feet
    Ground run: 890 feet
    Landing over 50-foot obstacle: 1350 feet
    Ground roll: 730 feet
Weights
    Gross: 2800 pounds
    Empty: 1645 pounds
Seats: Four
Dimensions
    Length: 27 feet 3 inches
    Height: 8 feet 7 inches
    Span: 35 feet 6 inches

Fig. 9-17. Cessna 1983 182 Skylane RG.

Make: Cessna   Model: 182-RG
Year: 1978-86
Engine
    Make: Lycoming
    Model: O-540-J3C5D
    Horsepower: 235
    TBO: 2000 hours
Speeds
    Maximum: 184 mph
    Cruise: 180 mph
    Stall: 58 mph
Fuel capacity: 56 gallons
Rate of climb: 1140 fpm
Transitions
    Takeoff over 50-foot obstacle: 1570 feet
    Ground run: 820 feet
    Landing over 50-foot obstacle: 1320 feet
    Ground roll: 600 feet
Weights
    Gross: 3100 pounds
    Empty: 1750 pounds
Seats: Four
Dimensions
    Length: 28 feet 7 inches
    Height: 8 feet 11 inches
    Span: 35 feet 10 inches

Lake

If the thought of having lunch in a quiet sheltered cove of a lake or a river is a turn-on, then perhaps a Lake amphibian is for you. Amphibian means that this plane is equally at home on land or on water.

Many pilots consider amphibian aircraft to be lack-luster in performance. Consider the size of the engine and the fact this is a four-place airplane, then look at the performance data: The Lake is no slouch. Plenty of land-bound airplanes can't do this well.

First produced with a 180-hp engine in 1960 as the LA-4, this aircraft was updated to 200 hp in 1970 and named the Buccaneer. The latest version is the Renegade, powered with a 250-hp engine.

Fig. 9-18. Lake Amphibian.

Make: Lake   Model: LA-4
Year: 1960-71
Engine
    Make: Lycoming
    Model: O-360-A1A
    Horsepower: 180
    TBO: 2000 hours
Speeds
    Maximum: 135 mph
    Cruise: 131 mph
    Stall: 51 mph
Fuel capacity: 40 gallons
Rate of climb: 800 fpm

Transitions (add 40 percent on water)
    Takeoff over 50-foot obstacle: 1275 feet
    Ground run: 650 feet
    Landing over 50-foot obstacle: 900 feet
    Ground roll: 475 feet
Weights
    Gross: 2400 pounds
    Empty: 1550 pounds
Seats: Four
Dimensions
    Length: 24 feet 11 inches
    Height: 9 feet 4 inches
    Span: 38 feet

Make: Lake   Model: LA-4 200 Buccaneer
Year: 1972-up
Engine
    Make: Lycoming
    Model: IO-360-A1B
    Horsepower: 200
    TBO: 1800 hours
Speeds
    Maximum: 154 mph
    Cruise: 150 mph
    Stall: 54 mph
Fuel capacity: 40 gallons
Rate of climb: 1200 fpm
Transitions (add 40 percent on water)
    Takeoff over 50-foot obstacle: 1100 feet
    Ground run: 600 feet
    Landing over 50-foot obstacle: 900 feet
    Ground roll: 475 feet
Weights
    Gross: 2690 pounds
    Empty: 1555 pounds
Seats: Four
Dimensions
    Length: 24 feet 11 inches
    Height: 9 feet 4 inches
    Span: 38 feet

Make: Lake   Model: LA-250 Renegade
Year: 1983-up
Engine
    Make: Lycoming
    Model: IO-540-C4B5

Horsepower: 250
TBO: 2000 hours
Speeds
    Maximum: NA
    Cruise: 140 mph
    Stall: 61 mph
Fuel capacity: 85 gallons
Rate of climb: 900 fpm
Transitions (add 40 percent on water)
    Takeoff over 50-foot obstacle: NA
    Ground run: NA
    Landing over 50-foot obstacle: NA
    Ground roll: NA
Weights
    Gross: 3050 pounds
    Empty: 1850 pounds
Seats: Six
Dimensions
    Length: 28 feet 1 inch
    Height: 10 feet
    Span: 38 feet

Mooney

Mooney airplanes always extract maximum performance from available horsepower with minimum fuel consumption.

All except a few very early versions have retractable landing gear. The first retractables had a Johnson bar to retract and extend the gear; later versions were equipped with electrically operated landing gear.

Mooney airplanes have undergone many power and name changes over the years, often leading to considerable confusion.

- M-20, 55-57, 150-hp (laminated wood wing and tail surfaces).
- M-20A, 58-60, 180-hp.
- M-20B/C Mark 21, 58-78, 180-hp, all-metal (Ranger).
- M-20E Chaparral, 64-75, 200-hp (Super 21).
- M-20F Executive, 21 67-77, 200-hp (10 inches longer than the M-20E).
- M-20G Mark 21, 68-70, 180-hp, all-metal (Statesman).
- M-20J Mooney 210, 77-up, 200-hp (sloped windshield).
- M-20K Mooney 231, 79-up, 210-hp (turbocharged).

Mooney built the M-22 Mustang, a pressurized five-seat plane, from 1967 to 1970. Approximately 26 were sold.

Fig. 9-19. Mooney M20.

Make: Mooney   Model: M-20
Year: 1955-57
Engine
    Make: Lycoming
    Model: O-320
    Horsepower: 150
    TBO: 2000 hours (fewer without modifications)

Speeds
    Maximum: 171 mph
    Cruise: 165 mph
    Stall: 57 mph
Fuel capacity: 35 gallons
Rate of climb: 900 fpm
Transitions
    Takeoff over 50-foot obstacle: 1150 feet
    Ground run: 850 feet
    Landing over 50-foot obstacle: 100 feet
    Ground roll: 600 feet
Weights
    Gross: 2450 pounds
    Empty: 1415 pounds
Seats: Four
Dimensions
    Length: 23 feet 1 inch
    Height: 8 feet 3 inches
    Span: 35 feet

Mooney Aircraft Corp.

Fig. 9-20. Mooney M20B.

Make: Mooney   Model: M-20 A/B/C/G
Year: 1958-78
Engine
    Make: Lycoming
    Model: O-360
    Horsepower: 180
    TBO: 2000 hours (fewer without modifications)
Speeds
    Maximum: 185 mph
    Cruise: 180 mph
    Stall: 57 mph

Fuel capacity: 52 gallons
Rate of climb: 1010 fpm
Transitions
    Takeoff over 50-foot obstacle: 1525 feet
    Ground run: 890 feet
    Landing over 50-foot obstacle: 1365 feet
    Ground roll: 550 feet
Weights
    Gross: 2575 pounds
    Empty: 1525 pounds
Seats: Four
Dimensions
    Length: 23 feet 2 inches
    Height: 8 feet 4 inches
    Span: 35 feet

Fig. 9-21. Mooney M20E.

Mooney Aircraft Corp.

Fig. 9-22. Mooney M20E Chaparral, post 1969.

Make: Mooney   Model: M-20 E/F
Year: 1965-77
Engine
    Make: Lycoming
    Model: IO-360-A1A
    Horsepower: 200
    TBO: 1800 hours (fewer without modifications)
Speeds
    Maximum: 190 mph
    Cruise: 184 mph
    Stall: 57 mph
Fuel capacity: 52 gallons
Rate of climb: 1125 fpm
Transitions
    Takeoff over 50-foot obstacle: 1550 feet
    Ground run: 760 feet
    Landing over 50-foot obstacle: 1550 feet
    Ground roll: 595 feet
Weights
    Gross: 2575 pounds
    Empty: 1600 pounds
Seats: Four
Dimensions
    Length: 23 feet 2 inches
    Height: 8 feet 4 inches
    Span: 35 feet

Make: Mooney   Model: M-20J 201
Year: 1977-up
Engine
    Make: Lycoming
    Model: IO-360-A3B6D
    Horsepower: 200
    TBO: 1800 hours (fewer without modifications)
Speeds
    Maximum: 202 mph
    Cruise: 195 mph
    Stall: 63 mph
Fuel capacity: 64 gallons
Rate of climb: 1030 fpm
Transitions
    Takeoff over 50-foot obstacle: 1517 feet
    Ground run: 850 feet
    Landing over 50-foot obstacle: 1610 feet
    Ground roll: 770 feet

Fig. 9-23. Mooney 201/231.

Mooney Aircraft Corp.

Weights
    Gross: 2740 pounds
    Empty: 1640 feet
Seats: Four
Dimensions
    Length: 24 feet 8 inches
    Height: 8 feet 4 inches
    Span: 36 feet 1 inch

Make: Mooney   Model: Mark 20K 231
Year: 1979-up
Engine
    Make: Continental
    Model: TSIO-360-GBA
    Horsepower: 210
    TBO: 1800 hours

Speeds
    Maximum: 231 mph
    Cruise: 220 mph
    Stall: 66 mph
Fuel capacity: 75 gallons
Rate of climb: 1080 fpm
Transitions
    Takeoff over 50-foot obstacle: 2060 feet
    Ground run: 1220 feet
    Landing over 50-foot obstacle: 2280 feet
    Ground roll: 1147 feet
Weights
    Gross: 2900 pounds
    Empty: 1800 pounds
Seats: Four
Dimensions
    Length: 25 feet 5 inches
    Height: 8 feet 4 inches
    Span: 36 feet 1 inch

Mooney Aircraft Corp.

Fig. 9-24. Mooney M-22 Mustang.

Make: Mooney   Model: Mark 22 Mustang
Year: 1967-70
Engine
    Make: Lycoming
    Model: TSIO-541-A1A
    Horsepower: 310
    TBO: 1300 hours

Speeds
    Maximum: 250 mph
    Cruise: 230 mph
    Stall: 69 mph
Fuel capacity: 92 gallons
Rate of climb: 1120 fpm
Transitions
    Takeoff over 50-foot obstacle: 2079 feet
    Ground run: 1142 feet
    Landing over 50-foot obstacle: 1549 feet
    Ground roll: 958 feet
Weights
    Gross: 3680 pounds
    Empty: 2380 pounds
Seats: Five
Dimensions
    Length: 26 feet 1 inch
    Height: 9 feet 1 inch
    Span: 35 feet

Navion

Of all the complex airplanes, there is no other like the Navion. It was placed into production by North American Aviation in 1946, just before the Beechcraft Bonanza. Sadly, though, the Navion has bounced around from one manufacturer to another in and out of production until 1976—and never enjoyed the popularity of the Bonanza.

The Navion is a strong and capable short-field plane; unimproved strips don't seem to bother it. Navions were built with 185-, 205-, and 225-hp engines. Rangemasters, a later model, were available with a 260- or 285-hp engine.

Few all-original Navions exist today because most have been modified. A wise purchaser will contact the American Navion Society (Appendix E) before making a choice; they can answer questions about modifications and difficulties.

Air Pix

Fig. 9-25. Navion 1947.

Make: Navion   Model: NA
Year: 1946-51
Engine
    Make: Continental
    Model: E-185-3
    Horsepower: 205
    TBO: 1500 hours
Speeds
    Maximum: 163 mph
    Cruise: 148 mph
    Stall: 60 mph
Fuel capacity: 40 gallons
Rate of climb: 750 fpm
Transitions
    Takeoff over 50-foot obstacle: 1500 feet
    Ground run: 670 feet
    Landing over 50-foot obstacle: 1300 feet
    Ground roll: 500 feet

Weights
    Gross: 2750 pounds
    Empty: 1700 pounds
Seats: Four
Dimensions
    Length: 27 feet 3 inches
    Height: 8 feet 7 inches
    Span: 33 feet 4 inches

Fig. 9-26. Navion 1968 Rangemaster.

Make: Navion   Model: Rangemaster
Year: 1961-75
Engine
    Make: Continental
    Model: IO-520-B
    Horsepower: 285
    TBO: 1700 hours
Speeds
    Maximum: 203 mph
    Cruise: 191 mph
    Stall: 55 mph
Fuel capacity: 40 gallons
Rate of climb: 1375 fpm
Transitions
    Takeoff over 50-foot obstacle: 950 feet
    Ground run: 740 feet
    Landing over 50-foot obstacle: 980 feet
    Ground roll: 760 feet
Weights
    Gross: 3315 pounds
    Empty: 2000 pounds
Seats: Four
Dimensions
    Length: 27 feet 3 inches
    Height: 8 feet 7 inches
    Span: 33 feet 4 inches

Piper

Piper entered the complex airplane market in 1958 with the PA-24 Comanche. It was an all-metal, low wing craft that became popular as a market trendsetter.

The PA-24 was built with several engines before production ceased in 1972 when the Lock Haven, Pennsylvania, manufacturing facility was flooded.

Piper's PA-28/235 is a rugged and honest airplane, yet easy to fly and quite inexpensive to maintain. The 235 will carry a load equivalent to its weight and, in later versions, do it in style.

The 235 was replaced by the 236 in 1979; the Dakota is a meld of the Warrior wing and the Archer fuselage.

The large success of the PA-28 series no doubt moved Piper—as it had Cessna—to install retractable landing gear and aim toward a different market: PA-28R Arrow series arose. Simplicity was desired in these new retractables. Even responsibility for actually controlling the landing gear was removed from the pilot; automatic landing gear.

Of course the basic airplane saw different configurations and names: 1969, 200-hp Arrow 200; 1973, Arrow II/200 (five-place); 1977, Arrow III/201 (turbo version is T201); and 1979, Arrow IV with T-tail.

In 1979 the PA-32R-300 Lance was introduced as a retractable version of the popular PA-32 Cherokee Six; Cherokee Six is covered in Chapter 10.

The Lance appeared with a conventional tail, and after the first half of 1978, with a Tee-tail.

The last complex entry from Piper is the Malibu, a cabin-class single.

International Comanche Society

Fig. 9-27. Piper PA-24 Comanche.

Make: Piper   Model: PA-24/180
Year: 1958-64
Engine
    Make: Lycoming
    Model: O-360-A1A
    Horsepower: 180
    TBO: 2000 (1200 without modifications)

Speeds
    Maximum: 167 mph
    Cruise: 150 mph
    Stall: 61 mph
Fuel capacity: 60 gallons
Rate of climb: 910 fpm
Transitions
    Takeoff over 50-foot obstacle: 2240 feet
    Ground run: 750 feet
    Landing over 50-foot obstacle: 1025 feet
    Ground roll: 600 feet
Weights
    Gross: 2550 pounds
    Empty: 1475 pounds
Seats: Four
Dimensions
    Length: 24 feet 9 inches
    Height: 7 feet 5 inches
    Span: 36 feet

Make: Piper   Model: PA-24/250
Year: 1958-64
Engine
    Make: Lycoming
    Model: O-540-A1A5
    Horsepower: 250
    TBO: 2000 (1200 without modification
Speeds
    Maximum: 190 mph
    Cruise: 181 mph
    Stall: 61 mph
Fuel capacity: 60 gallons
Rate of climb: 1350 fpm
Transitions
    Takeoff over 50-foot obstacle: 1650 fee
    Ground run: 750 feet
    Landing over 50-foot obstacle: 1025 fe
    Ground roll: 650 feet
Weights
    Gross: 2800 pounds
    Empty: 1690 pounds
Seats: Four
Dimensions
    Length: 24 feet 9 inches
    Height: 7 feet 5 inches
    Span: 36 feet

Make: Piper   Model: PA-24/260
Year: 1965-72
Engine
    Make: Lycoming
    Model: O-540 (IO-540 after 1969)
    Horsepower: 260
    TBO: 2000 (1200 without modifications)
Speeds
    Maximum: 195 mph
    Cruise: 185 mph
    Stall: 61 mph
Fuel capacity: 60 gallons
Rate of climb: 1320 fpm
Transitions
    Takeoff over 50-foot obstacle: 1400 feet
    Ground run: 820 feet
    Landing over 50-foot obstacle: 1200 feet
    Ground roll: 690 feet
Weights
    Gross: 3200 pounds
    Empty: 1773 pounds
Seats: Four
Dimensions
    Length: 25 feet 8 inches
    Height: 7 feet 3 inches
    Span: 36 feet

Fig. 9-28. Piper PA-28/235 Cherokee.

Make: Piper   Model: PA-28/235 Cherokee/Charger/Pathfinder
Year: 1964-77
Engine
    Make: Lycoming
    Model: O-540-B4B5

Horsepower: 235
TBO: 2000 hours (1200 without modifications)
Speeds
    Maximum: 166 mph
    Cruise: 156 mph
    Stall: 60 mph
Fuel capacity: 84 gallons
Rate of climb: 825 fpm
Transitions
    Takeoff over 50-foot obstacle: 1360 feet
    Ground run: 800 feet
    Landing over 50-foot obstacle: 1300 feet
    Ground roll: 680 feet
Weights
    Gross: 2900 pounds
    Empty: 1410 pounds
Seats: Four
Dimensions
    Length: 23 feet 6 inches
    Height: 7 feet 1 inch
    Span: 32 feet

Fig. 9-29. Piper PA-28/236 Dakota.

Make: Piper   Model: PA-28/236 Dakota
Year: 1979-up
Engine
    Make: Lycoming
    Model: O-540-J3A5D
    Horsepower: 235
    TBO: 2000 hours
Speeds
    Maximum: 170 mph
    Cruise: 159 mph

Stall: 64 mph
Fuel capacity: 72 gallons
Rate of climb: 1110 fpm
Transitions
    Takeoff over 50-foot obstacle: 1210 feet
    Ground run: 885 feet
    Landing over 50-foot obstacle: 1725 feet
    Ground roll: 825 feet
Weights
    Gross: 3000 pounds
    Empty: 1634 pounds
Seats: Four
Dimensions
    Length: 24 feet 8 inches
    Height: 7 feet 2 inches
    Span: 35 feet

Fig. 9-30. Piper PA-28R Arrow 200.

Make: Piper   Model: PA-28R/180 Arrow
Year: 1967-71
Engine
    Make: Lycoming
    Model: IO-360-B1E
    Horsepower: 180
    TBO: 2000 hours
Speeds
    Maximum: 170 mph
    Cruise: 162 mph
    Stall: 61 mph
Fuel capacity: 50 gallons
Rate of climb: 875 fpm
Transitions
    Takeoff over 50-foot obstacle: 1240 feet

Ground run: 820 feet
Landing over 50-foot obstacle: 1340 feet
Ground roll: 770 feet
Weights
Gross: 2500 pounds
Empty: 1380 pounds
Seats: Four
Dimensions
Length: 24 feet 2 inches
Height: 8 feet
Span: 30 feet

Make: Piper   Model: PA-28R/200 horsepower
Year: 1970-78
Engine
Make: Lycoming
Model: IO-360-C1C6
Horsepower: 200
TBO: 1800 hours (fewer without modifications)
Speeds
Maximum: 176 mph
Cruise: 162 mph
Stall: 63 mph
Fuel capacity: 50 gallons
Rate of climb: 831 fpm
Transitions
Takeoff over 50-foot obstacle: 1580 feet
Ground run: 780 feet
Landing over 50-foot obstacle: 1350 feet
Ground roll: 760 feet
Weights
Gross: 2750 pounds
Empty: 1601 pounds
Seats: Four
Dimensions
Length: 24 feet 2 inches
Height: 8 feet
Span: 30 feet

Make: Piper   Model: PA-28/200 Turbo Arrow
Year: 1977-78
Engine
Make: Continental
Model: TSIO-360-F
Horsepower: 200
TBO: 1400 hours

Fig. 9-31. Piper PA-28R Turbo Arrow IV.

Speeds
    Maximum: 198 mph
    Cruise: 172 mph
    Stall: 63 mph
Fuel capacity: 50 gallons
Rate of climb: 940 fpm
Transitions
    Takeoff over 50-foot obstacle: 1620 feet
    Ground run: 1120 feet
    Landing over 50-foot obstacle: 1555 feet
    Ground roll: 645 feet
Weights
    Gross: 2900 pounds
    Empty: 1638 pounds
Seats: Four
Dimensions
    Length: 24 feet 2 inches
    Height: 8 feet
    Span: 30 feet

Fig. 9-32. Piper PA-32R 300 Lance.

Make: Piper   Model: PA-32R8/300 Lance
Year: 1976-79
Engine
     Make: Lycoming
     Model: IO-540 (Turbocharging optional)
     Horsepower: 300
     TBO: 2000 hours
Speeds
     Maximum: 180 mph
     Cruise: 176 mph
     Stall: 60 mph
Fuel capacity: 98 gallons
Rate of climb: 1000 fpm
Transitions
     Takeoff over 50-foot obstacle: 1660 feet
     Ground run: 960 feet
     Landing over 50-foot obstacle: 1708 feet
     Ground roll: 880 feet
Weights
     Gross: 3600 pounds
     Empty: 1980 pounds
Seats: Seven
Dimensions
     Length: 27 feet 9 inches
     Height: 9 feet
     Span: 32 feet 9 inches

Fig. 9-33. Piper PA-46 Malibu.

Make: Piper   Model: PA-46 Malibu
Year: 1984-up
Engine
    Make: Continental
    Model: TSIO-520-BE
    Horsepower: 310
    TBO: 2000 hours
Speeds
    Maximum: 269 mph
    Cruise: 235 mph
    Stall: 67 mph
Fuel capacity: 120 gallons
Rate of climb: 1143 fpm
Transitions
    Takeoff over 50-foot obstacle: 2025 feet
    Ground run: 1440 feet
    Landing over 50-foot obstacle: 1800 feet
    Ground roll: 1070 feet
Weights
    Gross: 4100 pounds
    Empty: 2460 pounds
Seats: Six
Dimensions
    Length: 28 feet 10 inches
    Height: 11 feet 4 inches
    Span: 43 feet

Air Pix

Fig. 9-34. Republic SeaBee.

Republic

Republic Aviation was famous for its World War II P-47 Thunderbolt, and after the war produced the SeaBee, a four-place amphibian.

Few SeaBees were produced and in 1948 they disappeared from the market. Today the SeaBee commands a fairly high price. Docking is easy with a fully-reversible propeller—back out of a slip!

Many SeaBees have been extensively modified—some now twins—hence, performance data may not apply.

Make: Republic   Model: RC-3 Seabee
Year: 1948
Engine
    Make: Franklin
    Model: 6A-215-G8F
    Horsepower: 215
    TBO: 1200
Speeds
    Maximum: 120 mph
    Cruise: 100 mph
    Stall: 58 mph
Fuel capacity: 75 gallons
Rate of climb: 700 fpm
Transitions
    Takeoff over 50-foot obstacle: NA
    Ground run: NA
    Landing over 50-foot obstacle: NA
    Ground roll: NA
Weights
    Gross: 3000 pounds
    Empty: 2950 pounds
Seats: Four
Dimensions
    Length: NA
    Height: NA
    Span: NA

10

Heavy-Haulers

HEAVY-HAULER REFERS to capabilities of the described airplanes: carry heavy loads—often exceeding that which they are supposed to carry—ranging from people to livestock, and all the hardware and cargo in between.

These planes will be found doing their everyday work in the outer reaches of the lower 48 on ranches, reservations, or perhaps with the highway patrol. Alaska, Central America, Africa, and even the Australia outback are typically home to these airplanes.

Heavy-haulers are built beefy, with ample power and large lifting capabilities. Most are high-wing planes, for clearance reasons as well as easier loading. In short, these are bush planes, and may be found on wheels, skis, or floats.

Cessna

Cessna's 180 has become a legend: used everywhere that strength, reliability, and performance are required. Since 1953 the 180 has been unchanged, equipped with the Continental O-470 engine, and featuring conventional landing gear.

The 185 Skywagon, also with conventional gear, was introduced in 1961 with a 260-hp engine, updated in 1966 with a 300-hp engine. Both planes will accept an optional under-fuselage cargo carrier that will hold up to 300 pounds.

The 1963 Cessna 205 was introduced as a fixed-gear version of the 210. The 205 is basically a tricycle geared counterpart to the 185. It can also be fitted with the under-fuselage cargo carrier. The 205 was replaced in 1965 by the U206 Super Skywagon. The 206 has large double doors on the right side of the cabin to allow loading of awkardly shaped cargo items. It's powered with a 285-hp engine.

The P206 Super Skylane is a fancy version of the U206 that is designed for carrying passengers.

In 1969 the seven place 207 Skywagon was introduced. It's an outgrowth of the 206 series.

Cessna's latest entry to the heavy-hauler market is the Caravan, a turbo-prop single-engine plane designed for short hauls of light cargo. It is the largest and most costly of all the heavy-haulers.

Fig. 10-1. Cessna 1953 180.

Make: Cessna   Model: 180
Year: 1953-81
Engine
    Make: Continental
    Model: O-470-K
    Horsepower: 230
    TBO: 1500 hours
Speeds
    Maximum: 170 mph
    Cruise: 162 mph
    Stall: 58 mph
Fuel capacity: 55 gallons
Rate of climb: 1090 fpm
Transitions
    Takeoff over 50-foot obstacle: 1225 feet
    Ground run: 625 feet
    Landing over 50-foot obstacle: 1365 feet
    Ground roll: 480 feet
Weights
    Gross: 2800 pounds
    Empty: 1545 pounds
Seats: Four (Six after 1963)
Dimensions
    Length: 25 feet 9 inches
    Height: 7 feet 9 inches
    Span: 35 feet 10 inches

Make: Cessna   Model: 185 Skywagon (260)
Year: 1961-66
Engine
    Make: Continental
    Model: IO-470-F

Horsepower: 260
TBO: 1500 hours
Speeds
Maximum: 176 mph
Cruise: 167 mph
Stall: 62 mph
Fuel capacity: 65 gallons
Rate of climb: 1000 fpm
Transitions
Takeoff over 50-foot obstacle: 1510 feet
Ground run: 650 feet
Landing over 50-foot obstacle: 1265 feet
Ground roll: 610 feet
Weights
Gross: 3200 pounds
Empty: 1520 pounds
Seats: Six
Dimensions
Length: 25 feet 9 inches
Height: 7 feet 9 inches
Span: 35 feet 10 inches

Cessna Aircraft Co.

Fig. 10-2. Cessna 1983 185 Skywagon.

Make: Cessna   Model: 185 Skywagon (300)
Year: 1966-85
Engine
Make: Continental
Model: IO-520-D
Horsepower: 300
TBO: 1700 hours

Speeds
    Maximum: 178 mph
    Cruise: 169 mph
    Stall: 59 mph
Fuel capacity: 65 gallons
Rate of climb: 1010 fpm
Transitions
    Takeoff over 50-foot obstacle: 1365 feet
    Ground run: 770 feet
    Landing over 50-foot obstacle: 1400 feet
    Ground roll: 480 feet
Weights
    Gross: 3350 pounds
    Empty: 1585 pounds
Seats: Six
Dimensions
    Length: 25 feet 9 inches
    Height: 7 feet 9 inches
    Span: 35 feet 10 inches

Fig. 10-3. Cessna 1963 205.

Make: Cessna   Model: 205
Year: 1963-64
Engine
    Make: Continental
    Model: IO-470-S
    Horsepower: 260
    TBO: 1500 hours
Speeds
    Maximum: 167 mph

Cruise: 159 mph
Stall: 57 mph
Fuel capacity: 65 gallons
Rate of climb: 965 fpm
Transitions
    Takeoff over 50-foot obstacle: 1465 feet
    Ground run: 685 feet
    Landing over 50-foot obstacle: 1510 feet
    Ground roll: 625 feet
Weights
    Gross: 3300 pounds
    Empty: 1750 pounds
Seats: Six
Dimensions
    Length: 27 feet 3 inches
    Height: 9 feet 7 inches
    Span: 36 feet 6 inches

Cessna Aircraft Co.

Fig. 10-4. Cessna 1967 206 Super Skylane.

Make: Cessna   Model: U206/P206 Super Skylane/Skywagon
Year: 1965-86
Engine
    Make: Continental
    Model: IO-520 (turbocharging optional)
    Horsepower: 285
    TBO: 1700 hours (1400 if turbocharged)
Speeds
    Maximum: 174 mph
    Cruise: 164 mph
    Stall: 61 mph
Fuel capacity: 65 gallons

Rate of climb: 920 fpm
Transitions
    Takeoff over 50-foot obstacle: 1265 feet
    Ground run: 675 feet
    Landing over 50-foot obstacle: 1340 feet
    Ground roll: 735 feet
Weights
    Gross: 3600 pounds
    Empty: 1750 pounds
Seats: Six
Dimensions
    Length: 28 feet
    Height: 9 feet 7 inches
    Span: 35 feet 10 inches

Make: Cessna   Model: U206/P206 Super Skylane/Skywagon
Year: 1967-86
Engine
    Make: Continental
    Model: IO-520
    Horsepower: 300
    TBO: 1700 hours
Speeds
    Maximum: 179 mph
    Cruise: 169 mph
    Stall: 62 mph
Fuel capacity: 65 gallons
Rate of climb: 920 fpm
Transitions
    Takeoff over 50-foot obstacle: 1780 feet
    Ground run: 900 feet
    Landing over 50-foot obstacle: 1395 feet
    Ground roll: 735 feet
Weights
    Gross: 3600 pounds
    Empty: 2000 pounds
Seats: Six
Dimensions
    Length: 28 feet 3 inches
    Height: 9 feet 4 inches
    Span: 35 feet 10 inches

Fig. 10-5. Cessna 1982 207 Stationair.

Make: Cessna   Model: 207 Skywagon/Stationair
Year: 1969-84
Engine
    Make: Continental
    Model: IO-520 (turbocharging optional)
    Horsepower: 300
    TBO: 1700 (1400 is turbocharged)
Speeds
    Maximum: 168 mph
    Cruise: 159 mph
    Stall: 67 mph
Fuel capacity: 61 gallons
Rate of climb: 810 fpm
Transitions
    Takeoff over 50-foot obstacle: 1970 feet
    Ground run: 1100 feet
    Landing over 50-foot obstacle: 1500 feet
    Ground roll: 765 feet
Weights
    Gross: 3800 pounds
    Empty: 1890 pounds
Seats: Seven
Dimensions
    Length: 31 feet 9 inches
    Height: 9 feet 7 inches
    Span: 35 feet 10 inches

Fig. 10-6. Cessna Caravan I.

Make: Cessna   Model: 208 Caravan
Year: 1985-up
Engine
    Make: Pratt & Witney
    Model: PT6A-114
    Horsepower: 600 (shaft)
    TBO: 3500
Speeds
    Maximum: 210 mph
    Cruise: 200 mph
    Stall: 69 mph
Fuel capacity: 332 gallons
Rate of climb: 1215 fpm
Transitions
    Takeoff over 50-foot obstacle: 1665 feet
    Ground run: 970 feet
    Landing over 50-foot obstacle: 1550 feet
    Ground roll: 645 feet
Weights
    Gross: 7300 pounds
    Empty: 3800 pounds
Seats: Fourteen
Dimensions
    Length: 37 feet 7 inches
    Height: 14 feet 2 inches
    Span: 51 feet 8 inches

Helio

The Helio Courier originated with the Koppen-Bollinger Helioplane, built in 1949.

Couriers are STOL (short takeoff and landing) airplanes. To accomplish this task, yet retain good cruise speed, they feature various wing adaptations like full-span leading edge slats that deploy during slow flight and landings.

Fig. 10-7. Helio Courier.

Make: Helio   Model: H-295 Super Courier
Year: NA
Engine
    Make: Lycoming
    Model: GO-480-G1A6
    Horsepower: 295
    TBO: 1400 hours
Speeds
    Maximum: 167 mph
    Cruise: 165 mph
    Stall: 30 mph
Fuel capacity: 120 gallons
Rate of climb: 1150 fpm
Transitions
    Takeoff over 50-foot obstacle: 610 feet
    Ground run: 335 feet
    Landing over 50-foot obstacle: 520 feet
    Ground roll: 270 feet
Weights
    Gross: 3400 pounds
    Empty: 2080 pounds
Seats: Six
Dimensions
    Length: 31 feet
    Height: 8 feet 10 inches
    Span: 39 feet

Maule

Maules are simple, yet rugged, airplanes designed for short-field operation: Wings are all-metal and the tubular fuselage is covered with Fiberglass. They have few moving or complex parts and are therefore economically maintained.

Aileron and rudder controls are interconnected so there is little need to use the rudder pedals during normal flight.

Production started in 1962 with the M-4, eventually built under several model names, each designating a different engine rating: 145-hp (found in Chapter 9); 180-hp Astro Rocket; 210-hp Rocket; and 220-hp Strata Rocket.

Production of the M-4 series ceased in 1973 and in 1974 the M-5 Lunar Rocket series entered production with larger tail surfaces and a 30 percent increase in flap area. Both improvements and installation of a large engine allows these planes to carry large loads almost anywhere.

The M-6 was built from 1983 to 1985; M-6 has longer wings and a 235-hp engine was built. Performance is remarkable; takeoff ground run seems almost non-existent and approaches are incredibly slow.

Maule's recent entry is the M-7, which is powered by a 235-hp engine.

Make: Maule   Model: M-4/180 Astro Rocket
Year: 1970-71
Engine
      Make: Franklin
      Model: 6A-355B1
      Horsepower: 180
      TBO: 2000 hours
Speeds
      Maximum: 170 mph
      Cruise: 155 mph
      Stall: 40 mph
Fuel capacity: 42 gallons
Rate of climb: 1000 fpm
Transitions
      Takeoff over 50-foot obstacle: 700 feet
      Ground run: 500 feet
      Landing over 50-foot obstacle: 600 feet
      Ground roll: 450 feet
Weights
      Gross: 2300 pounds
      Empty: 1250 pounds
Seats: Four
Dimensions
      Length: 22 feet
      Height: 6 feet 2 inches
      Span: 30 feet 10 inches

Make: Maule   Model: M-4/210 Rocket
Year: 1965-73
Engine
    Make: Continental
    Model: IO-360-A
    Horsepower: 210
    TBO: 1500 hours
Speeds
    Maximum: 180 mph
    Cruise: 165 mph
    Stall: 40 mph
Fuel capacity: 42 gallons
Rate of climb: 1250 fpm
Transitions
    Takeoff over 50-foot obstacle: 650 feet
    Ground run: 430 feet
    Landing over 50-foot obstacle: 600 feet
    Ground roll: 390 feet
Weights
    Gross: 2300 pounds
    Empty: 1120 pounds
Seats: Four
Dimensions
    Length: 22 feet
    Height: 6 feet 2 inches
    Span: 30 feet 10 inches

Fig. 10-8. Maule M-4 220.

Fig. 10-9. Maule M-5 220C.

Make: Maule   Model: M-4/220 Strata Rocket
Year: 1967-73
Engine
    Make: Franklin
    Model: 6A-350-C1
    Horsepower: 220
    TBO: 1500 hours
Speeds
    Maximum: 180 mph
    Cruise: 165 mph
    Stall: 40 mph
Fuel capacity: 42 gallons
Rate of climb: 1250 fpm
Transitions
    Takeoff over 50-foot obstacle: 600 feet
    Ground run: 400 feet
    Landing over 50-foot obstacle: 600 feet
    Ground roll: 390 feet
Weights
    Gross: 2300 pounds
    Empty: 1220 pounds
Seats: Four
Dimensions
    Length: 22 feet
    Height: 6 feet 2 inches
    Span: 30 feet 10 inches

Make: Maule   Model: M-5/210 Lunar Rocket
Year: 1974-77

Engine
  Make: Continental
  Model: IO-360-D
  Horsepower: 210
  TBO: 1500 hours
Speeds
  Maximum: 180 mph
  Cruise: 158 mph
  Stall: 38 mph
Fuel capacity: 40 gallons
Rate of climb: 1250 fpm
Transitions
  Takeoff over 50-foot obstacle: 600 feet
  Ground run: 400 feet
  Landing over 50-foot obstacle: 600 feet
  Ground roll: 400 feet
Weights
  Gross: 2300 pounds
  Empty: 1350 pounds
Seats: Four
Dimensions
  Length: 22 feet 9 inches
  Height: 6 feet 4 inches
  Span: 30 feet 10 inches

Make: Maule   Model: M-5/235
Year: 1977-87
Engine
  Make: Lycoming
  Model: O-540-J1A5D
  Horsepower: 235
  TBO: 2000 hours
Speeds
  Maximum: 185 mph
  Cruise: 172 mph
  Stall: 38 mph
Fuel capacity: 40 gallons
Rate of climb: 1350 fpm
Transitions
  Takeoff over 50-foot obstacle: 600 feet
  Ground run: 400 feet
  Landing over 50-foot obstacle: 600 feet
  Ground roll: 400 feet
Weights
  Gross: 2300 pounds
  Empty: 1400 pounds

Seats: Four
Dimensions
    Length: 22 feet 9 inches
    Height: 6 feet 4 inches
    Span: 30 feet 10 inches

Fig. 10-10. Maule M-6 235C.

Make: Maule   Model: M-6/235 Super Rocket
Year: 1981-85
Engine
    Make: Lycoming
    Model: IO-540
    Horsepower: 235
    TBO: 2000 hours
Speeds
    Maximum: 180 mph
    Cruise: 148 mph
    Stall: 44 mph
Fuel capacity: 40 gallons
Rate of climb: 1900 fpm
Transitions
    Takeoff over 50-foot obstacle: 540 feet
    Ground run: 150 feet
    Landing over 50-foot obstacle: 440 feet
    Ground roll: 250 feet

Weights
    Gross: 2500 pounds
    Empty: 1450 pounds
Seats: Four
Dimensions
    Length: 23 feet 6 inches
    Height: 6 feet 4 inches
    Span: 33 feet 2 inches

Make: Maule   Model: M-7/235
Year: 1986-up
Engine
    Make: Lycoming
    Model: IO-540
    Horsepower: 235
    TBO: 2000 hours
Speeds
    Maximum: 180 mph
    Cruise: 170 mph
    Stall: 35 mph
Fuel capacity: 40 gallons
Rate of climb: 1350 fpm
Transitions
    Takeoff over 50-foot obstacle: 600 feet
    Ground run: 125 feet
    Landing over 50-foot obstacle: 600 feet
    Ground roll: 275 feet
Weights
    Gross: 2500 pounds
    Empty: 1500 pounds
Seats: Four
Dimensions
    Length: 22 feet 9 inches
    Height: 6 feet 4 inches
    Span: 33 feet 2 inches

Piper

Both Piper airplanes in this category defy the rule of "high wings only" for heavy haulers.

First is the low-winged Cherokee Six, which was manufactured from 1965 to 1979. Removable seats allow this craft to carry cargo, a stretcher, or livestock. A 260-hp or 300-hp engine is available.

Second, the PA-32-301 Saratoga replaced the Cherokee Six in 1980. It was built with a normally aspirated engine or with a turbo-charged engine.

Fig. 10-11. Piper PA-32/300 Cherokee Six.

Make: Piper   Model: PA-32/260 Cherokee Six
Year: 1965-78
Engine
    Make: Lycoming
    Model: O-540-E4B5
    Horsepower: 260
    TBO: 2000 hours (1200 without modifications)
Speeds
    Maximum: 168 mph
    Cruise: 160 mph
    Stall: 63 mph
Fuel capacity: 50 gallons
Rate of climb: 760 fpm
Transitions
    Takeoff over 50-foot obstacle: 1360 feet
    Ground run: 810 feet
    Landing over 50-foot obstacle: 1000 feet
    Ground roll: 630 feet

Weights
    Gross: 3400 pounds
    Empty: 1699 pounds
Seats: Seven
Dimensions
    Length: 27 feet 9 inches
    Height: 7 feet 11 inches
    Span: 32 feet 9 inches

Make: Piper   Model: PA-32/300 Cherokee Six
Year: 1966-79
Engine
    Make: Lycoming
    Model: IO-540-K1A5B
    Horsepower: 300
    TBO: 2000 hours
Speeds
    Maximum: 174 mph
    Cruise: 168 mph
    Stall: 63 mph
Fuel capacity: 50 gallons
Rate of climb: 1050 fpm
Transitions
    Takeoff over 50-foot obstacle: 1140 feet
    Ground run: 700 feet
    Landing over 50-foot obstacle: 1000 feet
    Ground roll: 630 feet
Weights
    Gross: 3400 pounds
    Empty: 1846 pounds
Seats: Seven
Dimensions
    Length: 27 feet 9 inches
    Height: 7 feet 11 inches
    Span: 32 feet 9 inches

Fig. 10-12. Piper PA-32/301 Saratoga.

Make: Piper   Model: PA-32/301 Saratoga
Year: 1979-up
Engine
     Make: Lycoming
     Model: IO-540-K1G5D (Turbocharging is optional)
     Horsepower: 300
     TBO: 2000 hours
Speeds
     Maximum: 175 mph
     Cruise: 172 mph
     Stall: 67 mph
Fuel capacity: 102 gallons
Rate of climb: 990 fpm
Transitions
     Takeoff over 50-foot obstacle: 1759 feet
     Ground run: 1183 feet
     Landing over 50-foot obstacle: 1612 feet
     Ground roll: 732 feet
Weights
     Gross: 3600 pounds
     Empty: 1940 pounds
Seats: Seven
Dimensions
     Length: 27 feet 8 inches
     Height: 8 feet 2 inches
     Span: 36 feet 2 inches

11

Affordable Twins

TWIN-ENGINE AIRPLANES OFFER the most in safety, speed, and comfort. The twin is well respected, is the ultimate in IFR operations, and makes positive impressions of the flying community for business purposes: snob appeal. (Well, at least that's what the manufacturers infer.)

It does make sense that when you have duplicity you have safety by sheer numbers. Unfortunately the safety margins do not always exist.

Flying a multi-engine airplane requires pilot expertise, an FAA multi-engine rating, and money. Sadly, many pilots obtain the rating and fly twins, yet don't maintain proficiency of required emergency procedures. This lulls the pilot into a sense of false security until the eventual engine-out and single-engine "games."

A twin-engine airplane is always expensive to own and operate. When selecting a used twin, realize that just about everything is doubled. There is two of almost everything and the airplane will be a retractable with other complexities, which equate with high maintenance costs.

Aero Commander

Aero Commander twin-engine airplanes have a high wing giving them a unique appearance, and also making them the easiest of all twins to board. They are excellent air taxis and have seen service all over the world doing just that, the mainstay for many small airlines.

An Aero Commander twin flew single-engine from Oklahoma to Washington, D.C., non-stop, and at maximum gross weight. This trip would be difficult for any small twin, but the Aero Commander took off and landed on one engine. The inoperative engine's propeller was carried as baggage, inside the airplane.

Aero Commanders may be found in used airplane listings under Aero Commander, Gulfstream, or Rockwell.

Fig. 11-1. Aero Commander 500.

Make: Aero Commander   Model: 500
Year: 1958-59
Engines
    Make: Lycoming
    Model: O-540-A2B
    Horsepower: 250
    TBO: 2000 hours (1200 without modifications)
Speeds
    Maximum: 218 mph
    Cruise: 205 mph
    Stall: 63 mph
Fuel capacity: 156 gallons
Rate of climb: 1400 fpm (290 single)
Transitions
    Takeoff over 50-foot obstacles: 1250 feet
    Ground run: 1000 feet
    Landing over 50-foot obstacles: 1350 feet
    Ground roll: 950 feet
Weights
    Gross: 6000 pounds
    Empty: 3850 pounds
Seats: Seven
Dimensions
    Length: 35 feet 1 inch
    Height: 14 feet 5 inches
    Span: 49 feet

Make: Aero Commander   Model: 500A
Year: 1960-63
Engines
    Make: Continental
    Model: IO-470-M
    Horsepower: 260
    TBO: 1500 hours
Speeds
    Maximum: 228 mph
    Cruise: 218 mph
    Stall: 62 mph
Fuel capacity: 156 gallons
Rate of climb: 1400 fpm (320 single)
Transitions
    Takeoff over 50-foot obstacles: 1210 feet
    Ground run: 970 feet
    Landing over 50-foot obstacles: 1150 feet
    Ground roll: 865 feet
Weights
    Gross: 6250 pounds
    Empty: 4255 pounds
Seats: Seven
Dimensions
    Length: 35 feet 1 inch
    Height: 14 feet 5 inches
    Span: 49 feet 5 inches

Beechcraft

The oldest Beech twin normally encountered is the Beech 18. It has radial engines and that makes the "right sounds." It is a small airliner that for many years were flown by small air carriers and corporations. Now they are old and expensive to maintain, including a very expensive wing spar AD.

The Twin Bonanza Model 50 was built for nearly 10 years. First production units had 260-hp engines. Later versions included 295- and 340-hp engines. The "T-Bone" went out of production in 1963.

In 1958, the Travelair 95 was introduced. It was powered with two 180-hp engines and seated four, eventually increased to six. Approximately 700 were built before the end of the line in 1968.

The first Beech Baron 55s were seen in 1961, seated six, and were powered by 260- to 340-hp engines. More than 5,700 were built.

The last Beech entry into the small-twin field was the Duchess Model 76, a T-tailed craft with counter-rotating engines. Counter-rotating propellers take some danger out of engine-out operations by eliminating most of the critical-engine factor.

Beech Aircraft Corp.

Fig. 11-2. Beechcraft E18S.

Make: Beechcraft   Model: D-18S
Year: 1946-69
Engines
    Make: Pratt & Whitney
    Model: R-985
    Horsepower: 450
    TBO: 1600 hours

Speeds
    Maximum: 230 mph
    Cruise: 214 mph
    Stall: 84 mph
Fuel capacity: 198 gallons
Rate of climb: 1410 fpm (255 single)
Transitions
    Takeoff over 50-foot obstacles: 1980 feet
    Ground run: 1445 feet
    Landing over 50-foot obstacles: 1850 feet
    Ground roll: 1036 feet
Weights
    Gross: 9700 pounds
    Empty: 5910 pounds
Seats: Seven-9 (and crew)
Dimensions
    Length: 35 feet 2 inches
    Height: 10 feet 5 inches
    Span: 49 feet 8 inches

Make: Beechcraft   Model: 50 and B/C-50
Year: 1952-62
Engines
    Make: Lycoming
    Model: GO-435
    Horsepower: 260 (275 on C)
    TBO: 1200 hours
Speeds
    Maximum: 203 mph
    Cruise: 183 mph
    Stall: 69 mph
Fuel capacity: 134 gallons
Rate of climb: 1450 fpm (300 single)
Transitions
    Takeoff over 50-foot obstacles: 1344 feet
    Ground run: 1080 feet
    Landing over 50-foot obstacles: 1215 feet
    Ground roll: 975 feet
Weights
    Gross: 6000 pounds
    Empty: 3940 pounds
Seats: Six
Dimensions
    Length: 31 feet 5 inches
    Height: 11 feet 5 inches
    Span: 45 feet 2 inches

Fig. 11-3. Beechcraft D50 Twin Bonanza.

Beech Aircraft Corp.

Make: Beechcraft   Model: D-50
Year: 1956-61
Engines
    Make: Lycoming
    Model: GO-480
    Horsepower: 295
    TBO: 1400 hours
Speeds
    Maximum: 214 mph
    Cruise: 203 mph
    Stall: 71 mph
Fuel capacity: 134 gallons
Rate of climb: 1450 fpm (300 single)
Transitions
    Takeoff over 50-foot obstacles: 1260 feet
    Ground run: 1000 feet
    Landing over 50-foot obstacles: 1455 feet
    Ground roll: 1010 feet
Weights
    Gross: 6300 pounds
    Empty: 4100 pounds
Seats: Seven
Dimensions
    Length: 31 feet 5 inches
    Height: 11 feet 5 inches
    Span: 45 feet 9 inches

Make: Beechcraft   Model: E/F-50
Year: 1957-58
Engines
    Make: Lycoming
    Model: GSO-480
    Horsepower: 340
    TBO: 1400 hours
Speeds
    Maximum: 240 mph
    Cruise: 212 mph
    Stall: 83 mph
Fuel capacity: 180 gallons
Rate of climb: 1320 fpm (325 single)
Transitions
    Takeoff over 50-foot obstacles: 1250 feet
    Ground run: 975 feet
    Landing over 50-foot obstacles: 1840 feet
    Ground roll: 1250 feet
Weights
    Gross: 7000 pounds
    Empty: 4460 pounds
Seats: Seven
Dimensions
    Length: 31 feet 5 inches
    Height: 11 feet 5 inches
    Span: 45 feet 9 inches

Fig. 11-4. Beechcraft 1959 Travel Air 95.

Make: Beechcraft   Model: 95 Travelair
Year: 1958-68
Engines
    Make: Lycoming
    Model: O-360-A1A (fuel injection after 1960)

Horsepower: 180
TBO: 2000 (1200 without modifications)
Speeds
    Maximum: 210 mph
    Cruise: 200 mph
    Stall: 70 mph
Fuel capacity: 80 gallons
Rate of climb: 1250 fpm (205 single)
Transitions
    Takeoff over 50-foot obstacles: 1280 feet
    Ground run: 1000 feet
    Landing over 50-foot obstacles: 1850 feet
    Ground roll: 1015 feet
Weights
    Gross: 4200 pounds
    Empty: 2635 pounds
Seats: Four (6 after 1960)
Dimensions
    Length: 25 feet 3 inches
    Height: 9 feet 6 inches
    Span: 37 feet 9 inches

Fig. 11-5. Beechcraft B55.

Make: Beechcraft   Model: 55 (all)
Year: 1961-82
Engines
    Make: Continental
    Model: IO-470

Horsepower: 260
TBO: 1500 hours
Speeds
    Maximum: 236 mph
    Cruise: 225 mph
    Stall: 78 mph
Fuel capacity: 112 gallons
Rate of climb: 1670 fpm (320 single)
Transitions
    Takeoff over 50-foot obstacles: 1664 feet
    Ground run: 1339 feet
    Landing over 50-foot obstacles: 1853 feet
    Ground roll: 945 feet
Weights
    Gross: 5100 pounds
    Empty: 3070 pounds
Seats: Six
Dimensions
    Length: 27 feet
    Height: 9 feet 7 inches
    Span: 37 feet 10 inches

Beech Aircraft Corp.

Fig. 11-6. Beechcraft 1978 Duchess 76.

Make: Beechcraft   Model: 76 Duchess
Year: 1978-82
Engines
    Make: Lycoming
    Model: O-360-A1G6D
    Horsepower: 180
    TBO: 2000 hp

Speeds
    Maximum: 197 mph
    Cruise: 182 mph
    Stall: 69 mph
Fuel capacity: 100 gallons
Rate of climb: 1248 fpm (235 single)
Transitions
    Takeoff over 50-foot obstacles: 2119 feet
    Ground run: 1017 feet
    Landing over 50-foot obstacles: 1880 feet
    Ground roll: 1000 feet
Weights
    Gross: 3900 pounds
    Empty: 2460 pounds
Seats: Four
Dimensions
    Length: 29 feet
    Height: 9 feet 6 inches
    Span: 38 feet

Cessna

Modern Cessna light twins have always been marked by their graceful lines, speed, and reliability. Two basic versions of the conventional Cessna twin are the original 310 and sister ship 320.

The 310 was introduced in 1954 with two 240-hp engines. Since that date numerous changes have been made: 1956, additional window space; 1959, 260-hp engines; 1960, swept tail; 1963, six seats; and 1969, 285-hp engines.

The model 320 with turbocharged engines (260-hp each) entered production in 1962; 285 hp and a sixth seat in 1966.

The second twin from Cessna is the Model 336. It has centerline thrust with one engine in front and one in the rear. It was built to be a simple twin to fly with very easy engine-out procedures; it even had fixed landing gear. Cessna thought easy handling would make it a great seller. It wasn't! The next year, 1965, Cessna introduced the 337 with better cooling, quieter operation, and retractable landing gear.

Make: Cessna   Model: 310 and A-B
Year: 1955-58
Engines
    Make: Continental
    Model: O-470-B
    Horsepower: 240 hp
    TBO: 1500 hours
Speeds
    Maximum: 232 mph
    Cruise: 213 mph
    Stall: 74 mph
Fuel capacity: 102 gallons
Rate of climb: 1660 fpm (450 single)
Transitions
    Takeoff over 50-foot obstacles: 1410 feet
    Ground run: 810 feet
    Landing over 50-foot obstacles: 1720 feet
    Ground roll: 620 feet
Weights
    Gross: 4700 pounds
    Empty: 2900 pounds
Seats: Five
Dimensions
    Length: 26 feet
    Height: 10 feet 6 inches
    Span: 35 feet 9 inches

Fig. 11-7. Cessna 1962 310.

Make: Cessna   Model: 310 C-Q
Year: 1959-74
Engines
    Make: Continental
    Model: IO-470-D
    Horsepower: 260
    TBO: 1500 hours
Speeds
    Maximum: 240 mph
    Cruise: 223 mph
    Stall: 76 mph
Fuel capacity: 102 gallons
Rate of climb: 1690 fpm (380 single)
Transitions
    Takeoff over 50-foot obstacles: 1545 feet
    Ground run: 920 feet
    Landing over 50-foot obstacles: 1900 feet
    Ground roll: 690 feet
Weights
    Gross: 5100 pounds
    Empty: 3063 pounds
Seats: Six
Dimensions
    Length: 29 feet 5 inches
    Height: 9 feet 11 inches
    Span: 36 feet 11 inches

Fig. 11-8. Cessna 1981 310.

Make: Cessna   Model: 310 P-R
Year: 1969-81
Engines
    Make: Continental
    Model: IO-520-M (Turbocharging optional)
    Horsepower: 285
    TBO: 1700 hours
Speeds
    Maximum: 238 mph
    Cruise: 223 mph
    Stall: 81 mph
Fuel capacity: 102 gallons
Rate of climb: 1662 fpm (370 single)
Transitions
    Takeoff over 50-foot obstacles: 1700 feet
    Ground run: 1335 feet
    Landing over 50-foot obstacles: 1790 feet
    Ground roll: 640 feet
Weights
    Gross: 5500 pounds
    Empty: 3603 pounds
Seats: Six
Dimensions
    Length: 31 feet 11 inches
    Height: 10 feet 8 inches
    Span: 36 feet 11 inches

Make: Cessna   Model: 320 (through C)
Year: 1962-65
Engines
    Make: Continental
    Model: TSIO-470

Fig. 11-9. Cessna 1962 320.

Horsepower: 260
TBO: 1400 hours
Speeds
    Maximum: 265 mph
    Cruise: 235 ph
    Stall: 78 mph
Fuel capacity: 102 gallons
Rate of climb: 1820 fpm (400 single)
Transitions
    Takeoff over 50-foot obstacles: 1890 feet
    Ground run: 870 feet
    Landing over 50-foot obstacles: 2056 feet
    Ground roll: 640 feet
Weights
    Gross: 4990 pounds
    Empty: 3190 pounds
Seats: Six
Dimensions
    Length: 29 feet 5 inches
    Height: 10 feet 3 inches
    Span: 36 feet 9 inches

Make: Cessna   Model: 320 D-F
Year: 1966-68
Engines
    Make: Continental
    Model: TSIO-520
    Horsepower: 285
    TBO: 1400 hours

Speeds
  Maximum: 275 mph
  Cruise: 260 mph
  Stall: 74 mph
Fuel capacity: 102 gallons
Rate of climb: 1924 fpm (475 single)
Transitions
  Takeoff over 50-foot obstacles: 1515 feet
  Ground run: 1190 feet
  Landing over 50-foot obstacles: 1736 feet
  Ground roll: 614 feet
Weights
  Gross: 5300 pounds
  Empty: 3273 pounds
Seats: Six
Dimensions
  Length: 29 feet 5 inches
  Height: 10 feet 3 inches
  Span: 36 feet 9 inches

Make: Cessna   Model: 336
Year: 1964
Engines
  Make: Continental
  Model: IO-360-C
  Horsepower: 210
  TBO: 1500 hours
Speeds
  Maximum: 183 mph
  Cruise: 173 mph
  Stall: 60 mph
Fuel capacity: 93 gallons
Rate of climb: 1340 fpm (355 single)
Transitions
  Takeoff over 50-foot obstacles: 1145 feet
  Ground run: 625 feet
  Landing over 50-foot obstacles: 1395 feet
  Ground roll: 655 feet
Weights
  Gross: 3900 pounds
  Empty: 2340 pounds
Seats: Four (6 optional)
Dimensions
  Length: 29 feet 7 inches
  Height: 9 feet 4 inches
  Span: 38 feet

Fig. 11-10. Cessna 1965 337.

Make: Cessna   Model: 337 (all)
Year: 1965-80
Engines
    Make: Continental
    Model: IO-360-C
    Horsepower: 210
    TBO: 1500 hours
Speeds
    Maximum: 199 mph
    Cruise: 190 mph
    Stall: 70 mph
Fuel capacity: 93 gallons
Rate of climb: 1100 fpm (235 single)
Transitions
    Takeoff over 50-foot obstacles: 1675 feet
    Ground run: 1000 feet
    Landing over 50-foot obstacles: 1650 feet
    Ground roll: 700 feet
Weights
    Gross: 4360 pounds
    Empty: 2695 pounds
Seats: Six
Dimensions
    Length: 29 feet 9 inches
    Height: 9 feet 4 inches
    Span: 38 feet 2 inches

Piper

Piper entered the light twin market in 1954 with the PA-23 Apache: a poor performer with ungainly looks. When operating single-engine the pilot had to look for a place to land because landing was soon to come. Although the specifications provide single-engine climb numbers, it does not climb.

Several changes improved the Apache seating and engine power: 1958, 160-hp engines; 1960, five seats; and 1963, 235-hp engines.

Apaches can be acquired cheap and while the low-powered models have poor performance, they do represent a lot of plane for the money. The last year of production was 1963.

Piper introduced the Aztec in 1960 as a PA-23 (same as the Apache). It was a sleeker looking plane than the Apache and had a swept tail. Originally powered with 250-hp engines and seating five, it was soon updated to seat six. The Aztec is an excellent instrument plane and some are equipped with de-ice equipment.

The Twin Comanche PA-30 was introduced in 1963. It was similar in appearance to the Cessna 310, powered by 160-hp engines, sat low to the ground, and was docile in flight. It became the PA-39 in 1970 with the addition of counterrotating propellers. Twin Comanche production ceased in 1972.

Seneca was introduced in 1970 (a Cherokee Six with two engines) as the PA-34. The PA-44 Seminole was built from 1979 to 1982 as an entry level twin, similar to the Beech Duchess.

Fig. 11-11. Piper PA-23 Apache (150 hp).

Make: Piper   Model: PA-23 (through C) Apache
Year: 1954-57
Engines
    Make: Lycoming

Model: O-320-A1A
Horsepower: 150
TBO: 2000 hours (1200 without modifications)
Speeds
Maximum: 180 mph
Cruise: 170 mph
Stall: 59 mph
Fuel capacity: 72 gallons
Rate of climb: 1250 fpm (240 single)
Transitions
Takeoff over 50-foot obstacles: 1600 feet
Ground run: 900 feet
Landing over 50-foot obstacles: 1360 feet
Ground roll: 670 feet
Weights
Gross: 3500 pounds
Empty: 2180 pounds
Seats: Five
Dimensions
Length: 27 feet 4 inches
Height: 9 feet 6 inches
Span: 37 feet 1 inch

Make: Piper   Model: PA-23 D/E/F Apache
Year: 1957-61
Engines
Make: Lycoming
Model: O-320-B3B
Horsepower: 160
TBO: 2000 hours (1200 without modifications)
Speeds
Maximum: 183 mph
Cruise: 173 mph
Stall: 61 mph
Fuel capacity: 72 gallons
Rate of climb: 1260 fpm (240 single)
Transitions
Takeoff over 50-foot obstacles: 1550 feet
Ground run: 1190 feet
Landing over 50-foot obstacles: 1360 feet
Ground roll: 750 feet
Weights
Gross: 3800 pounds
Empty: 2230 pounds
Seats: Five

Dimensions
    Length: 27 feet 4 inches
    Height: 9 feet 6 inches
    Span: 37 feet 1 inch

Fig. 11-12. Piper PA-23 Apache (late model).

Make: Piper   Model: PA-23 235 Apache
Year: 1962-65
Engines
    Make: Lycoming
    Model: O-540-B1A5
    Horsepower: 235
    TBO: 2000 hours (1200 without modifications)
Speeds
    Maximum: 202 mph
    Cruise: 191 mph
    Stall: 62 mph
Fuel capacity: 144 gallons
Rate of climb: 1450 fpm (220 single)
Transitions
    Takeoff over 50-foot obstacles: 1280 feet
    Ground run: 830 feet
    Landing over 50-foot obstacles: 1360 feet
    Ground roll: 880 feet
Weights
    Gross: 4800 pounds
    Empty: 2735 pounds

Seats: Five
Dimensions
    Length: 27 feet 7 inches
    Height: 10 feet 3 inches
    Span: 37 feet 1 inch

Fig. 11-13. Piper PA-23 Aztec.

Make: Piper   Model: PA-23 Aztec
Year: 1960-81
Engines
    Make: Lycoming
    Model: IO-540-C4B5 (turbocharging optional)
    Horsepower: 250
    TBO: 2000 hours (1200 without modifications - 1800 if turbocharged)
Speeds
    Maximum: 215 mph
    Cruise: 205 mph
    Stall: 62 mph
Fuel capacity: 144 gallons
Rate of climb: 1650 fpm (365 single)
Transitions
    Takeoff over 50-foot obstacles: 1100 feet
    Ground run: 750 feet
    Landing over 50-foot obstacles: 1260 feet
    Ground roll: 900 feet
Weights
    Gross: 4800 pounds
    Empty: 2900 pounds
Seats: Six
Dimensions
    Length: 27 feet 7 inches
    Height: 10 feet 3 inches
    Span: 37 feet 1 inch

Fig. 11-14. Piper PA-39 Twin Comanche.

Make: Piper   Model: PA-30/39 Twin Comanche
Year: 1963-72
Engines
    Make: Lycoming
    Model: IO-320-B1A (turbocharging optional)
    Horsepower: 160
    TBO: 2000 hours (1800 if turbocharged)
Speeds
    Maximum: 205 mph
    Cruise: 198 mph
    Stall: 70 mph
Fuel capacity: 90 gallons
Rate of climb: 1460 fpm (260 single)
Transitions
    Takeoff over 50-foot obstacles: 1530 feet
    Ground run: 940 feet
    Landing over 50-foot obstacles: 1870 feet
    Ground roll: 700 feet
Weights
    Gross: 3600 pounds
    Empty: 2270 pounds
Seats: Four (6 after 1965)
Dimensions
    Length: 25 feet 2 inches
    Height: 8 feet 3 inches
    Span: 36 feet

Make: Piper   Model: PA-34 200 Seneca
Year: 1972-74
Engines
    Make: Lycoming

Fig. 11-15. Piper 1984 PA-34 Seneca.

    Model: IO-360-C1E6
    Horsepower: 200
    TBO: 1800 hours
Speeds
    Maximum: 196 mph
    Cruise: 187 mph
    Stall: 67 mph
Fuel capacity: 100 gallons
Rate of climb: 1460 fpm (190 single)
Transitions
    Takeoff over 50-foot obstacles: 1140 feet
    Ground run: 750 feet
    Landing over 50-foot obstacles: 1335 feet
    Ground roll: 705 feet
Weights
    Gross: 4000 pounds
    Empty: 2586 pounds
Seats: Six
Dimensions
    Length: 28 feet 6 inches
    Height: 9 feet 10 inches
    Span: 38 feet 10 inches

Make: Piper   Model: PA-34 200T Seneca
Year: 1975-up
Engines
    Make: Lycoming
    Model: TSIO-360
    Horsepower: 220
    TBO: 1800 hours

Speeds
    Maximum: 225 mph
    Cruise: 205 mph
    Stall: 74 mph
Fuel capacity: 93 gallons
Rate of climb: 1400 fpm (240 single)
Transitions
    Takeoff over 50-foot obstacles: 1210 feet
    Ground run: 920 feet
    Landing over 50-foot obstacles: 2160 feet
    Ground roll: 1400 feet
Weights
    Gross: 4750 pounds
    Empty: 2852 pounds
Seats: Seven
Dimensions
    Length: 28 feet 7 inches
    Height: 9 feet 11 inches
    Span: 38 feet 11 inches

Make: Piper   Model: PA-44 Seminole
Year: 1979-82
Engines
    Make: Lycoming
    Model: IO-360-E1A6D (turbocharging optional)
    Horsepower: 180
    TBO: 2000 hours
Speeds
    Maximum: 193 mph
    Cruise: 185 mph
    Stall: 63 mph
Fuel capacity: 108 gallons
Rate of climb: 1340 fpm (217 single)
Transitions
    Takeoff over 50-foot obstacles: 1400 feet
    Ground run: 880 feet
    Landing over 50-foot obstacles: 1400 feet
    Ground roll: 595 feet
Weights
    Gross: 3800 pounds
    Empty: 2406 pounds
Seats: Four
Dimensions
    Length: 27 feet 7 inches
    Height: 8 feet 6 inches
    Span: 38 feet 7 inches

Part III
Tall Tales, Tidbits, and Hot Information

12

Hangar Flying
Used Airplanes

THE FOLLOWING PAGES ARE DEVOTED to comments, statements, rumors, and facts that are often heard about used airplanes. (Attribution in parenthesis.)

Beechcraft

"Beechcraft 19, 23, Sport, and Musketeer airplanes have speed-to-horsepower ratios that are low when compared to other planes in their class. The 150-hp versions take off and climb marginally on hot days, and at high altitudes. Stalls are abrupt and complete, unlike the Cessna and Piper stalls. Resale prices are poor on these planes and there is little demand for them. Additionally, Beech parts are notoriously expensive." (Broker)

"My [Bonanza] Vee tail has never worried me. I know there was a speed limit, but I never worried. When I had the AD modification done, cracks were found. Next time some problem indicates a need to slow down, you can bet I'll do what I am told." (Owner)

"I prefer the three-piece tail over the Vee. It seems more stable laterally." (Owner)

"Resale on lower models of Beech, such as the 19 and 23 series, are poor." (Dealer)

"The Musketeers have wonderfully large cabins. Much bigger than Piper or Cessna." (Wife)

"My Musketeer has two doors, many don't." (Owner)

"Many Model 33, 35, ad 36 planes are not equipped with dual controls." (Broker)

"Those Vee-tails are the classiest planes out there." (Sunday driver)

"If you need AD work on D-18 wings you might as well junk it." (Mechanic)

"The gear on the Model 23 is about the stoutest in the industry." (Mechanic)

Cessna

"The Cessna 150 is probably the most two-place airplane for the money in today's market. The 172 is the same for four-placers. Either will take care of you, as long as you take care of it." (Author)

"The Lycoming O-320-H2AD engine is the worst thing that ever happened to general aviation. It is only found in 1977 through 1980 Cessna 172s. It is an engine capable of self destruction and has been the subject of many very expensive ADs." (Mechanic)

"The Cessna 172 is so good that one even got past the Russian Air Defense system in May 1987 when a 19-year-old German pilot flew hundreds of miles over the USSR and landed in Red Square." (History)

"Before purchasing a used 182 check the firewall for damage from hard landings. The nosegear can cause the firewall to buckle if the airplane is landed wheel-barrow fashion." (Broker)

"The 182 is a true four-place plane. It will carry four people and all their luggage." (Owner)

"Insuring the Cessna 172 is easy, with no real secrets to them. They are reliable, easy to fly, and replacement parts are available." (Underwriter)

"Cessna gives very poor support to small airplane owners." (Owner)

"I just paid over $600 for a set of seat tracks for my Cessna 182. I feel ripped off, they couldn't possibly be worth more than $20 or $30." (Owner)

"The 150 hp Cardinal is an under-powered dog!" (Instructor)

"I see all kinds of planes, and some are real expensive, but I really like to see an old 172 that has been all fixed up. The pilot is usuallly the guy who fixed it, and he's real proud of it." (Lineboy)

"I could afford to buy a retractable if I wanted it, but why pay for all the extra maintenance for a little extra speed? Slow down and enjoy life." (Owner)

"The 172 flies like a 150, just bigger." (Owner)

"I just had a 180-hp engine installed in my 172, wow! What get-up and-go! This really helps, as the ranch strip is kinda' bad in the spring." (Rancher)

"The visibility in a busy traffic pattern is poor, but that's the same for all high-wingers." (Instructor)

"Love the barn door flaps because they can really save a high approach." (Rancher)

"I have a '63 model with manual flaps, and plan to keep it. I don't like the electric flaps because there's too much that can break on them." (Owner)

"I have Deemers wingtips on the plane, and they allow me to make it into my farm strip easier. The strip is only 990 feet long, but clear on both ends." (Farmer)

"I use mogas in my '64 Hawk. Seems okay, and it saves me money. I wish the FBO would pump it because the gas in the trunk of the car scares me." (Owner)

"Cessna 172s sell themselves. They are roomy, look good, and are reasonable in price. They're just real good value: something you don't often see these days." (Broker)

"I have rarely seen a bargain 172; generally, you get what you pay for." (Mechanic)

Ercoupe

"Cute, but glides like a piano." (Instructor)

"Watch for corrosion in the wing root." (Mechanic)

"I like to fly with the window open." (Owner)

"Sure am glad Univair is around to supply parts." (Owner)

Gulfstream (Grumman) American

"The nose wheel is a swivel affair. You have no control of it except by differential brake steering. It is very good in close quarters." (Owner)

"Watch for delamination of the control and wing surfaces. There is an AD about this problem." (Mechanic)

"The laminated Fiberglass landing gear will save most botched landings. They are great mistake absorbers." (Instructor)

Luscombe

"A pilot's airplane. Keeps you in shape on crosswind landings." (Instructor)

"Luscombes have a poor reputation for ground loops." (FBO)

"Too bad they didn't keep going. The Sedan was way ahead of everyone else." (Owner)

Maule

"Most pilots will tell you they are good performers for the market they are built for. That is utility use. They are noisy and drafty." (Patrol Pilot)

"The specification numbers given for Maule airplanes are somewhat optimistic." (Owner)

Piper

"The PA-22 Tri-Pacer is probably the last of the four-place affordable airplanes. Just remember it is fabric covered. Like a Maule, the PA-22 is noisy and drafty." (FBO)

"Some PA-28s are not true four-place planes: a two-place with the rear seat added." (Instructor)

"The Warrior is very stable for instrument work." (Owner)

"Any Cub is an investment, if you take care of it." (FBO)

"Watch the lift struts on all older Pipers. They tend to rust and crack. There is an AD out about this problem." (Mechanic)

"The PA-28 180 is a true four-place airplane." (Owner)

"That great big throttle quadrant and only 112 horses." (Tomahawk owner)

"The first Apaches flew like a rock on one engine." (FBO)

"I bought a Super Cub that had been a sprayer. Had to rebuild most of the airframe. Those chemicals ate it all up. Think what they do to people." (Owner)

"It is very easy to overload the Seneca. It's just so big!" (Rancher)

"The tail shakes like it will fall off when a stall breaks." (Tomahawk student)

"The Tee tailed Lance doesn't fly as well as the straight tailed version. It lacks authority on takeoff and requires a faster and longer roll." (Owner)

"Wish Piper had put two doors on like the Skipper." (Instructor)

"I had a bug get caught in the gear sensor and couldn't get the gear up on my Arrow." (Owner)

"I have had nothing but trouble with my cabin door. It never wants to stay closed." (Owner)

Stinson

"The barn door fin on the Stinson will become a weathercock in heavy winds." (Owner)

"My wagon is metalized. Nice, but I wonder what's going on under there." (Owner)

"On my next major I'm going to get an STC for a 200-hp Lycoming or Continental to replace the Franklin. It'll give better performance and be cheaper to maintain in the long run." (Owner)

Swift

"There is only room for two people in my Swift. The luggage compartment is a joke. You can take your toothbrush if you pack it carefully." (Owner)

"The landing felt super smooth as I flared, then I realized the gear wasn't down." (Past owner)

Taylorcraft

"T-Crafts are good performers, just remember they are fabric covered." (FBO)

"Kind of light in heavy winds, but enough control to handle it though." (Owner)

"The 0-200 engine is very reliable." (Patrol pilot)

13

Alternative Aircraft

EVERYONE IS NOT THE TYPICAL AIRPLANE BUYER, in fact most are very individual: interests, finances, and skills will vary. Fortunately there is considerable flexibility in flying, allowing for individual pursuit.

Floatplanes

Ever wish you could go someplace and really get away from it all? Perhaps the answer to your dream is a floatplane. (Fig. 13-1). The fun of float flying attracts many people and such planes offer a means of transportation to otherwise inaccessible locations.

You will need a seaplane rating which is relatively easy to obtain because many flying schools around the country offer seaplane training. The training is practical and involves flying skills only, nothing written. Often the price is fixed and the rating guaranteed. Check *Trade-A-Plane* and other publications for appropriate advertising.

Insurance rates will go up drastically, unless you have extensive floatplane experience with no accident history. Even then, rates will be higher for a float-equipped airplane than for a land-only plane. The reasoning behind the higher rates is the higher loss ratio with floatplanes compared to land planes.

For example, a typical ground loop in a land-based aircraft can result in several hundred dollars damage. The damaged aircraft can often be taxied to a repair facility. The same type of mishap on the water could mean a sunken aircraft, resulting in difficult or impossible recovery, and thousands of dollars in damages.

Extensive maintenance is required on floatplanes, mainly corrosion control.

Areas of Float Plane Activity

Floatplane flying is found in every state of the union, however, some states have more activity than others. The following states have excellent float flying: Alaska, California, Florida, Louisiana, Maine, Massachusetts, Minnesota, Washington, and Wisconsin.

Fig. 13-1. Float equipped planes open new vistas of enjoyment and utility.

Canada offers some of the best floatplane flying in the world because many locations are accessible only by floatplane.

Association

AOPA sponsors the Seaplane Pilots Association (SPA). The group was formed in 1972 and now claims several thousand members. SPA's objective is to assist seaplane pilots with technical problems, provide a national lobbying effort, and more. Membership includes the quarterly magazine *Water Flying*. *Water Flying Annual*, and other written communications that include timely tips and safety measures. SPA sponsors numerous fly-ins annually. Contact:

Seaplane Pilot's Association
421 Aviation Way
Frederick, MD 21701
(301) 695-2000

Homebuilts

Airplane home-building has been with us since the Wright brothers. It is really the grass roots of general aviation. Today there is still constant activity in the homebuilt airplane field.

Home-builders construct an airplane most suitable to their needs and tastes: utility, speed, maneuverability, or individuality.

Airplanes built by their owners may be constructed of tube-and-fabric, metal, or composite. The latter is a method of construction similar to that found in Fiberglass power boats. Generally the builder is building to make the plane his and his alone. If there was a motive to save money, he would have most likely purchased a factory-built airplane (Figs. 13-2 and 13-3).

Home-building is not cheap, but rewards are plentiful. No one is prouder than the builder pointing to an airplane and saying: "I built that." This will make up for the years spent constructing the plane (Fig. 13-4).

Contact:

Experimental Aircraft Association
Wittman Field
Oshkosh, WI 54903

Fig. 13-2. Homebuilt tube and fabric aircraft.

Fig. 13-3. Homebuilt composite airplane, the Lancair.

256

Fig. 13-4. Thousands come to see the homebuilt airplanes each year at Oshkosh.

Gliders

Most pilots have heard at one time or another that obtaining a glider rating makes a better pilot. No doubt there is some truth to that statement. After all, the glider pilot gets only one shot at a landing; the "power" pilot can always go around and do it again.

We "power pilots" tend to only think of getting there in a hurry. Glider flying is more back to the basics, more attuned to the surroundings. Make no mistake, gliders are very sophisticated aircraft. (Figs. 13-5 and 13-6).

The powered glider, first brought to popularity in Europe, is perhaps one of the most interesting aircraft ever. It offers good glider flight characteristics, yet can be flown under power over long distances. They are new to the United States and costs are quite high. (Fig. 13-7). Contact:

Soaring Society of America
P.O. Box E
Hobbs, NM 88241

Fig. 13-5. This entry level glider offers loads of performance.

Fig. 13-6. Hi-performance gliders set world class records.

War Birds

World War II saw the greatest use of air power the world has ever seen. The airplanes were reeky with sight and sound; this appeal has fostered interest in war birds.

The fighters, bombers, and patrol airplanes can be seen at many air shows around the country. Some are small, like the Army L-3 (Aeronca) and L-4 (Piper), which are also known as Aeronca 7AC and Piper J3. Others are big and powerful like the famous Mustang, Bearcat, and B17 (Fig. 13-8).

Fig. 13-7. This powered glider offers interest from both worlds of sport aviation.

Fig. 13-8. P-51.

Some small aircraft, like the Cessna T-41, can also be claimed as war birds. These planes were used for training and logistical work. Korean era jet fighters are coming into their own.

Unfortunately most war birds are not for the average pilot. They drink fuel at a rate only OPEC could appreciate but the direct operating costs are quite nominal when compared to the very costly maintenance required. This is to say nothing of purchase and insurance costs. The larger fighters and bombers require pilot skills few general aviation pilots possess.

Many are owned by the CAF (Confederate Air Force) and Warbirds of America (a division of the EAA). (Fig. 13-9).

Contact:

Warbirds of America, Inc.
Wittman Airfield
Oshkosh, WI 54903

Fig. 13-9. EAA Aviation Center where many warbirds are on display.

Appendix A:

Airworthiness Directives

WARNING: This listing of ADs is incomplete and should not be used for mainte-nance or inspection purposes. It is intended to act as a guide for the prospective purchaser, as an aid in determining values and choices. Some ADs might not apply to every airplane of a particular model. Some ADs are not included in this list. Serial number checks must be made for specific aircraft. Consult with an A&P mechanic for additional information.

Note that some manufacturers appear to have many ADs listed: the more air-planes built, the more ADs issued. The list is formatted to include aircraft make, AD number, AD procedure, and aircraft model(s) affected.

Aero Commander

61-14-1, reinforce the engine mounts: **500s**.
65-6-1, reinforce the front spar cap: **500s**.
(Check Gulfstream and Rockwell for additional information.)

Aeronca

61-16-1, periodic inspection of the lift strut fittings: **15-series**.
(Check Bellanca for additional Aeronca and Champion information.)

Beechcraft

47-33-5, reinforce the horizontal spar: **35 (1-378)**.
57-18-1, inspect the fuselage bulkhead for cracks: **35 (D1-D1500)**.
68-13-2, 400 hrs inspect Hartzell propeller: **S35/V35/V35A/C33A/E33A**.
68-17-6, modify the master brake cylinder: **23 series**.
70-12-2, modify the seat tracks: **36/36A (E1-201)**.
73-20-7, inspect the wing brackets: **23/24 series**.
73-23-3, replace the carb induction system: **23/24 series**.
73-23-6, inspect/replace the throttle assembly: **23 series**.
76-4-5, each 1,000 hrs inspect the stabilizer: **35 series**.

76-25-5, install strap in the wing trailing edge: **23/24 series**.
77-3-5, dye inspect the main landing gear housing: **23/24 series**.
77-11-3, dye check/replace the prop pitch control: **35H/J/K/M/N/P**.
78-4-1, replace the flap control weld assembly: **23/24 series**.
79-23-5, inspect the wing attach bolts: **77 series**.
80-7-7, replace the aileron bearings: **77 series**.
80-21-10, rework the engine mount and bolts: **77 series**.
83-23-3, reinforce the rudder balance weight bracket: **77 series**.
86-21-7, install a speed limit placard: **all V-tail through V35B**.
87-2-8, inspect the stabilator hinge: **most 23/24 series**.

Bellanca

63-6-2, each 100 hrs inspection/replace rudder bellcrank: **14 series**.
68-23-8, modify the elevator trim tab system: **14-19-3A/17-30**.
69-12-4, each 25 hrs inspect/replace rear strut clevises: **14-19-3A/17-30**.
72-20-6, replace control cables: **7ECA/GCAA/GCBS/KCAB**.
73-5-2, replace the rudder shaft assemblies: **17-30/31**.
74-23-4, inspect the wing ribs for cracks: **8KCAB (4-159)**.
75-17-16, replace the carb air valves: **7/8 series**.
75-20-6, inspect the fuselage tubes for cracks: **14-19-3A/17-30/31**.
76-8-4, annual check for wood deterioration in wood wing: **14/17 series**.
76-20-7, inspect the wood wing spar for moisture/decay: **14 series**.
76-23-3, each 100 hrs inspect the exhaust system: **17 series**.
77-22-5, replace the wing front lift struts: **7 series**.
79-19-5, inspect the aileron rigging: **14 series**.
79-22-1, inspect the exhaust system for cracks: **7ECA/8KCAB**.
86-25-6, install a fuel drain valve: **17-30/31**.

Cessna

47-50-2, reinforce the fuselage bulkhead: **120/140**.
50-31-1, reinforce the fin spar: **120/140**.
51-11-2, reinforce the elevator spar: **190/195**.
68-7-9, modify the flap system: **177**.
71-1-3, inspect/rework the stabilator attach points: **177**.
71-22-2, each 1,000 hrs inspect or replace the nose gear fork: **most tricycle-gear planes**.
72-3-3, each 100 hrs inspect the flap screw jack: **many 100/200 series**.
72-7-9, check for cracks & loose bolts on fin and rudder: **182**.
73-23-7, replace the wing attach fitting: **100 series**.
74-4-1, inspect for cracks in aft bulkhead: **172**.
76-14-7, each 1,000 hrs replace the landing gear saddle: **210 series**.
77-2-9, replace the flap actuator ball nut assembly: **150/172/182/206/207**.
78-1-13, inspect the rear prop hub: **T-337**.
78-7-1, replace the turbocharger housing: **T206/207/210**.

78-25-7, replace the vertical fin brackets: **A150/A152**.

79-2-6, inspect/replace the heater muffler: **152/A152**.

79-3-3, inspect/replace the turbo charger housing: **TU206G/T207A/T210M**.

79-8-3, remove the cigarette lighter wiring: **most models**.

79-25-7, modify the alternator installation: **many from 180 up**.

80-1-6, modify the flap actuator assembly: **152/A152/172RG**.

80-11-4, replace the nut plates in the tail assembly: **150/152 series**.

81-14-6, replace the rudder trim/nose gear bungees: **172RG (1-769)**.

82-27-2, dye check the prop blade: **most from 172RG up**.

83-22-6, modify/replace the aileron hinges: **152-185 series**.

83-24-11, dye check the prop blades: **180/206/210 series**.

84-10-1, install quick fuel drains/inspect tanks: **180 and up**.

85-11-7, replace the turbo oil reservoir: **210 series**.

85-17-7, inspect and install the doubler in the rear wing spar: **206/207 series**.

86-19-11, modify the fuel quick drain system: **172 and up**.

86-24-7, modify the engine control rod ends: **most single-engine aircraft**.

87-20-3, inspect and replace the seat rails on practically every airplane.

Ercoupe

46-49-1, replace the nose wheel: **415**.

47-20-5, reinforce the belly skin: **415**.

47-20-6, reinforce the aileron skin: **415**.

47-42-20, inspect and replace control column shaft: **415**.

59-5-4, reinforce the rear spar: **415**.

59-25-5, reinforce the rudder: **415**.

60-9-2, replace the nose gear bolts: **all**.

67-6-3, modify the rudder control: **415**.

Gulfstream

70-25-5, replace the bungee mounting plate: **AA-1**.

75-9-7, replace the mixture control wires: **AA-1/A/B**.

76-1-2, replace the engine cowl hinge: **AA-5 series**.

76-17-3, rework some bonded skins: **AA-1/AA-5 series**.

76-22-9, replace the oil cooler: **AA-5 series**.

77-7-4, replace the carb heat valve: **AA-5/AA-5A**.

78-13-4, replace the fuel gauge floats: **AA-1**.

79-22-4, rework the aileron control system: **AA-5 series**.

Lake

65-15-3, rework the nosegear drag strut bolt: **LA-4**.

74-26-2, each 100 hours and replace the rudder bellcrank: **LA-4/200**.

76-24-2, replace the oil cooler: **LA-4-200**.

78-14-5, inspect and replace the wing beam fittings: **LA-4-200**.

79-6-1, replace the engine mount straps: **LA-4-200**.

Luscombe

48-49-1, reinforce the vertical stabilizer spar: **8 series**.
79-25-5, each 100 hours inspect the stabilizer attachments: **8 series**.

Maule

65-18-1, reinforce the fuselage fabric: **M-4 series**.
69-20-2, replace the aileron control pulley: **M-4 series**.
71-6-6, rework the seat tracks: **M-4 180C/220C**.
79-12-1, modify the tail and fuselage attachment: **M-4/5**.
81-14-2, modify the rudder bar: **M-4/5**.
84-9-7, replace the fuel drain fittings: **M-4/5 series**.

Mooney

63-10-5, replace the empenage brackets: **M20/A**.
67-11-5, replace the tail truss: **M20/M20A**.
73-21-1, rework flight controls and landing gear: **M20/A/B/C/D/E/F/G**.
75-9-8, inspect the engine mount for cracks: **M20C/D/E/F/G**.
77-17-4, each 1,000 hours check the control wheel shaft: **M20/A/B/C/D/E/F/G**.
77-18-1, check and replace the oil cooler: **M20E/F/J**.
78-15-2, replace the landing gear brace bolts: **M20F/J**.
80-13-3, replace the Duke fuel pump: **M20E/F/J**.
85-24-3, inspect the fuel tanks: **M20/22 series**.
86-19-10, each 12 months perform a load test on wooden wings: **M20/A**.

Navion

64-4-5, each 100 hours inspect/replace outer wing panel: **all through G**.

Piper

59-13-2, reinforce the aileron balance weight: **PA-24**.
62-26-5, rework the exhaust system: **PA-24**.
62-26-6, rework the exhaust system: **PA-28 150-/160-hp**.
64-6-6, dye check and replace the control wheel: **PA-28**.
64-21-5, replace the Hartzell propeller governor relief valve: **PA-23/30**.
66-20-5, modify the propeller spinner: **PA-28**.
67-20-4, replace the torque links: **PA-28/32**.
68-12-4, rework the gear retraction system: **PA-28R**
69-22-2, inspect the control wheel: **PA-28/32**.
70-18-5, replace the landing gear bolts: **PA-28/32**.
70-26-4, dye inspect and replace the stabilator tube: **PA-28/32**.
74-6-1, rework the turbo chargers: **PA-23**.
74-16-8, rework to prevent cracking in aft bulkhead: **PA-30/39**.
74-24-12, rebuild the aileron centering assembly: **PA-28**.

75-2-3, heat treat and replace the nose wheel fork: **PA-28/32**.

75-12-6, each 100 hours magnify inspect the fin spar attach point: **PA-24**.

75-16-4, rework the carburetor air box: **PA-28-151**.

76-18-5, inspect the forward fin channel for cracks: **PA-30/39**.

76-19-7, replace the stabilator weight tube assembly: **PA-24**.

77-1-3, modify the air filter box: **PA-28-151**.

77-3-8, inspect the lift struts: **most tube and fabric series**.

77-13-21, each 500 hours inspect the landing gear/replace bungee cords: **PA-24**.

78-2-3, each 100 hours inspect the stabilator system: **PA-23-250**.

78-8-3, dye and magnify inspect the rudder hinges: **PA-23-150/160**.

78-22-1, install rudder kit: **PA-28**.

78-22-7, replace the control column stop sleeve: **PA-32RT**.

78-23-1, each 100 hours inspect the fuel drain: **PA-28-235/PA-32**.

78-23-4, modify the rear wing spar attachment fittings: **PA-38**.

78-23-9, modify and replace the control wheels: **PA-38**.

78-26-6, dye check and replace the fin spar plate: **PA-38**.

79-3-2, install rudder hinge kit: **PA-38**.

79-8-2, dye inspect the stabilizer fittings: **PA-38**.

79-11-6, replace the gear selector lever: **PA-23**.

79-13-4, install a steel fuel line: **PA-32RT**.

80-19-1, inspect and repair muffler leaks: **PA-28R-180/200/201/RT201**.

80-22-13, replace the rudder hinge brackets: **PA-38**.

81-12-4, modify the rudder system: **PA-28RT/201T**.

81-23-7, modify and replace the engine mount: **PA-38**.

81-24-7, modify the nose gear: **PA-32R series**.

81-25-5, replace the strut forks: **J3/PA-11/12/14/16/18/20/22**.

82-2-1, install an aileron balance reinforcement kit: **PA-38**.

82-19-1, dye check the wing spar caps and plates: **PA-24** series.

82-27-8, dye check and replace the fin spar: **PA-38**.

83-5-4, replace the landing gear bolts: **PA-38**.

83-14-8, install kit and replace airspeed indicator: **PA-38**.

83-19-1, each 100 hours inspect and modify the fin spars: **PA-38**.

83-19-3, inspect the spar cap: **PA-24 series**.

85-11-6, modify the control wheel shaft: **PA-38**.

86-17-1, replace the ammeter: **PA-28/32 series**.

87-8-8, inspect the lower spar caps and upper skin: **PA-28/32 series**.

Rockwell

68-12-5, modify the rudder control arms: **100/100A**.

68-21-2, inspect and replace the aileron cable assembly: **100 series**.

73-1-1, inspect and repair the exhaust system: **100 series**.

Stinson

51-15-2, inspect for cracked crankcase: **6A4-165-B3 Franklin engines**.

Taylorcraft

75-18-5, 100 hours inspect and replace the engine mount bolts: **F-19**.
79-4-4, rewire the starter solenoid to switch: **F-19 (1-132)**.

Varga

80-2-8, check for bolts in rudder balance weight: **2150/A**.
80-13-8, install a throttle stop: **2150/A**.
82-8-4, replace the elevator balance arm: **2150A/2180**.

All Small Airplanes

84-26-2, each 500 hours replace paper air filter element: **all aircraft**.

Airborne-brand Equipment

86-1-6, replace dry vacuum pumps: **many aircraft**.

Bendix-brand Equipment

82-11-5, comply with service bulletin: **many engines**.
82-20-1, inspect impulse couplers: **many engines**.

Brackett-brand Equipment

81-15-3, replace inlet air filter: **most small aircraft**.

Slick-brand Equipment

80-6-5, test the magneto impulse coupling: **many engines**.
81-16-5, inspect the magneto coil: **many engines**.

Continental Engines

60-12-1, replace the piston pins: **E-185/E-225/O-470**.
63-15-1, replace the exhaust valves: **E-165/E-185/E-225/O-470**.
72-20-2, inspect/replace the cylinders: **O-470 engines**.
77-13-22, inspect the crankcase for cracks: **O-520 series**.
81-7-6, inspect/replace the fuel pump: **A-65/75/C-75/85/90/C-125/O-200**.
81-13-10, rework the oil pump drive: **IO-360 series**.
85-8-2, replace the exhaust valves: **O-470 series**.

Lycoming Engines

71-11-2, replace the tappet plungers: **IO-360 A/C series**.
75-8-9, replace the oil pump shaft and impeller: **O-235/320/360/540**.
77-7-7, modify the oil filter: **O-320-H series**.

77-20-7, replace the tappets: **O-320-H series**.

78-12-8, replace the oil pump impeller: **O-320-H series**.

78-12-9, replace the crankshaft: **O-320-H series**.

78-25-1, replace the Slick magneto: **PA-38**.

80-4-3, replace valve springs, seats, and lifters: **O-320**.

80-14-7, inspect the exhaust valve springs and seats: **O-320-H/O-360-E**.

80-25-2, inspect the valve pushrods: **O-235 series**.

81-18-4, replace the oil pump impeller & shaft: **most engines**.

83-22-4, replace the fuel diaphram: **IO-540 series**.

87-10-6, inspect and replace the rocker arm assembly: **many engines**.

Appendix B:

NTSB Accident Ranking of Small Airplanes

The National Transportation Safety Board (NTSB) and FAA investigates airplane accidents. Based upon thousands of investigations, the board has reached interesting conclusions and published charts comparing aircraft accidents with makes and types of aircraft. **The charts are based on an adjusted rate of 100,000 hours flying time**.

Placement of an aircraft make and model on NTSB charts is determined by the frequency of accidents compared to other aircraft listed on the same chart: aircraft with poor accident records at the top, aircraft with better records at the bottom.

An airplane might not appear on a chart because too few records were available for analysis.

Fatal Accident By Manufacturer

	Rate per 100,000 hours
Bellanca	4.84
Grumman	4.13
Beech	2.54
Mooney	2.50
Piper	2.48
Cessna	1.65

Accidents Caused By Engine Failure

	Rate per 100,000 hours
Globe GC-1	12.36
Stinson 108	10.65
Ercoupe	9.50
Grumman AA-1	8.71
Navion	7.84
Piper J-3	7.61
Luscombe 8	7.58
Cessna 120/140	6.73
Piper PA-12	6.54
Bellanca 14-19	5.98
Piper PA-22	5.67
Cessna 195	4.69
Piper PA-32	4.39
Cessna 210/205	4.25
Aeronca 7	4.23
Aeronca 11	4.10
Taylorcraft	3.81
Piper PA-24	3.61
Beech 23	3.58
Cessna 175	3.48
Mooney M-20	3.42
Piper PA-18	3.37
Cessna 177	3.33
Cessna 206	3.30
Cessna 180	3.24

	Rate per 100,000 hours
Cessna 170	2.88
Cessna 185	2.73
Cessna 150	2.48
Piper PA-28	2.37
Beech 33, 35, 36	2.22
Grumman AA-5	2.20
Cessna 182	2.08
Cessna 172	1.41

Accidents Caused by In-flight Airframe Failure

	Rate per 100,000 hours
Bellanca 14-19	1.49
Globe GC-1	1.03
Ercoupe	0.97
Cessna 195	0.94
Navion	0.90
Aeronca 11	0.59
Beech 33, 35, 36	0.58
Luscombe 8	0.54
Piper PA-24	0.42
Cessna 170	0.36
Cessna 210/205	0.34
Cessna 180	0.31
Piper PA-22	0.30
Aeronca 7	0.27
Beech 23	0.27
Cessna 120/140	0.27
Piper PA-32	0.24
Tayorcraft	0.24
Piper J-3	0.23
Mooney M-20	0.18
Piper PA-28	0.16
Cessna 177	0.16
Cessna 182	0.12
Cessna 206	0.11
Grumman AA-1	0.09
Cessna 172	0.03
Cessna 150	0.02

Accidents Resulting from a Stall

	Rate per 100,000 hours
Aeronca 7	22.47
Aeronca 11	8.21
Taylorcraft	6.44

	Rate per 100,000 hours
Piper J-3	5.88
Luscombe 8	5.78
Piper PA-18	5.49
Globe GC-1	5.15
Cessna 170	4.38
Grumman AA-1	4.23
Piper PA-12	3.27
Cessna 120/140	2.51
Stinson 108	2.09
Navion	1.81
Piper PA-22	1.78
Cessna 177	1.77
Grumman AA-5	1.76
Cessna 185	1.47
Cessna 150	1.42
Beech 23	1.41
Ercoupe	1.29
Cessna 180	1.08
Piper PA-24	0.98
Beech 33, 35, 36	0.94
Cessna 175	0.83
Piper PA-28	0.80
Mooney M-20	0.80
Cessna 172	0.77
Cessna 210/205	0.71
Bellanca 14-19	0.60
Piper PA-32	0.57
Cessna 206	0.54
Cessna 195	0.47
Cessna 182	0.36

Accidents Caused by Hard Landings

	Rate per 100,000 hours
Beech 23	3.50
Grumman AA-1	3.02
Ercoupe	2.90
Cessna 177	2.60
Globe GC-1	2.58
Luscombe 8	2.35
Cessna 182	2.17
Cessna 170	1.89
Beech 33, 35, 36	1.45
Cessna 150	1.37
Cessna 120/140	1.35
Cessna 206	1.30

Piper PA-24	1.29
Aeronca 7	1.20
Piper J-3	1.04
Grumman AA-5	1.0-3
Cessna 175	1.00
Cessna 180	0.93
Cessna 210/205	0.82
Piper PA-28	0.81
Cessna 172	0.71
Piper PA-22	0.69
Taylorcraft BC	0.48
Cessna 195	0.47
Piper PA-18	0.43
Piper PA-32	0.42
Cessna 185	0.42
Navion	0.36
Mooney M-20	0.31
Piper PA-12	0.23
Stinson 108	0.19

Piper PA-28	1.36
Piper PA-24	1.29
Cessna 210/205	1.08
Cessna 182	1.06
Cessna 172	1.00
Mooney M-20	0.65
Beech 33, 35, 36	0.55
Navion	0.36
Cessna 175	0.17

Accidents Resulting from a Ground Loop

	Rate per 100,000 hours
Cessna 195	22.06
Stinson 108	13.50
Luscombe 8	13.00
Cessna 170	9.91
Cessna 120/140	8.99
Aeronca 11	7.86
Aeronca 7	7.48
Cessna 180	6.49
Cessna 185	4.72
Piper PA-12	4.67
Piper PA-18	3.90
Taylorcraft BC	3.58
Globe GC-1	3.09
Grumman AA-1	2.85
Piper PA-22	2.76
Ercoupe	2.74
Beech 23	2.33
Bellanca 14-19	2.10
Piper J-3	2.07
Cessna 206	1.73
Cessna 177	1.61
Grumman AA-5	1.47
Piper PA-32	1.42
Cessna 150	1.37

Accidents Caused by Undershot Landings

	Rate per 100,000 hours
Ercoupe	2.41
Luscombe 8	1.62
Piper PA-12	1.40
Globe GC-1	1.03
Cessna 175	0.99
Grumman AA-1	0.95
Taylorcraft BC	0.95
Piper PA-22	0.83
Piper PA-32	0.70
Bellanca 14-19	0.60
Aeronca 11	0.59
Piper PA-28	0.59
Aeronca 7	0.59
Piper PA-24	0.57
Piper J-3	0.57
Stinson 108	0.57
Cessna 120/140	0.53
Cessna 195	0.47
Grumman AA-5	0.44
Piper PA-18	0.43
Beech 23	0.43
Cessna 185	0.41
Mooney M-20	0.37
Cessna 170	0.36
Navion	0.36
Cessna 150	0.35
Cessna 210/205	0.33
Cessna 206	0.32
Cessna 172	0.26
Cessna 182	0.24
Beech 33, 35, 36	0.21
Cessna 180	0.15
Cessna 177	0.10

Accidents Resulting from Landing Overshoot

	Rate per 100,000 hours
Grumman AA-5	2.35
Cessna 195	2.34
Beech 23	1.95
Piper PA-24	1.61
Piper PA-22	1.33
Cessna 175	1.33
Stinson 108	1.33
Cessna 182	1.21
Aeronca 11	1.17
Luscombe 8	1.08
Piper PA-32	1.03
Globe GC-1	1.03
Mooney M-20	1.01
Cessna 172	1.00
Cessna 170	0.99
Grumman AA-1	0.95
Piper PA-12	0.93
Cessna 210/205	0.89
Cessna 177	0.88
Piper PA-18	0.81
Cessna 206	0.81
Piper PA-28	0.80
Cessna 120/140	0.71
Piper PA-28	0.80
Cessna 120/140	0.71
Ercoupe	0.64
Bellanca 14-19	0.60
Cessna 180	0.56
Navion	0.54
Aeronca 7	0.48
Cessna 150	0.35
Piper J-3	0.34
Cessna 185	0.31
Beech 33, 35, 36	0.23

Appendix C:

FAA GADO and FSDO Locations

Whenever you need a question about general aviation answered, or if you have a question about general aviation aircraft, you can always turn to the Federal Aviation Administration. They have many offices spread around the country with experts to serve the public.

In the many years that I have been associated with general aviation I have never been disappointed with help received from the FAA. When a problem arises, contact them.

ALABAMA

GADO 2
6500 43rd Avenue, North
Birmingham, AL 35206
(205) 254-1557

ALASKA

GADO 1
510 West Int'l Airport Road, Suite 216
Anchorage, AK 99502
(907) 243-1902

FSDO 61
3788 University Avenue
Fairbanks, AK 99701
(907) 474-0276

FSDO 62
1910 Alex Holden Way
Juneau, AK 99701
(907) 789-0231

ARIZONA

GADO 9
15041 Airport Drive
Scottsdale, AZ 85260
(602) 241-2561

ARKANSAS

GADO 6
1701 Bond Street
Little Rock, AR 72202
(501) 378-5565

CALIFORNIA

GADO 1
7120 Hayvenhurst Avenue, Suite 316
Van Nuys, CA 91406
(818) 904-6291

GADO 2
1387 Airport Boulevard
San Jose, CA 95110
(408) 291-7681

GADO 3
8665 Gibbs Drive, Suite 110
San Diego, CA 92123
(619) 557-5281

GADO 4
Fresno Air Terminal
4955 East Anderson, Suite 110
Fresno, CA 93727
(209) 487-5306

GADO
Santa Monica Municipal Airport
3200 Airport Avenue, Suite 3
Santa Monica, CA 90405
(213) 391-6701

GADO 8
Riverside Municipal Airport
6961 Flight Road
Riverside, CA 92504
(714) 351-6701

GADO 12
Executive Airport
Sacramento, CA 95822
(916) 551-1721

FSDO 64
P.O. Box 2397
Airport Station
Oakland, CA 94614
(415) 273-7155

FSDO 65
2815 East Spring Street
Long Beach, CA 90806
(213) 426-7134

COLORADO

GADO 3
10455 East 25th Avenue, Room 202
Aurora, CO 80010
(303) 340-5400

GADO 3S
764 Horizon Drive
Grand Junction, CO 81501
(303) 243-9518

CONNECTICUT

GADO 19
(See Massachusetts)

DELAWARE

GADO 9
North Philadelphia Airport
Philadelphia, PA 19114
(215) 597-9708

DISTRICT OF COLUMBIA

FSDO 62
GT Bldg., Suite 112
Box 17325
Dulles International Airport
Washington, D.C. 20041
(202) 557-5360

FLORIDA

GADO 5
P.O. Box 592336
Miami, FL 33159
(305) 526-2572

GADO 7
FAA Building
Craig Field
855 Saint John's Bluff Road
Jacksonville, FL 32211
(904) 641-7311

FSDO 64
Saint Petersburg/Clearwater Airport
Clearwater, FL 33520
(813) 531-1434

GEORGIA

GADO 1
FAA Building
3400 Norman Berry Drive, Room 361
Atlanta, GA 30336
(404) 763-7265

HAWAII

FSDO 61
FAA-FSDO -13 90 Nakolo Place
Room 215
Honolulu, HI 96819
(808) 836-0615

IDAHO

GADO 1
3975 Rickenbacker Street
Boise, ID 83705
(203) 334-1238

ILLINOIS

GADO 3
Post Office Box H
DuPage County Airport
West Chicago, IL 60185
(312) 377-4500

GADO 19
Capitol Airport
Springfield, IL 62708
(217) 492-4238

INDIANA

GADO 10
Indianapolis International Airport
6801 Pierson Drive
Indianapolis, IN 46241
(317) 247-2491

GADO 18
1843 Commerce Drive
South Bend, IN 46628
(219) 236-8480

IOWA

GADO 4
3021 Army Post Road
Des Moines, IA 50321
(515) 285-9895

KANSAS

GADO 11
Administration Building
Fairfax Municipal Airport
Kansas City, KS 66115
(913) 281-3491

GADO 22
Flight Standards Building
Mid-Continent Airport
Wichita, KS 67209
(316) 946-4462

KENTUCKY

GADO 13
FAA Building
Bowman Field
Louisville, KY 40205
(502) 582-6116

LOUISIANA

GADO 8
FAA Building
Lakefront Airport
New Orleans, LA 70126
(504) 241-2506

GADO 8 South
FAA Office
Lafayette Airport
Lafayette, LA 70508
(318) 234-2321

GADO 11
Terminal Building
Room 137
Downtown Airport
Shreveport, LA 71107
(318) 226-5379

MAINE

GADO 15
Portland International Jetport
Portland, ME 04102
(207) 780-3263

MARYLAND

GADO 21
Elm Road
BWI International Airport
Baltimore, MD 21240
(301) 859-5780

MASSACHUSETTS

GADO 13
Norwood Municipal Airport
Norwood, MA 02062
(617) 769-1845

GADO 19
Barnes Municipal Airport
Westfield, MA 01085
(413) 562-4582

MICHIGAN

GADO 8
Kent County International Airport
5500 44th Street SE
Grand Rapids, MI 49508
(616) 456-2427

GADO 20
Flight Standards Building
Willow Run Airport
880 Beck Road
Belleville, MI 48111
(313) 485-2550

MINNESOTA

GADO 14
6201 34th Avenue South
Minneapolis, MN 55450
(612) 725-4211

MISSISSIPPI

GADO 4
120 North Hangar Drive, Suite C
Jackson Municipal Airport
Jackson, MS 39208
(601) 960-4633

MISSOURI

FSDO 62
9275 Genaire Drive
Burkley, MO 63134
(314) 731-2121

MONTANA

FSDO 61
Administration Building
Room 216
Billings Logan International Airport
Billings, MT 59101
(406) 245-6179

FSDO 65
FAA Building
Room 3
Helena Airport
Helena, MT 59601
(406) 499-5270

NEBRASKA

GADO 12
General Aviation Building
Lincoln Municipal Airport
Lincoln, NE 68524
(402) 437-5485

NEVADA

GADO 11
601 South Rock Blvd.
Suite 102
Reno, NV 89502
(702) 784-5321

FSDO 66
241 East Reno Avenue, Suite 200
Las Vegas, NV 89119
(702) 388-6482

NEW HAMPSHIRE

GADO 15
(See Maine)

NEW JERSEY

FSDO 61
150 Fred Wehran Drive, Room 5
Teterboro Airport
Teterboro, NJ 07608
(201) 288-4340

NEW MEXICO

GADO 1
1601 Randolph Road, SE, Suite 200N
Albuquerque, NM 87106
(505) 247-0156

NEW YORK

GADO 1
Albany County Airport
Albany, NY 12211
(518) 869-8481

GADO 11
Building 53
Republic Airport
Farmingdale, NY 11735
(516) 694-5530

GADO 17
Rochester-Monroe Airport
Rochester, NY 14624
(716) 263-5880

NORTH CAROLINA

GADO 3
FAA Building
5318 Morris Field Drive, Municipal Airport
Charlotte, NC 28208
(704) 392-3214

GADO 11
Route 1, Box 486A
Morrisville, NC 27560
(919) 856-4240

NORTH DAKOTA

FSDO 64
1801 23rd Ave. N.
Fargo, ND 58105
(701) 232-8949

OHIO

GADO 5
4242 Airport Road
Lunken Executive Building
Cincinnati, OH 45226
(513) 533-8110

GADO 6
Federal Facilities Building
Cleveland Hopkins International Airport
Cleveland, OH 44135
(216) 267-0220

GADO 7
3939 East 17th Avenue
Port Columbus International Airport
Columbus, OH 43219
(614) 469-7476

OKLAHOMA

GADO 9
FAA Building
Wiley Post Airport
Bethany, OK 73008
(405) 789-5220

FSDO 65
General Aviation Terminal Building
Room 103
Tulsa International Airport
6501 E. Apache
Tulsa, OK 74115
(918) 835-2378

OREGON

GADO 2
Mahlon Sweet Airport
90606 Greenhill Road
Eugene, OR 97402
(503) 688-9721

GADO 3
Portland/Hillsboro Airport
3355 NE Cornell Road
Hillsboro, OR 97124
(503) 221-2104

PENNSYLVANIA

GADO 3
Allentown-Bethlehem-Easton Airport
Allentown, PA 18103
(215) 264-2888

GADO 9
Scott Plaza 2, Fourth Floor
Philadelphia, PA 19113
(215) 596-0673

GADO 10
Room 201
Administration Building
Capitol City Airport
New Cumberland, PA 17070
(717) 782-4528

GADO 14
Allegheny County Airport
West Mifflin, PA 15122
(412) 462-5507

RHODE ISLAND

GADO 13
(See Massachusetts)

SOUTH CAROLINA

GADO 9
Columbia Metropolitan Airport
2819 Aviation Way
West Columbia, SC 29169
(803) 765-5931

SOUTH DAKOTA

FSDO 66
Rural Route 2, Box 633B
Rapids City, SD 57701
(605) 393-1359

TENNESSEE

FSDO 62
322 Knapp Blvd.
Room 101
Nashville Metropolitan Airport
Nashville, TN 37217
(615) 251-5661

FSDO 63
2488 Winchester
Room 137
Memphis, TN 38116
(901) 345-0600

TEXAS

GADO 2
8032 Aviation Place
Love Field Airport
Dallas, TX 75235
(214) 357-0142

GADO 3
FAA NWS Building
Room 202
6795 Convair Road
El Paso, TX 79925
(915) 778-6389

FSDO 61
Administration Building
Room 240
Meacham Field
Fort Worth, TX 76106
(817) 624-4911

FSDO 62
8800 Paul B Koonce Drive
Room 152
Houston, TX 77061
(713) 643-6504

GADO 7
Route 3, Box 51
Lubbock, TX 79401
(806) 762-0335

FSDO 4
10100 Reunion Place, Suite 200
San Antonio, TX 78216
(512) 314-4371

UTAH

FSDO 67
116 North 2400 West
Salt Lake City, UT 84116
(801) 524-4247

VERMONT

GADO 15
(See Maine)

VIRGINIA

GADO 16
Byrd International Airport
Sandstone, VA 23150
(804) 222-7494

FSDO 62
GT Building, Suite 112
Box 17325
Dulles International Airport
Washington, D.C. 20041
(703) 557-5360

WASHINGTON

GADO 5
5620 East Rutter Avenue
Spokane, WA 99206
(509) 456-4618

FSDO 61
7300 Perimeter Road South
Seattle, WA 98108
(206) 431-1354

WEST VIRGINIA

GADO 22
Yeager Airport, 301 Eagle Mountain Road
Room 144
Kanawha Airport
Charleston, WV 25311
(304) 343-4689

WISCONSIN

FSDO 61
General Mitchell Field
4915 South Howell Avenue
Milwaukee, WI 53207
(414) 747-5531

WYOMING

FSDO 62
Natrona County International Airport
FAA/WB Building
Casper, WY 82601
(307) 234-8959

Appendix D:

State Aviation Agencies

When it comes to daily living it seems that everyone wants to make a regulation. Aviation is no exception, just look at the FARs. Most states have an aviation agency of one type or another that has additional regulations.

Contact your state's aviation agency and see what they might offer to pilots and what they might require form pilots. Some agencies provide many services, while others are nothing but a taxing agency.

ALABAMA
Department of Aeronautics
817 South Court St.
Montgomery, AL 36130
(205) 261-4480

ALASKA
Department of Transportation
Post Office Box 6900
Anchorage, AK 99502
(907) 266-1462

ARIZONA
Division of Aeronautics
1801 West Jefferson, Rm 426
Phoenix, AZ 85007
(602) 255-7691

ARKANSAS
Department of Aeronautics
1 Airport Drive, 3rd Floor
Little Rock, AR 72202
(501) 376-6781

CALIFORNIA
Division of Aeronautics
P.O. Box 942874
Sacramento, CA 94272-0001
(916) 322-3090

COLORADO
Airport Planning Staff
1313 Sherman St., Suite 520
Denver, CO 80203
(303) 866-3004

CONNECTICUT
Bureau of Aeronautics
P.O. Drawer A
Wethersfield, CT 06109
(203) 566-4417

DELAWARE
Aeronautics Administration
P.O. Box 778
Dover, DE 19903
(302) 736-3264

FLORIDA
Bureau of Aviation
605 Swannee St., M.S. 46
Tallahassee, FL 32301-8064
(904) 488-8444

GEORGIA
Bureau of Aeronautics
20175 Flightway Drive
Chamblee, GA 30341
(404) 986-1350

HAWAII
Airports Division
Honolulu International Airport
Honolulu, HI 96819
(808) 836-6432

IDAHO
Bureau of Aeronautics & Public Transportation
3483 Rickenbacker St.
Boise, ID 83705
(208) 334-3183

ILLINOIS
Division of Aeronautics
1 Langhorne Bond Dr.
Springfield, Il 62707-8415
(217) 785-8515

INDIANA
Division of Aeronautics
143 West Market St., Suite 300
Indianapolis, IN 46204
(317) 232-1470

IOWA
Air and Transit Division
International Airport
Des Moines, IA 50321
(515) 281-4280

KANSAS
Aviation Division
State Office Building
Topeka, KS 66612-1586
(913) 296-2553

KENTUCKY
Office of Aeronautics
US 127 South
Frankfort, KY 40622
(502) 564-4480

LOUISIANA
Office of Aviation and Public Transportation
P.O. Box 94245
Baton Rouge, LA 70804
(504) 379-1235

MAINE
Division of Aeronautics
State Office Building
Augusta, ME 04333
(207) 289-3185

MARYLAND
State Aviation Administration
P.O. Box 8766
Baltimore, MD 21240
(301) 859-7060

MASSACHUSETTS
Aeronautics Commission
10 Park Plaza, Rm 6620
Boston, MA 02116-3966
(617) 973-7350

MICHIGAN
Aeronautics Commission
Capital City Airport
Lansing, MI 48906
(517) 373-1834

MINNESOTA
Aeronautics Division
Transportation Building
St. Paul, MN 55155
(612) 296-8202

MISSISSIPPI
Aeronautics Commission
P.O. Box 5
Jackson, MS 39205
(601) 359-1270

MISSOURI
Department of Highways & Transportation
P.O. Box 272
Jefferson City, MO 65101
(314) 751-2589

MONTANA
Aeronautics Division
P.O. Box 5178
Helena, MT 59604
(406) 444-2506

NEBRASKA
Department of Aeronautics
P.O. Box 82088
Lincoln, NE 68510
(402) 471-2371

NEVADA
Department of Transportation
1263 S. Stewart St.
Carson City, NV 89712
(702) 885-5510

NEW HAMPSHIRE
Aeronautics Commission
65 Airport Road
Concord, NH 03301-5298
(603) 271-2551

NEW JERSEY
Division of Aeronautics
1035 Parkway Ave.
Trenton, NJ 08625
(609) 530-2900

NEW MEXICO
Aviation Division
P.O. Box 579
Sante Fe, NM 87504-0579
(505) 827-0332

NEW YORK
Aviation Bureau
1220 Washington Ave.
Albany, NY 12232
(518) 457-2820

NORTH CAROLINA
Division of Aviation
P.O. Box 25201
Raleigh, NC 27611
(919) 787-9618

NORTH DAKOTA
North Dakota Aeronautics Commission
Bismark Airport
P.O. Box 5020
Bismark, ND 58502
(701) 224-2748

OHIO
Division of Aviation
2829 West Dublin-Granville Rd.
Worthington, OH 43235
(614) 466-7120

OKLAHOMA
Aeronautics Commission
200 NW 21st St., Rm B-7 (1st flr)
Oklahoma, OK 73105
(405) 521-2377

OREGON
Division of Aeronautics
3040 25th St. SE
Salem, OR 97301
(503) 378-4880

PENNSYLVANIA
Bureau of Aviation
Transportation & Safety Bldg, Rm 716
Harrisburg, PA 17120
(717) 783-2280

RHODE ISLAND
Division of Airports
Theodore Francis Green State Airport
Warwick, RI 02886
(401) 737-4000

SOUTH CAROLINA
Aeronautics Commission
Drawer 1987
Columbia, SC 29202
(803) 734-1700

SOUTH DAKOTA
Department of Transportation
700 Broadway Ave.
Pierre, SD 57501-2586
(605) 773-3574

TENNESSEE
Office of Aeronautics
P.O. Box 17326
Nashville, TN 37217
(615) 741-3208

TEXAS
Texas Aeronautics Commission
P.O. Box 12607
Austin, TX 78711
(512) 476-9262

UTAH
Aeronautical Operation Division
135 North 2400 West
Salt Lake City, UT 84116
(801) 328-2066

VERMONT
Agency of Transportation
120 State Street
Montpelier, VT 05603-0001
(802) 828-2828

VIRGINIA
Department of Aviation
P.O. Box 7716
Richmond, VA 23231
(804) 786-1364

WASHINGTON
Division of Aeronautics
8600 Perimeter Rd., Boeing Field
Seattle, WA 98108
(206) 764-4131

WEST VIRGINIA
Office of Community & Industrial Development
Building 6, Rm B-553
State Capitol Complex
Charleston, WV 25305
(304) 348-4010

WISCONSIN
Bureau of Aeronautics
P.O. Box 7914
Madison, WI 53707
(608) 266-3351

WYOMING
Aeronautics Commission
Cheyenne, WY 82002-0090
(307) 777-7481

Appendix E:

Owner Organizations

Finding owner support for most airplanes is only a phone call or a letter away. In some cases you would contact the manufacturer, however, in a number of instances this is impossible because they are no longer in business. In a few cases manufacturers do not want to be bothered. A club often becomes the sole source of owner and pilot information.

Most of the popular makes and models of small planes have a club; some planes have more than one club. Clubs generally publish a newsletter, host national or regional gatherings, and can answer questions about their particular airplanes. I strongly recommend that you join and support the club that features your airplane.

AERONCA

Aeronca Aviators Club
511 Terrace Lake Road
Columbus, IN 47201
(812) 342-6878

The Aeronca Club
1432 28th Court
Kenosha, WI 53140
(414) 552-9014

Aeronca Lover's Club
401 1st St. East
Clark, SD 57225
(605) 532-3862

Aeronca Sedan Club
2311 E. Lk. Sammamish Pl. S.E.
Issaquah, WA 98027
(206) 392-1024

BEECH

American Bonanza Society
Mid-Continent Airport
P.O. Box 12888
Wichita, KS 67277
(316) 945-6913

Twin Bonanza Association
19684 Lakeshore Dr.
Three Rivers, MI 49093
(616) 279-2540

Staggerwing Club
1885 Millsboro Road
Mansfield, OH 44906
(419) 529-3822

Western Bonanza Beech Owners Society
1436 Muirlands Dr.
La Jolla, CA 92037
(619) 459-5901

BELLANCA

Bellanca Contact
1820 N. 166 St.
Brookfield, WI 53005
(414) 784-0318

CESSNA

Cardinal Club
1701 St. Andrew's Dr.
Lawrence, KS 66044
(913) 842-7016

Cessna 150/152 Club
P.O. Box 15388
Durham, NC 27704
(919) 471-9492

Cessna Owners Organization
P.O. Box 75068
Birmingham, AL 35253
(205) 822-8035

Cessna Pilots Association
P.O. Box 12948
Wichita, KS 67277
(316) 946-4777

International Cessna 120/140 Association
P.O. Box 830092
Richardson, TX 75083-0092
(612) 652-2221

International Cessna 170 Association
P.O. Box 1667
Lebanon, MO 65536
(417) 532-4847

International 180/185 Club
4539 N. 49th Ave.
Phoenix, AZ 85031
(602) 846-6236

National 210 Owners Association
9959 Glenoaks Blvd.
Sun Valley, CA 91352
(213) 875-2820

West Coast Cessna 120/140 Club
Post Office Box 727
Rosebud, OR 97470
(503) 672-5046

ERCOUPE/ALON/FORNEY

Ercoupe Owners Club
P.O. Box 15388
Durham, NC 27704
(919) 471-9492

GRUMMAN

American Yankee Association
3232 Western Drive
Cameron Park, CA 95682
(919) 676-2022

LUSCOMBE

Continental Luscombe Association
5736 Esmar Road
Ceres, CA 95307
(209) 537-9934

Luscombe Association
6438 W. Millbrook
Remus, MI 49340
(517) 561-2393

MAULE

Maule Newsletter
5630 S. Washington
Lansing, MI 48910
(517) 882-8433

MEYERS

Meyers Aircraft Owners Association
5852 Boque Road
Yuba City, CA 95991
(916) 673-2724

MOONEY

Mooney Aircraft Pilots Association
314 Stardust Dr.
San Antonio, TX 78228
(512) 434-5959

NAVION

American Navion Society
P.O. Box 1175
Municipal Airport
Banning, CA 92220
(714) 849-2213

PIPER

Cherokee Pilots Association
P.O. Box 716
Safety Harbor, FL 34695
(813) 791-3255

Cub Club
P.O. Box 2002
Mt. Pleasant, MI 48858
(517) 561-2393

Flying Apache Association
1 South 300 Dillon Lane
Villa Park, IL 60181
(312) 627-8027

International Comanche Society Inc.
P.O. Box 400
Grant, NE 69140
(308) 352-4275

Piper Owner Society
P.O. Box 75068
Birmingham, AL 35253
(800) 247-8360

Short Wing Piper Club Inc.
32 West End Ave.
Brentwood, NY 11717
(516) 273-5072

Super Cub Pilot's Association
P.O. Box 9823
Yakima, WA 98909
(509) 248-9491

Tomahawk Pilots Association
P.O. Box 15388
Durham, NC 27704
(919) 471-9492

SEABEE

Seabee Club International
6761 N.W. 32nd Avenue
Ft. Lauderdale, FL 33309
(305) 979-5470

STINSON

National Stinson Club (108s)
117 Lanford Rd.
Spartanburg, SC 29301
(803) 576-9698

Northwest Stinson Club
29804 179th Pl. SE
Kent, WA 98042
(206) 631-9644

Southwest Stinson Club
3619 Nortree Street
San Jose, CA 95148
(408) 274-9179

SWIFT

International Swift Association
P.O. Box 644
Athens, GA 37303
(615) 745-9547

TAYLORCRAFT

International Taylorcraft Owners Club
12809 Greenbower Road
Alliance, OH 44601
(216) 823-9748

Appendix F:

Used Airplane Prices

Prices fluctuate depending upon market demands. Newer planes will see yearly drops, until a plateau is reached, generally at about 15 years. Drastic price reductions will be noted on planes experiencing expensive maintenance problems or costly ADs. Some late-model aircraft actually increase slightly in value, on paper, due to the increased costs of new airplanes.

Average airplane asking prices might vary as much as 30 percent from those contained in this list. Variations can be caused by the geogaphical location of the aircraft, condition of the airplane, or how badly the owner wishes to sell the airplane.

In practice the selling price can be defined as the sum mutually agreed upon by the seller and the buyer, with regard to the need to sell, and the need to buy, and the value of the airplane. The latter is often the least significant figure.

AERO COMMANDER

Darter	$8,300
Lark	$11,000
112	$26,000
112TC	$35,500
114	$45,000
Meyers 200	$50,000
500/500A	$32,000

AERONCA

7AC	$8,000
11AC	$7,500
Champ 7ACA	$N/A
Traveler 7EC	$8,000
Tri-Traveler 7FC	$9,500
Citabria 7ECA	$12-29,000
Citabria 7KCAB	$19,000
Champ 7GC	$9-24,000
Scout 8GCBC	$24,000
Decathlon 8KCAB	$15-36,000

BEECHCRAFT

Staggerwing 17	$90,000
Twin Beech 18	$16-40,000
Sport 19	$13,000
Musketeer 23	$14,000
Musketeer 24-23	$16,500
Sundowner 23 73-79	$25,000
Sundowner 23 80-82	$36,000
Sierra 24 70-75	$23,000
Sierra 24 76-79	$31,000
Sierra 24 80-82	$45,000
Debonair 33	$34,000
Bonanza 33	$43,000 and up

Mentor T34	$60-100,000
Bonanza 35 47-56	$19,000
Bonanza 35 57-65	$26,500
Bonanza 35 66-74	$34-60,000
Bonanza 36 68-69	$55,000
Bonanza A36 70-77	$60-90,000
Twin Bonanza 50	$17-48,000
Baron B55 61-68	$27-44,000
Baron B55 69-73	$46-88,500
Dutchess 76	$50-70,000
Skipper 77	$13,000
Travelair 95 58-65	$29,500
Travelair 95 66-68	$42,000

BELLANCA

14-13	$13,000
14-19	$18,000
Viking 17-30/31 67-71	$24,000
Viking 17-30/31 72-78	$36,500

CESSNA

120/140	$9,500
150 59-72	$9,500
150 73-77	$11,500
152 78-80	$16,000
152 81-82	$18-30,000
170	$14,000
172 56-68	$9-16,000
172 69-76	$15-24,000
172 77-80	$22-36,000
172 81-82	$37,000
172-RG	$38,000
175	$13,000
177 68-75	$22,000
177 76-78	$31,000
177-RG	$33,000
180 53-65	$23,000
180 66-70	$28,000
180 71-75	$32,000
180 76-80	$44,000
182 56-66	$20,000
182 67-75	$32,000
182 76-80	$49,000
182-RG	$58,000
185 61-66	$26,000

185 67-75	$28-40,000
185 76-80	$46,000
195	$18-40,000
205	$24,000
P206	$25,000
U206 64-70	$30,000
U206 71-75	$35,000
U206 76-80	$46,000
207 69-75	$34,000
207 76-80	$46,000
210 60-70	$27,000
210 71-75	$37,000
310 55-65	$16- $28,500
310 66-74	$28-50,000
310 75-78	$50-75,000
320	$24-38,000
336	$12,000
337 65-74	$18-38,000
337 75-77	$43,000

ERCOUPE

415	$8,500
Alon A2	$11,000
Mooney Cadet	$12,800

GULFSTREAM

AA1 series	$9,500
AA5 150 hp	$14,000
AA5 180 hp	$26,000

HELIO

H-295	$30-90,000

LAKE

LA-4 60-70	$30,000
LA-4 200 hp 70-80	$23-49,000
LA-250	$160,000

LUSCOMBE

8A	$9,000
8E	$12,000
8F	$14,000
Sedan	$22,000

MAULE

M4 145 hp	$10,000
M4 180 hp	$12,000
M4 210 hp	$15,000
M4 220 hp	$16,000
M5 210 hp	$20,000
M5 235 hp	$26,000
M6 235 hp	$34,000
M7 235 hp	$40,000

MOONEY

M10	$10,000
M20C	$18-32,000
M20E	$18-30,000
M20F	$30,000
201	$46-80,000
231	$52-90,000
M22	$42,000

PIPER

J3	$13,500
J4	$10,000
J5	$13,000
PA-11	$14,000
PA-12	$11,000
PA-15/17	$9,500
PA-16	$10,000
PA-18	$8-40,000
PA-20	$12,000
PA-22 Colt	$9,500
PA-22 Tri-Pacer	$10,000
PA-23 150 hp	$9-15,000
PA-23 160 hp	$18,000
PA-23 225 hp	$21,000
PA-23 Aztec 60-65	$24,000
PA-23 66-72	$30,000
PA-23 73-75	$55,000

PA-24 250 hp	$26,000
PA-24 260 hp	$30,000
PA-28 140 Cherokee	$11,000
PA-28 140 Cruiser	$14,000
PA-28 150 Cherokee	$12,000
PA-28 180 Archer	$22,000
PA-28 235 Pathfinder	$17-29,000
PA-28 151 Warrior	$27,000
PA-28 161 Warrior II 77-81	$38,000
PA-28 181 Archer II 76082	$25-60,000
PA-28 236 Dakota 79-81	$49,000
PA-28R Arrow 69-76	$28,000
PA-30 Twin Comanche	$34,000
PA-32 Cherokee Six	$32,000
PA-32R-300 Lance 76-79	$48,500
PA-32-301 Saratoga 80-83	$60-90,000
PA-38 Tomahawk 78-80	$12,000
PA-39 Twin Comanche	$44,000

REPUBLIC

SeaBee	$15-25,000

STINSON

108 series	$8-12,000

SWIFT

GC-1B	$12,000

TAYLORCFAFT

BC-12	$7,500
F19	$12,500
F21	$15-18,500

VARGA

150 hp	$18,000
180 hp	$25,000

Index